The Pentateuch

D1596126

Other Titles in the Cornerstones Series

The Israelite Woman by Athalya Brenner-Idan
Paul and the Hermeneutics of Faith by Francis Watson
Jews in the Mediterranean Diaspora by John M. G. Barclay
One God, One Lord by Larry Hurtado
Archaeology, History and Society in Galilee by Richard Horsley
Q and the History of Early Christianity by Christopher M. Tuckett
Messianism Among Jews and Christians by William Horbury
Ancient Israel by Niels Peter Lemche
Jesus: Miriam's Child, Sophia's Prophet by Elisabeth Schüssler-Fiorenza
Solidarity and Difference by David G. Horrell
Neither Jew nor Greek by Judith Lieu
In Search of 'Ancient Israel' by Philip R. Davies
Fragmented Women by J. Cheryl Exum

The Pentateuch
A Social-Science Commentary

Second Edition

John Van Seters

Bloomsbury T&T Clark
An imprint of Bloomsbury Publishing Plc

B L O O M S B U R Y
LONDON • NEW DELHI • NEW YORK • SYDNEY

Bloomsbury T&T Clark

An imprint of Bloomsbury Publishing Plc

Imprint previously known as T&T Clark

50 Bedford Square	1385 Broadway
London	New York
WC1B 3DP	NY 10018
UK	USA

www.bloomsbury.com

BLOOMSBURY, T&T CLARK and the Diana logo are trademarks of Bloomsbury Publishing Plc

First published 1999, reprinted 2004. This edition published 2015.

© John Van Seters, 2015

John Van Seters has asserted his right under the Copyright, Designs and Patents Act, 1988, to be identified as Author of this work.

All rights reserved. No part of this publication may be reproduced or transmitted in any form or by any means, electronic or mechanical, including photocopying, recording, or any information storage or retrieval system, without prior permission in writing from the publishers.

No responsibility for loss caused to any individual or organization acting on or refraining from action as a result of the material in this publication can be accepted by Bloomsbury or the author.

British Library Cataloguing-in-Publication Data
A catalogue record for this book is available from the British Library.

ISBN: PB: 978-0-56765-879-1
          ePDF: 978-0-56765-880-7

Library of Congress Cataloging-in-Publication Data
Van Seters, John.
The Pentateuch : a social-science commentary / by John Van Seters—Third edition.
pages cm
Includes bibliographical references and indexes.
ISBN 978-0-567-65879-1 (paperback)—ISBN 978-0-567-65880-7 (edpf)   1. Bible.
Pentateuch—Criticism, interpretation, etc.   I. Title.
BS1225.52.V357 2015
222'.1067—dc23
2014048280

Typeset by RefineCatch Limited, Bungay, Suffolk
Printed and bound in India

Contents

Preface to the Second Edition

Since the first edition of this book fifteen years ago there have been some significant new trends in the study of the Pentateuch as they relate to its social and historical context, i.e. in what period of time and under what social circumstances and conditions did the writers of the Pentateuch produce their histories and laws? For a long time scholars identified three basic collections, a 'Priestly' work dominated by the concerns of temple and sacrifice (P), a 'non-Priestly corpus' (J) that was primarily focused on the people's origins and history from creation to their eventual arrival in the promised land, and the third in the book of Deuteronomy (D), construed as a long speech by Moses, consisting of laws and exhortation, given just before his death and their preparations for entrance into the promised land. Were there just three authors of these three collections, or many more? What was the order of these works and in what particular time period and circumstances were they written? Were they originally separate and individual books put together by editors (the Documentary Hypothesis), or were the later works additions made to the earlier ones (the Supplementary Hypothesis), or some complex combination of both (Redaction Criticism)? The first edition attempted to lay out, in this guidebook, a history of the critical study of the Pentateuch up to the time of its publication in 1999, in Chapters 3 and 4.

However, in the time that followed that earlier edition there has been a radicalization of views with little serious communication between them, and it is this present situation in Pentateuchal scholarship that I have attempted to address in my addition at the end of Chapter 4. On the one hand, among a number of European scholars there is the tendency to completely abolish any notion of authors in biblical literature and to speak only of 'traditions', Priestly and non-Priestly, that have been combined with each other and with other blocks of tradition by editors or redactors in a supplementary fashion over an extended period of time. This reflects a strong attack on the Documentary Hypothesis and its authors, while preserving its notion of editors. At the other extreme, especially in America, is the renewed attempt to defend the Documentary Hypothesis with its authors and redactors against any such changes. My position since the mid-1970s has been, and still is, to retain the notion of authors, but to reject completely the very existence of editors in antiquity, for which there is no clearly documented evidence. Authors, on the other hand, are present with great abundance in antiquity, and many of their works resemble the anonymous authors of the Pentateuch. This means that the combination of these authors was the result of one author expanding the work of an earlier author, and this combination was then expanded by a still later author. No editor is necessary to account for such a combination.

The question may well be asked, what is the point of setting out in such a guidebook, so many pages dedicated to this debate about sources and how they came together? There are two primary reasons for doing so. First of all, in the first four books of the Pentateuch (Genesis to Numbers) there are two dominant sources. The one is completely non-Priestly in which the relationship between humanity and the deity is not mediated in any way by a priest or temple institutions, but by direct personal access to the deity through prayer or lay sacrifice; the other source is completely dominated by priests who perform the only means of access to God through the rituals of the temple; the laity are completely passive. The combination of these two sources produces a complete contradiction of each other, and this must be accounted for both literarily and socially. The entire debate about the sources and the nature of their combination with each other arises out of a close study of just this phenomenon within the one Bible, which tradition associated with a single author, Moses.

The second reason for my spending so much time and space in this guidebook on these problems, is to give to the reader enough tools so that he/she may be able to develop his or her own judgment on what is the most reasonable or rational explanation for the nature of the text as we have it. This includes the ability to engage in a critical reading of my own presentation in the rest of the book, as compared with the other possibilities to which I refer. All too often a charismatic scholar attracts a group of novices around him or her and creates a school, such as the famous 'Albright school', much to the detriment of the discipline as a whole. As Gerhard von Rad once said to his students in a class I attended at Princeton Seminary in 1961, 'never belong to a "school"'. So the object of this book is for the student to learn to think critically.

With respect to critical thinking, one should constantly apply this to one's own work as well as the works of others. In this respect, the reader will find in Chapter 6 on the Yahwist (J) two significant changes. The one reflects a correction of my earlier view regarding the story of Abraham's encounter with the king of Gerar in Gen. 20.1-7; 21.25-31a, which I had argued was earlier than the parallel episode in the Isaac story in Gen. 26. Others offered some arguments for the view that the Isaac version of the story was earlier than the one in Gen. 20, but I resisted making that change. However, recently I came across new evidence that proved clearly that they were right, and this correction is reflected in the current edition. The other change in this edition has to do with my recent investigation into the origin of the synagogue, which I now associate with the Jewish community in exile in Babylonia, and which is reflected in the Yahwist's simple "Tent of Meeting" that Moses set up in the wilderness as a place of prayer and where he would communicate with the deity (Exod. 33.1-7). This raises a whole new set of issues regarding the relationship between this completely lay institution of the synagogue (= place of meeting) that arose prior to the rebuilding of the Temple. After the re-establishment of Temple worship in Jerusalem, an attempt was made by the Priestly source to counter this non-Priestly source, by his addition of the wilderness tabernacle/temple to the earlier J narrative. This represents a long-standing tension between the Judaism of the Second Temple priesthood and the synagogue of the diaspora, down to the ultimate destruction of the Temple by the Romans.

This guidebook on the Pentateuch is not presented as the last word on the Pentateuch, but rather as an open invitation to the reader to get involved in this form of social and historical study of the Bible as it reflects those formative years of Judaism's origins.

Preface to the First Edition

Within the last decade there have been a number of introductions or guidebooks to the study of the Pentateuch and it is reasonable to ask whether yet another one is necessary. Quite apart from the place that this introduction has within the larger scheme of the Social-Scientific Commentary series as outlined by the editors, I would like to make a case for this guidebook to the Pentateuch. One of the reasons for the flurry of student guidebooks on the Pentateuch has been the need to take account of the major changes that have come about in Pentateuchal studies, whether in sympathy with the new literary approaches or in defense of the older consensus. I myself have been engaged in Pentateuchal studies for over three decades and deeply involved in the changes that have come about. These have challenged the historical, social and literary understanding of what many regarded as the older sources and traditions of the Pentateuch. The publications resulting from my research have been more narrowly focused to the issues of the debate. What I have therefore attempted to do in the present work is to sketch in broad outline the implications of my method and results for the whole of the Pentateuch. This gives rise to a quite different picture of the compositional history of the Pentateuch and its major components, especially as they relate to one another, from those reflected in other introductions and guidebooks.

I have attempted to write this book for the student and the novice, to keep it short and to make few assumptions about prior knowledge in biblical studies. At the same time I have tried to remain faithful to the complexity of the discussion on method and fair to opposing viewpoints. The limitations of the guidebook format have restricted the scholarly debate and footnote citations, but much of that can be found in the works that are listed at the beginning of each chapter. Having taught the Pentateuch to large numbers of students at all levels over many years, I hope that I have been able to strike the right balance between the articulation of general principles and particular examples to illustrate them.

Publication on the Pentateuch has been so prolific in recent years that it is always difficult to keep up with it and to include comments on the latest work before the book goes to press. In particular, E. W. Nicholson's *The Pentateuch in the Twentieth Century* came to my attention too late to receive the attention that it deserves. His defense of the older consensus and his discussion of my views will have to wait for my response at another time.

I wish to thank the editors, Brian Schmidt and Diana Edelman, for inviting me to write an introduction for this series and for the many comments and corrections on the manuscript. However, I take sole responsibility for the views expressed in the finished product. I also wish to thank Kristy Irish, my graduate research assistant, for her help in preparing the indexes. The staff at Sheffield Academic Press has likewise been most helpful and careful in editing and production and special thanks to the editor, Vicky Acklam, for her diligent work. As always, I am grateful to my wife Elizabeth who has been patient and supportive throughout the process of my writing this book.

In the 1950s my brother Arthur and I were undergraduate students together in Near Eastern studies at the University of Toronto. Since then our paths have diverged, but we have both remained in academic life and have continued to be students of the Bible. Now we are at the end of our formal academic careers and I hope that he will have a little leisure to sit back and read this book and enjoy this latest effort in Pentateuchal studies. To him I dedicate this book with much fraternal affection.

Abbreviations

AB	Anchor Bible
ABD	David Noel Freedman (ed.), *The Anchor Bible Dictionary* (New York: Doubleday, 1992)
AnBib	Analecta biblica
ANET	James B. Pritchard (ed.), *Ancient Near Eastern Texts Relating to the Old Testament* (Princeton, NJ: Princeton University Press, 1950)
APAPM	American Philological Association Philological Monographs
ARCE	American Research Center in Egypt
ATANT	Abhandlungen zur Theologie des Alten und Neuen Testaments
ATSAT	Arbeiten zu Text und Sprache im Alten Testament
BASOR	*Bulletin of the American Schools of Oriental Research*
BETL	Bibliotheca ephemeridum theologicarum lovaniensium
Bib	*Biblica*
BO	*Bibliotheca Orientalis*
BWANT	Beiträge zur Wissenschaft vom Alten und Neuen Testament
BZAW	Beihefte zur *ZAW*
ConBOT	Coniectanea biblica, Old Testament
CBQ	*Catholic Biblical Quarterly*
EncRel	M. Eliade (ed.), *The Encyclopaedia of Religion* (16 vols.; London: Macmillan, 1987)
ErFor	Erträge der Forschung
ETL	*Ephemerides theologicae lovanienses*
FOTL	The Forms of the Old Testament Literature
FRLANT	Forschungen zur Religion und Literatur des Alten und Neuen Testaments
HAR	*Hebrew Annual Review*
HKAT	Handkommentar zum Alten Testament
HSM	Harvard Semitic Monographs
HUCA	*Hebrew Union College Annual*
ICC	International Critical Commentary
JAOS	*Journal of the American Oriental Society*
JBL	*Journal of Biblical Literature*
JSOTSup	*Journal for the Study of the Old Testament*, Supplement Series
JTS	*Journal of Theological Studies*

LÄ	W. Helck and E. Otto (eds.), *Lexikon der Ägyptologie* (Wiesbaden: Otto Harrassowitz, 1975–86)
NCBC	New Century Bible Commentary
OBO	Orbis biblicus et orientalis
OTL	Old Testament Library
OTS	*Oudtestamentische Studiën*
RGG	F. M. Schiele *et al.* (eds.), *Die Religion in Geschichte und Gegenwart* (5 vols.; Tübingen: J.C.B. Mohr, 1909–13; 2nd edn; 5 vols.; ed. H. Gunkel *et al.*; 1927–31; 3rd edn; 6 vols.; ed. K. Galling *et al.*; 1956–62)
SBLMS	Society of Biblical Literature Monograph Series
SBT	Studies in Biblical Theology
SJOT	*Scandinavian Journal of the Old Testament*
ST	Studia Theologica
TBü	Theologische Bücherei
TDOT	G. J. Botterweck and H. Ringgren (eds.), *Theological Dictionary of the Old Testament*
Tru	*Theologische Rundschau*
VT	*Vetus Testamentum*
VTSup	*Vetus Testamentum*, Supplements
WMANT	Wissenschaftliche Monographien zum Alten und Neuen Testament
ZAW	*Zeitschrift für die alttestamentliche Wissenschaft*

1

Introduction

Bibliography

Barr, J., *Holy Scripture, Canon, Authority, Criticism* (Philadelphia: Westminster Press, 1983).

Barton, J., *Oracles of God* (Oxford: Oxford University Press, 1986).

—— *Reading the Old Testament* (Philadelphia, PA: Westminster Press, 2nd edn, 1997 [1984]).

Blenkinsopp, J., *The Pentateuch* (New York: Doubleday, 1992).

Childs, B. S., *Introduction to the Old Testament as Scripture* (Philadelphia: Fortress Press, 1979).

Houtman, C., *Der Pentateuch* (Kampen: Kok, 1994).

McKenzie, S. L., and S. R. Haynes (eds.), *To Each its Own Meaning: An Introduction to Biblical Criticisms and their Meanings* (Louisville, KY: Westminster/John Knox Press, 1993).

Nicholson, E. W., *The Pentateuch in the Twentieth Century: The Legacy of Julius Wellhausen* (Oxford: Oxford University Press, 1998).

Pury, A. de, and T. Römer, 'Le pentateuque en question: Position du problème et brève histoire de la recherche', in A. de Pury (ed.), *Le pentateuque en question* (Geneva: Labor et Fides, 1989), pp. 9–90.

Whybray, R. N., *The Making of the Pentateuch: A Methodological Study* (JSOTSup, 53; Sheffield: Sheffield Academic Press, 1987).

—— *Introduction to the Pentateuch* (Grand Rapids: Eerdmans, 1995).

Zenger, E., *et al.*, *Einleitung in das Alte Testament* (ST, 1.1; Stuttgart: W. Kohlhammer, 1995).

The term 'Pentateuch', which is the subject of this book, is used by scholars to refer to the first five books of the Old Testament: Genesis, Exodus, Leviticus, Numbers and Deuteronomy. In the Christian Bible, the first five books are not set apart in any way from the rest of the books. This arrangement reflects the layout of the Septuagint, the translation of the Hebrew Scriptures into Greek. In the Hebrew Bible, by contrast, these five books constitute the first of three divisions: *Torah* (the Law), *Nevi'im* (the Prophets), and *Kethuvim* (the Writings). Nevertheless, early Christian writers coined the term 'Pentateuch' (derived from the Greek *pentateuchos*, meaning 'five-part book') as the equivalent of the first division of the Law in the Hebrew Bible. The Law (*Torah*) or Pentateuch was ascribed to Moses and was regarded by all branches and groups within early Judaism (including

Christianity) as the most complete revelation and authoritative religious document handed down from ancient Israel.

Biblical scholarship, at least since the seventeenth century, has increasingly rejected Moses' authorship of the Pentateuch and has long struggled to account for the peculiar literary nature of these early books of the Bible. As we will see below, scholars have identified a number of reasons pointing to multiple authors or literary strata and they have labored to find an explanation for how such diverse works came together in the Pentateuch. The division into books does not correspond to the works of the different authors and is entirely secondary.

Furthermore, the Hebrew term *Torah*, 'Law', is a little misleading as a description of the content of the Pentateuch, since it consists of about one half law and the other half narrative. Most of the laws are concentrated in large blocks within Exodus 19–Numbers 10 and Deuteronomy 5 and 12–26 and are closely associated with the figure of Moses and his reception of the laws at Mount Sinai. Hence, the whole of the Pentateuch came in time to be known as the Law of Moses. However, some laws are imbedded in narrative outside of these blocks, such as at the time of the exodus from Egypt in Exodus 12–13, or during the wilderness journey in Numbers 15–19, 26–31, 34–36; and some are found in Genesis in connection with Noah (Gen. 9) and Abraham (Gen. 17). Within the Old Testament the terms 'book of the law' or 'the law of Moses' have a much more limited reference to a particular set of laws and not to a larger composition.

The theological process by which the term Law and the common authorship and authority of Moses was attached to the whole corpus of the Pentateuch is known as canonization. While it seems fairly certain that, by the first century CE, the Pentateuch or Law was a fixed collection of five books, our direct evidence for any Pentateuch earlier than this remains conjectural. There has been a widely accepted view that the recognition of the Pentateuch as a distinct corpus goes back to the late fifth or early fourth century BCE and is coterminus with the end of its compositional development. It is this theory of the Pentateuch's canonicity that underlies the limits and approach of introductions to the Pentateuch.

However, such an understanding of the Pentateuch's canonicity has become increasingly problematic in recent years.[1] In my view, there is good reason to believe that the process by which the Pentateuch became divided into five books and then was regarded as distinct from the books that followed is separated in time from the composition of the Pentateuch's content by perhaps several centuries. This makes problematic the whole notion of a 'Pentateuch' for a number of reasons. First, as we shall see below, there are many scholars who do not view Deuteronomy as the conclusion to a literary corpus but a work that continues on into Joshua and perhaps beyond. For this reason, scholars coined the term 'Hexateuch' to include at least Joshua as well. Another tendency that has gained much support is to see a radical division between Genesis–Numbers, a 'Tetrateuch', and the whole corpus from Deuteronomy to 2 Kings. Both approaches make the Pentateuch problematic from the perspective of a literary history. It is only the highly speculative notion of a 'Pentateuchal editor', who, in the final stage of literary development, created a division at the end of Deuteronomy, that unites the canonical Pentateuch with its literary history.

Secondly, this convergence of canonicity with the final stage of literary history has led increasingly in recent years to the literary study of the Pentateuch in its final canonical form.[2] The assumption is that it is a unity to which various postmodern literary methods may be applied.[3] However, the unity implied in the Law of Moses or the Pentateuch is not a literary one, but a theological one. It is the unity of authority by the attribution of these books to Moses as the medium of divine inspiration. This cannot be the basis for any literary analysis of the Pentateuch or part of it. The Pentateuch does not have a final 'form' because the division at the end of Deuteronomy was not based upon literary considerations. Unless one can convincingly demonstrate such a design by careful critical analysis, the concept of a Pentateuch remains problematic for any literary analysis of the Hebrew Bible or Old Testament.

Nevertheless, the term Pentateuch remains as the subject of this introduction because it is the term used in scholarship for a field of academic inquiry, even when its unity and limits are in question. Indeed, this book intends to show how the literary and historical-critical study of the Pentateuch has made the very concept of the Pentateuch problematic. Once the decision is made to separate the question of canon from the literary history of the Bible, then a literary history of the biblical text cannot arrive at the final form of the Pentateuch. What we will be concerned with is the development of the literary strata that we discover in the Pentateuch, their relationship to each other and to the rest of the books that follow the Pentateuch in the Hebrew Bible.

The purpose of this book is to introduce the student to the historical-critical method of Pentateuchal study, which is the indispensable basis for a social-scientific commentary of the five books within the Pentateuch. There are many hermeneutical methods applied to the interpretation of the Bible, many different ways of reading the texts of the Pentateuch.[4] The limits of 'social-scientific' preclude the inclusion of many of these and virtually require that any Pentateuchal texts under consideration be compatible with a historical understanding of the literature's literary development. Therefore, the first task will be to identify those features and problems within the Pentateuch that call for some explanation by way of a historical/literary theory and the basic compositional models that are used in such explanations. This will be followed by a brief survey of the rise of the historical-critical method from the mid-nineteenth to the mid-twentieth centuries and the dominant methods and schools of the literary, form-critical and traditio-historical methods. Limitations of space will only permit rather selective treatment of major figures. The emphasis will be on the continuing impact of these figures and their views in current Pentateuchal study. It will also address how the historical and social setting of these scholars and interpreters affected their perspectives of the Bible's literary development.

It has been frequently stated that Pentateuchal studies have been in a state of flux and upheaval since the mid-1970s. As one who has been among those at the center of this state of affairs, I will give an account, as I see it, of how this upheaval came about. I will try to sort out the current issues under discussion and the models of literary criticism that are now being used. In spite of the apparent chaos rendered by the demise of the older consensus, there is greater attention to basic methodological issues than ever before.[5]

The second half of the book will be an attempt to construct a history of the literary development of the Pentateuch. It will advocate the view that the Pentateuch as we now have it was the product of literary activity in a few clearly identifiable stages, leaving distinct literary strata, over a period of a little more than two centuries from the late monarchy to the late Persian periods. The proposal will be made in dialogue with the other literary methods set out in the previous chapters, but space limitations will mean that I will need to rely on more detailed argument in other publications. A major point of contention will be the relative chronological order of the literary strata and the dating of these strata within the larger history of Israel. Yet as we shall see, there can be no serious discussion of the social setting of the various parts of the Pentateuch without such chronological decisions.

Notes

1 Barr, *Holy Scripture, Canon, Authority, Criticism*; Barton, *Oracles of God*.
2 Childs, *Introduction to the Old Testament as Scripture*; Barton, *Oracles of God*.
3 Barton, *Reading the Old Testament*.
4 Barton, *Reading the Old Testament*; McKenzie and Haynes (eds.), *To Each its Own Meaning*.
5 There have been a number of recent introductions to the Pentateuch that may be consulted with benefit. These include Blenkinsopp, *The Pentateuch*; Whybray, *The Making of the Pentateuch*; *idem*, *Introduction to the Pentateuch*; Houtman, *Der Pentateuch*; de Pury and Römer, 'Le pentateuque en question'; Zenger *et al., Einleitung in das Alte Testament*; Nicholson, *The Pentateuch in the Twentieth Century*. These works represent a range of perspectives with which the present work will dialogue.

2

The Pentateuch as a Whole: Basic Features and Problems

Bibliography

Berge, K., *Reading Sources in a Text: Coherence and Literary Criticism in the Call of Moses* (ATSAT, 54; St Ottilien: EOS Verlag, 1997).

Carr, D. M., *Reading the Fractures of Genesis: Historical and Literary Approaches* (Louisville, KY: Westminster/John Knox Press, 1996).

Fishbane, M., *Biblical Interpretation in Ancient Israel* (Oxford: Oxford University Press, 1985).

1. The Pentateuch in outline

In order to consider some basic features of the Pentateuch as a whole, it will be useful to have an outline of its content for ready reference. For the first four books I will make a distinction between blocks of material that are obviously parallel to each other by italicizing one stratum that may be compared with the other. This is only intended as a preliminary distinction of strata, because there are other places where the literary strata are combined in the same unit. An asterisk (*) indicates those units that betray a substantial mixture of literary strata.

a. Genesis 1–11: The primeval history

1.1–2.4a	*The creation of the world and human beings*
2.4b–3.24	A second account of creation and the origin of evil
4.1-16	The story of Cain and Abel and the first murder
4.17-26	The genealogies of Cain and Seth
5	*A second genealogy of Seth (from Adam to Noah) with precise chronology*
6.1–8.22*	The story of the flood and Noah's ark
9.1-17	*The covenant of Noah, a second promise by God not to bring another flood*
9.18-27	Noah's discovery of wine and the curse of Ham

10*	The table of nations and the origins of the world's peoples
11.1-9	The tower of Babel (Babylon)
11.12-32	*A second genealogy of Shem with chronology down to Abraham*

b. Genesis 12–50: the story of the patriarchs of Israel

12.1–25.11	Stories in the lives of Abram (Abraham)
12–13*	Abraham's call in Harran, migration to Canaan, brief sojourn in Egypt, separation from Lot and renewed promise of the land of Canaan
[14	War with four eastern kings]
15	Covenant with Abraham
16	The flight of Hagar, birth of Ishmael
17	*A second covenant with Abraham*
18–19	The promised birth of Isaac, the destruction of Sodom and Gomorrah
20	Abraham and Sarah in Gerar
21	Birth of Isaac, expulsion of Hagar, Abraham's covenant with the king of Gerar
22	The binding of Isaac
23	*The death and burial of Sarah*
24	The marriage of Isaac
25.1-11	The offspring of Keturah and the death of Abraham
25.12-18	*The genealogy of Ishmael*
26	Story of Isaac in Gerar
25.19-33; 27-35	The adventures of Jacob, including the rivalry with Esau, his brother (*a second blessing of Jacob by Isaac, 28.1-9*), the flight and revelation at Bethel, and the sojourn with his uncle Laban in Harran and marriage to his cousins, Leah and Rachel, and his return to Canaan
35.9-15	*A second revelation to Jacob*
36	*The genealogy of Esau*
37, 39–50*	The story of Joseph and his brothers
38	The story of Judah

c. Exodus 1–15: The sojourn in Egypt and the liberation from slavery

1*	The oppression of the Hebrews
2–4	The birth, youth and calling of Moses
5	The first audience with Pharaoh
6.2–7.13	*A second call of Moses (with genealogy) with a second introduction to Pharaoh—contest of magicians*

7–11*	Plagues
12–13*	The death of the first-born and the departure from Egypt combined with the institution of the passover and feast of unleavened bread
14–15*	The crossing and rescue at the Red Sea

d. Exodus 15–Numbers 10: The revelation of the Law at Sinai

15–18*	The journey through the wilderness to Sinai
19*	The theophany at Sinai
20.1-17	*The giving of the Ten Commandments*
20.18–23.33	The giving of a code of laws
24.3-8	A covenant-making ceremony ratifying the code
24.1-2, 9-11	*A second covenant ceremony*
24.12-18*	Moses ascends the mountain to receive the tablets
25.1–31.17	*Moses receives instructions about building the Tabernacle*
32	The violation of the covenant through the making of the Golden Calf (in Moses' absence)
33	The presence of God among his people, the making of the Tent of Meeting (vv. 7-11)
34	Covenant renewal
35–40	*The construction of the Tabernacle*
Leviticus 1–7	*Laws for sacrifice*
8–10	*Investiture of Aaron and sons as priests*
11–16	*Regulations on purity and the ritual of atonement*
17–26	*The Holiness code*
Lev. 27–Num. 10	*Various laws and regulations*

e. Numbers 10–36: The journey through the wilderness from Sinai to Moab

10.11-36*	Departure from Sinai
11	Two episodes of 'murmurings' and the appointment of elders to help Moses
12	Aaron and Miriam contest Moses' authority
13–14*	The failed southern campaign to capture Canaan
15	*Various priestly laws and regulations*
16–17*	The rebellion of Korah, Dathan and Abiram
18–19	*Various priestly regulations*
20.1-13	*Moses' and Aaron's sin at Meribah*
20.14-21	The journey around Edom
20.22-29	*The death of Aaron and installation of Eleazar as high priest*

21	The war against the kings of Sihon and Og to gain possession of the Transjordanian territory for Israel
22–24	The story of Balaam
25*	The sin of Baal of Peor
26–30	*The census of the people, the inheritance of the daughters of Zelophehad, the inauguration of Joshua as successor to Moses, the regulations regarding feast and holy days, vows of women*
31	*War against Midian*
32*	The distribution of the territory east of the Jordan
33	*The record of the desert itinerary*
34–36	*Further preparations for entering Canaan*

f. Deuteronomy: The 'second law'

1–3	A recapitulation of the wilderness journey from Horeb (Sinai) to Moab by Moses
4	Recapitulation of the Horeb (Sinai) theophany
4.44-49	A new introduction to the book
5	Another version of the giving of the Ten Commandments (cf. Exod. 20.1-17)
6–11	Prologue of exhortations on keeping the laws
12–26	The Deuteronomic code
27–28	Blessings and curses
29–33	Final instructions in the land of Moab
34	The death of Moses

2. General observations on the Pentateuch as a whole

From the above outline of the content of the Pentateuch certain features that govern the present study of this corpus will be obvious. First, there is a fundamental difference between the first four books from Genesis to Numbers, often referred to as the Tetrateuch, and Deuteronomy. The Tetrateuch is a continuous story in historical sequence from creation to the end of the wilderness journey in anticipation of the people of Israel's invasion of the promised land. Deuteronomy does not continue this story but consists of a long peroration by Moses that includes the giving of another set of laws in addition to those already given in the previous historical narration before Moses ascends Mount Nebo to die. Not only is Deuteronomy a 'second law' but it is also a second telling of various events about Sinai/Horeb and the wilderness journey from the sacred mountain to the edge of the Jordan as a recapitulation in the speech of Moses. So different is Deuteronomy (henceforth designated D) in the presentation of its laws, in the account of the events, and in its style, language and form that it has long been a field of investigation largely separate from the rest.

Turning to the Tetrateuch, we observe a feature that I have highlighted by the use of italics, in which parallel blocks of material have been set side by side. Thus, there are two accounts of creation, two genealogies of Seth, two genealogies of Shem, two covenants between Abraham and his god, two revelations to Jacob at Bethel, two calls of Moses to rescue his people, two sets of laws given at Sinai, two Tents of Meeting/Tabernacles set up at Sinai. Within many of the narrative units there is often evidence of duplication of some of the features and details. This is particularly evident in the flood story (Gen. 6–9), the story of the plagues, the death of the first-born and the sea crossing (Exod. 7–14), the spy story (Num. 13–14), the rebellion of Korah, Dathan and Abiram (Num. 16–17), the sin of Baal of Peor (Num. 25) and the distribution of the land (Num. 32).

3. Pentateuchal sources

When one has separated these two strands of material from each other, they display a number of features that identify them as distinct literary works:

a. The Priestly/non-Priestly content dichotomy

Comparison of these two major literary strands in terms of content and religious interest, especially in Exodus to Numbers, has led to the designation of the one as 'Priestly' (P) because of its strong concern for all matters that have to do with priests, the sacrificial cult and formal regulations of worship. In addition it has strong interests in chronology and genealogy, matters that impinge on the legitimation of priestly families and the regulation of holy days. This interest is extended to include the genealogies of families, clans and tribes within Israel as well as the genealogy of peoples and nations going back to the creation of the first pair. In similar fashion a precise chronological structure from creation to the time of Moses' death is also included in this work.

The 'non-Priestly' strand is markedly different in character from P. It has no interest in priests and, while some individuals may offer sacrifices, such as Cain, Abel, Noah, Abraham and Jacob, and Moses, there is little concern for details. There are a few regulations having to do with some festivals and the sabbath, but it reflects a minimal amount of lay observance. For the most part the non-P material consists of a long series of stories narrated in lively fashion, set in an imprecise chronological sequence of successive generations. At times when these non-P stories are taken together with the precise chronological framework of the P material, the combination produces a conflict between the chronology and the stories themselves. Thus, in the story of the expulsion of the slave woman Hagar and her child Ishmael from the household of Abraham (Gen. 21.7-20), Ishmael is viewed as quite young. However, according to the chronology of P (Gen. 12.4; 16.3; 17.1; 21.5) Ishmael is about sixteen years old. This produces the ridiculous picture of the mother carrying her teenaged son as she set out into the desert (Gen. 21.4) and a further conflict with the subsequent scene of the crying child being rescued by God.

b. Doublets within non-P

The division of the Tetrateuch into two literary strands is complicated by the presence within the non-P corpus of doublets and parallels that do not fit the characteristics of P. This is particularly true of the patriarchal stories but is not obviously the case for the whole of the non-P corpus of Exodus–Numbers. Thus, there are three cases in which the patriarch pretends that his wife is his sister for his own benefit, twice with Abraham (Gen. 12.10-20; 20) and once with Isaac (Gen. 26.1-11). There are close parallels between the story of Hagar's flight in Genesis 16 and Hagar's expulsion with her son (Gen. 21.8-21). All of the episodes in the life of Isaac in Genesis 26 have their parallels in the Abraham story. The episode of Esau's selling his birthright to Jacob for a lentil stew (Gen. 25.27-34) has its parallel in Jacob's theft of his brother's blessing (Gen. 27). In all these instances, however, it is not so easy to see how these parallels can be related to distinct literary strands within non-P in any comprehensive fashion. A different solution will be suggested below.

c. The use of the divine name

Another major difference in the two literary strands is in the choice of designation for the deity. In non-P there is a preference for the use of the divine name 'Yahweh' (= 'the LORD' in English versions), while P uses the generic term for deity, 'Elohim' (God) or the divine title 'El Shaddai' (God Almighty) in Genesis and in the first part of Exodus. P actually gives an explanation for his particular usage in Exod. 6.2-3: 'God [Elohim] said to Moses, "I am Yahweh. I appeared to Abraham, to Isaac and to Jacob as El Shaddai, but by my name Yahweh I did not make myself known to them". Now in the Abraham story there are two accounts of a divine covenant between the deity and Abraham in Genesis 15 and 17. In the one the deity says to Abraham, 'I am Yahweh' (15.7), which contradicts Exod. 6.3. But in the parallel text the deity tells him, 'I am El Shaddai' (Gen. 17.1), and this agrees with Exod. 6.3. The Jacob story contains the same kind of parallel divine appearances at Bethel, the one using Yahweh to identify the deity (Gen. 28.13), the other El Shaddai (Gen. 35.9-11). In the Isaac story we do not have parallel revelations of the divine name, although it is clear from Genesis 26 that Yahweh appears to Isaac and that he subsequently invokes the name of Yahweh (vv. 24-25). However, there are two parallel blessings of Jacob by Isaac: in the first Isaac blesses him by Yahweh (27.27) and in the second one by El Shaddai (28.3).

Since this usage of the divine name Yahweh/El Shaddai coincides so completely with a number of major parallel blocks, it strongly commends the separation of these literary strands by using the criterion of the designation for deity. Thus, in the two creation accounts, the first uses Elohim throughout and the second uses Yahweh, but in combination with Elohim, since, as the author later explains, it was only in the third generation that mankind began to invoke the name of Yahweh (Gen. 4.26). However, at least for the P material prior to Exod. 6.2-3, one may expect to find only Elohim and El Shaddai, but not Yahweh.

This distinction in the use of the divine name is further supported by the use of other differences in vocabulary and stereotyped language and formulae that clearly set them apart. Scholars have made lists of such typical usage, based upon the obvious blocks, and then extended their application to the places where the two strands have become mixed together. To give one illustration among many, in the P creation story there is a statement by the deity in which he blesses the human pair with the injunction to 'be fruitful and increase and fill the earth' (Gen. 1.28). This injunction occurs again in the flood story where the same blessing is repeated as a renewal of creation (Gen. 9.2, 7) in which the two accounts are linked together. The same blessing occurs in the three patriarchal texts in which El Shaddai is used for the deity (17.2, 6, 16; 28.3; 35.9, 11). It then appears in the more mixed contexts of Gen. 47.27 and 48.3-4; Exod. 1.7. In these three cases the phraseology combines with other criteria. Thus, in 47.27 it is followed by a statement of the chronology of Jacob's sojourn in Egypt and age at death, standard features of P texts. In 48.3-4 the blessing formula is combined with another about Joseph's descendants becoming a 'host of nations' and receiving the land of Canaan that occurs in the P covenant of Abraham (Gen. 17.4-8; cf. 28.3-4; 35.11-12). Exod. 1.7 follows closely a genealogical summary in Exod. 1.1-4 that is, in turn, linked to the longer P genealogy in Gen. 46.8-27. The point is that the special language and phraseology, combined with the evidence of the divine name and the blocks of parallel material and other stylistic criteria, all intermesh and converge to confirm the distinction and separation of P and non-P material.[1]

The matter is complicated, however, by the fact that within the non-P material there is some fluctuation in the use of Yahweh and Elohim. In a few cases where doublets are present in Genesis 20–21, the designation Elohim is used, whereas in the parallels elsewhere Yahweh is the name for the deity. Yet this distinction does not cover all of the parallels in the patriarchal stories and may have an explanation that does not relate to literary strands. The effort to see distinct terminology within these parallels and thus extend the separation of strands to other parts of non-P is problematic.

d. Ideology of the separate strands

The ideology or theology of the various strands or 'documents' is reflected in the distinctive language and formulae as well as in the different treatment of parallel texts. This is particularly true in the case where one text is dependent upon an earlier text and seeks fundamentally to modify or change the perspective or narrative treatment of the earlier version of a story, a discourse, a law. How one reconstructs the ideology of a 'source' will depend very much on the degree to which there is clear and conscious intertextual dependence and the direction of that dependence.[2] That is a matter that must be taken up in the later discussion.

e. Consistency, coherence and cohesion in the unity of a text

Up to this point I have suggested making a distinction among three strands or blocks of material that are labeled D, non-P and P, and this distinction is not disputed among the large majority of biblical scholars. Problems arise, however, when Pentateuchal experts begin to debate the degree to which these three strands or sources are unified works and how they are related to each other. A particular text-unit or a larger 'source' is the work of a single author only if it manifests a fairly high degree of consistency. Blatant contradiction, therefore, suggests that a second hand is at work. This is especially true if the work is wholly the invention of the author. If the author is using certain traditions or sources for his/her composition, he/she may not be able to eliminate all of the differences between them. But the very idea of authorship demands consistency. In like fashion, an author is required to be coherent so that his/her thoughts and ideas are presented in such a way that one can follow what is being presented. Radical breaks in the chain of presentation, even if they do not contradict what has gone before, suggest the intervention of another hand. A unified work must also be grammatically and structurally cohesive, although the application of any principles of cohesiveness has often lacked rigor.[3]

What makes the use of the criteria of consistency, coherence and cohesiveness difficult is any agreement on the limits of the strands or sources and their relationship to each other. This is especially true for P and non-P. Even if P is consistently viewed as later than non-P, it still leaves open whether they are two complete and independent documents or whether one is dependent upon, and supplemental to, the other. In the case of the first option one will look for the criteria of unity in both, whereas in the second case the dependent source will need the earlier source to make it coherent and structurally complete. In the past the non-P material has been judged to be the most disunified and therefore divided into two or more sources. P, on the other hand, at least in the narrative portion and in its relationship to the non-P, has been viewed as the most unified, a unity that has come at the expense of the non-P material. Thus, in the case of a text like the flood story, which is viewed as a combination of P and non-P, if the attribution of a particular verse to one source or the other is in question, it is given to P to make it coherent and non-P remains incoherent as a result, because it is not possible to reconstruct two totally unified P and non-P texts.

4. Basic models for compositional reconstruction

There are basically three kinds of explanations that have been used to account for the evidence of disunity in the Pentateuch. These are the following:

a. The fragmentary/story-cycle/block model

In this model the basic component of composition is the individual narrative unit that may have been brought together by one or more collectors or editors, or which may have come together as story-cycles, or developed over time as blocks of tradition that were combined only in the final stages of the Pentateuch's 'redaction'. The same could apply to the laws as well, with each 'code' having its own history of development before its combination with the narrative framework. Inconsistencies, lack of coherence between smaller or larger units and lack of cohesion in the process of redaction could be accounted for by this model.

b. The supplementation or expansion of a basic text model

This compositional model suggests that one can recover a basic Pentateuchal or Tetrateuchal text that was supplemented and expanded from time to time and that it was primarily the additions that created inconsistencies and destroyed the coherence and cohesiveness of the earlier text.

c. The source/document/literary strata model

The notion of sources or documents corresponding to the multiple authorship of the Pentateuch has been the model that has dominated Pentateuchal research in modern times. This model seeks to recover a number of extensive narrative sources running throughout the Pentateuch that are largely parallel but originally independent from one another. These were combined with each other by a series of redactors. The inconsistencies in the Pentateuch are the evidence for the sources, while the breaks in coherence and cohesion point to the redactional activity of combining them.

These three compositional models, used as explanations of the literary complexity of the Pentateuch, are frequently found in combination with each other in the case of any particular scholar's treatment of Pentateuchal problems. This means that the number of explanatory models is greatly increased with some confusion as to how to classify the work of any particular scholar. Yet the three modes of compositional explanation will prove useful in looking at the work of individual scholars.

Notes

1   For an excellent extended discussion of the principles of source division see Carr, *Reading the Fractures of Genesis*.
2   See especially Fishbane, *Biblical Interpretation in Ancient Israel*.
3   An excellent discussion of these principles may be found in Berge, *Reading Sources in a Text*, Chapter 2.

3

A Survey of Historical-Critical Research
on the Pentateuch

Bibliography

(See also Chapter 1.)

Albright, W. F., *From the Stone Age to Christianity* (Baltimore: The Johns Hopkins University Press, 1940).

—— *Yahweh and the Gods of Canaan* (Garden City, NY: Doubleday, 1968).

Alt, A., 'The Origin of Israelite Laws' (1934), in *idem, Essays on Old Testament History and Religion* (Oxford: Basil Blackwell, 1966), pp. 79–132.

—— 'The God of the Fathers' (1929), in *idem, Essays*, pp. 1–66.

Cross, F. M., *Canaanite Myth and Hebrew Epic* (Cambridge, MA: Harvard University Press, 1973).

Eissfeldt, O., *The Old Testament, an Introduction* (trans. P. R. Ackroyd; New York: Harper & Row, 1965 [1964]).

Engnell, I., *A Rigid Scrutiny: Critical Essays on the Old Testament* (trans. John T. Willis; Nashville: Vanderbilt University Press, 1969).

Fohrer, G., *Introduction to the Old Testament* (trans. D. E. Green; Nashville: Abingdon Press, 1968 [1965]).

Gressmann, H., *Mose und seine Zeit* (FRLANT, 1; Göttingen: Vandenhoeck & Ruprecht, 1913).

Gunkel, H., *Genesis* (HKAT, 1.1; Göttingen: Vandenhoeck & Ruprecht, 3rd edn, 1910); ET *Genesis* (trans. M. E. Bittle; Macon, GA: Mercer University Press, 1997).

Kaufmann, Y., *The Religion of Israel: From its Beginnings to the Babylonian Exile* (trans. and abr. M. Greenberg; Chicago: University of Chicago Press, 1960).

Kirkpatrick, P. G., *The Old Testament and Folklore Study* (JSOTSup, 62; Sheffield: Sheffield Academic Press, 1988).

Mowinckel, S., *Erwägungen zur Pentateuch Quellenfrage* (Oslo: Universitetsforlaget, 1964).

Noth, M., *Überlieferungsgeschichtliche Studien* (Tübingen: Max Niemeyer, 2nd edn, 1957); pp. 1–110 were translated as *The Deuteronomistic History* (JSOTSup, 15; Sheffield: JSOT Press, 1981).

—— *Überlieferungsgeschichte des Pentateuch* (Stuttgart: W. Kohlhammer, 1948); ET *A History of Pentateuchal Traditions* (trans. B. W. Anderson; Englewood Cliffs, NJ: Prentice-Hall, 1972).

Perlitt, L., *Bundestheologie im Alten Testament* (Neukirchen-Vluyn: Neukirchener Verlag, 1969).

Pfeiffer, R. H., *Introduction to the Old Testament* (New York: Harper & Brothers, 1941).

Rad, G. von, *Das formgeschichtliche Problem des Hexateuchs* (BWANT, 4.26; Stuttgart: W. Kohlhammer, 1938); ET 'The Form-Critical Problem of the Hexateuch', *in idem, The Problem of the Hexateuch and Other Essays* (trans. E. W. T. Dicken; Edinburgh: Oliver & Boyd, 1966), pp. 1–78.

—— *Old Testament Theology* (trans. D. M. G. Stalker; 2 vols.; New York: Harper & Row, 1962).

Rogerson, J., *Old Testament Criticism in the Nineteenth Century: England and Germany* (London: SPCK, 1984).

Rudolph, W., *Der 'Elohist' von Exodus bis Joshua* (BZAW, 68; Berlin: W. de Gruyter, 1938).

Thompson, T. L., *The Historicity of the Patriarchal Narratives* (BZAW, 133; Berlin: W. de Gruyter, 1974).

Van Seters, J., *Abraham in History and Tradition* (New Haven: Yale University Press, 1975).

Volz, P., and W. Rudolph, *Der Elohist als Erzähler: Ein Irrweg der Pentateuchkritik?* (BZAW, 63; Berlin: W. de Gruyter, 1933).

Wahl, H., *Die Jakob Erzählungen* (BZAW, 258; Berlin: W. de Gruyter, 1997).

Wellhausen, J., *Prolegomena to the History of Ancient Israel* (Edinburgh: A. & C. Black, 1885).

Winnett, F. V., *The Mosaic Tradition* (Toronto: University of Toronto Press, 1949).

—— 'Reexamining the Foundations', *JBL* 84 (1965), pp. 1–19.

1. The rise of the Documentary Hypothesis to Wellhausen

There is little need for the purpose of this study-guide to deal in detail with the history of Pentateuchal research. That may be obtained from a number of recent publications.[1] I will merely outline those aspects of research in the nineteenth and twentieth centuries that are necessary as a prelude to understanding the current situation in Pentateuchal studies. By the nineteenth century, the rise of the scientific and historical methods of the seventeenth century and the Enlightenment of the eighteenth century had already firmly established the principle in academic circles that the Bible was to be subject to the same kind of critical scrutiny as that of other ancient works. Since the Mosaic authorship for most of the Pentateuch had been rejected, much of it was left anonymous, and this meant ascertaining the limits of any individual works within it and setting these works within their true historical and social framework. The analytic model most amenable to such a program of research was the documentary method, and various versions of the Documentary Hypothesis were in vogue. For the early documentarians of the eighteenth century the most important clue for distinguishing between sources or documents was the distinction between the use of Yahweh and Elohim as the designation for the deity. A refinement of this was the effort to distinguish between two Elohistic sources. This distinction between two Elohistic sources alongside a Yahwistic source was first observed in Genesis by Karl David Ilgen (*The Documents of the Jerusalem Temple Archives in their Original Form as a Contribution to the Correct Understanding of the History of its Religion and Politics*, 1798)[2] and later by Hermann Hupfeld (*The Sources of Genesis and the Manner of their Conflation*, 1853) and only subsequently extended to the rest of the Pentateuch. By the mid-nineteenth century, the Elohistic source that contained both narrative and law of a Priestly kind (later labeled P) was regarded as the earliest of the sources and the basic document for the rest, because it provided a clear chronological framework for the Pentateuch as a whole.

A major development in the Documentary Hypothesis was made by W. M. L. de Wette (*Contributions to Old Testament Introduction*, 2 vols., 1806–1807), who identified the 'book of the law' that was reported to have been discovered in the temple in the time of Josiah as Deuteronomy.[3] He drew from this the conclusion that it was a work that was written in the time of Josiah for the purpose of encouraging and legitimizing the reform program of the king and the Jerusalem temple priesthood. He also concluded that it was a source distinct from the rest of those in Genesis to Numbers and the latest of them. This firm dating of one of the sources (D) created a fixed point to which the other sources could then be related.

At the same time that most Pentateuchal scholars were proposing various modifications to the Documentary Hypothesis, there were a few attempts to give support to the other models of composition. Early advocates of a fragmentary approach, such as Alexander Geddes (*Critical Remarks on the Holy Scriptures . . . I. Containing Remarks on the Pentateuch*, 1800) and Johann Vater (*Commentary on the Pentateuch*, 3 vols., 1802–1805), proposed that the Pentateuch consisted of numerous independent units or fragments, some of which were of great antiquity, perhaps from the time of Moses, that were only brought together at a rather late stage. Geddes saw this time of collection as the reign of Solomon with the possibility of later expansions. Vater considered the Pentateuch as arising in the late monarchy. They accounted for the difference in the use of divine name as the result of traditions coming from different circles of tradents. The difference between these scholars and the documentarians should not be too sharply drawn, because a number of those who supported the model of parallel sources also identified a number of fragments or independent units behind their sources, especially in Genesis. This combination of fragments and documents, with varying emphasis from one scholar to another, played an important role in much of the subsequent debate on Pentateuchal problems.

The supplementary model that suggested the idea of a basic source to which other material was later added is associated with the names of J. J. Stähelin (*Critical Research concerning Genesis*, 1830) and Heinrich Ewald (*History of Israel*, vols. 1–2, 1843–1859). The latter gave Stähelin a favorable review of his work and then went on to develop an elaborate version of his own that had considerable impact on the discussion of the day. His view was that the base document was an Elohistic work (= P) that contained some older pieces, such as the Decalogue and the Covenant Code (Exod. 20–23). At a later period a Yahwistic writing that contained many more stories, especially of the patriarchs, was used by a redactor to fill out the Elohistic work. To this other pieces were also added. This work also included Joshua, hence, the term Hexateuch became a standard designation in place of

Pentateuch. Again, this approach of Ewald (who himself tended to change his mind a number of times) is not a radical departure from the Documentary Hypothesis, merely a difference in emphasis, and continued to be reflected in the later formulations of the documentarians, as we shall see.

Another major shift in the Documentary Hypothesis came about when a number of scholars, Edouard Reuss (1834),[4] Karl Graf (*The Historical Books of the Old Testament*, 1865) and Abraham Kuenen (*An Historico-Critical Inquiry into the Origin and Composition of the Pentateuch*, 1866), argued that the Priestly source was not the earliest but the latest source. It represented the reconstruction of the priestly cult in the time of the Second Temple in the Persian period and therefore subsequent to Deuteronomy. It was pointed out that there is little hint of the kind of religion represented in the P code of the Pentateuch within the pre-exilic prophets or the historical books of Joshua to 2 Kings. Only with Ezekiel does it begin to come to the fore, and it is especially prominent in works of the Persian and Hellenistic periods. Thus, the book of Chronicles, which parallels the books of Samuel and Kings, restores to his presentation of the monarchy the cultic religion of P that was missing from the earlier history. This redating of P became known as the Newer Documentary Hypothesis.

It was Kuenen in particular who gave to the Documentary Hypothesis its classical form of JE, D, P, the three main components. The JE component consisted of a ninth-century Yahwistic document and an eighth-century Elohistic document, both from North Israel, that were combined by a Judahite redactor at the end of the monarchy. This work was in turn combined with the D core by an exilic redactor (with its recapitulations of material in JE). P, which consisted of at least three levels, was put together in the time of Ezra and subsequently combined with JED by another redactor at the end of the fifth century, with later additions made down to the Hellenistic period. Kuenen's historical-critical work went hand in hand with his work on the history of Israelite religion. Thus, for him, JE reflected a strong prophetic influence prior to the reforms of Deuteronomy. P, on the other hand, was nowhere reflected in D, and in its earliest level, P[1] (= Holiness Code, Lev. 17–26), was close to the time of Ezekiel in the exile. Kuenen's work, written in Dutch, did not get very wide circulation and it was only through his influence upon Wellhausen that it made a major impact on biblical studies.

It was the great scholar Julius Wellhausen who took up this new position and supported it so brilliantly in his two works, *The Composition of the Hexateuch and the Historical Books of the Old Testament* (1889) and *Prolegomena to the History of Israel* (1883, with English version in 1885), that it became the classical statement of the Documentary Hypothesis. In it he retained the four sources of the Yahwist (J = Jahvist in German), Elohist (E), Deuteronomy (D) and the Priestly Writer (P). Wellhausen labeled P as Q for *quattuor* (four), standing for the source that contains four covenants from creation to Moses. Wellhausen often refrained from making any clear distinction between J and E and referred to them jointly as Jehovist (JE).

In *The Composition of the Hexateuch*, Wellhausen sets out his careful literary and exegetical studies in commentary form with results very similar to those of Kuenen. One concession to the older view, reflected in his teacher Ewald, was to retain the notion that the final redactor retained P as the basic document and framework for the whole to which the rest of the combined JED was accommodated. This meant that the literary reconstruction of P as the *Grundschrift* for the whole by the earlier scholars was not seriously reconsidered when it was placed at the end of the compositional process, a rather contradictory position that has persisted within the Documentary Hypothesis.

As with Kuenen and others of his day, Wellhausen's primary interest in the historical-critical reconstruction of the Pentateuch's sources was for the purpose of developing a history of Israelite religion, the subject of his *Prolegomena*. In this work he tried to show that the three major divisions, JE, D and P, reflected in both the laws and the narrative three major phases in the development of Israel's religion from a natural, spontaneous, family and local village form of worship in JE, through a reform to centralize and purify the cult in D, to a highly regulated, hierarchical and remote cultus in P. This whole scheme has been criticized as Hegelian, but such a characterization is overdrawn and hardly necessary.[5] The nineteenth century was greatly preoccupied with biological, social and cultural evolution and would remain so well into the twentieth century. There was great interest in the evolution of religion as a major aspect of human, cultural evolution, and Wellhausen's notions fitted the current models and patterns of the day. One of the leading scholars of the day in the history of religions was W. Robertson Smith, who was also an Old Testament scholar, and who published a series of lectures on *The Religion of the Semites* (1889). It was this scholar who was responsible for the translation and dissemination of Wellhausen's views in the English-speaking world.[6]

It is primarily in the milieu of the discussion of primitive religion as preserved in the vestiges of primitive societies, and efforts to find such vestiges in the Old Testament as well, that one must understand Wellhausen's views of primitive religion in JE. When Wellhausen, as a historian of religion, endeavored to place the religion of P or the reform of D in their historical contexts, he at least had the possibility of comparing this corpus with other datable biblical texts. That part of the argument has not changed in spite of what one might think of his general scheme of religious evolution. However, when he came to place the JE texts in their historical context he accepted the earlier view that they at least contained some ancient materials, vestiges of earlier times for which there would not be any datable biblical documents for comparison. It is at this point that he resorts to contemporary notions about primitive naturalistic religion and its fit with J.[7] E was viewed as more strongly influenced by the rise of prophetic religion and, therefore, closer in time to the eighth-century prophets. It is that assumption about the nature of Israelite religion in J that has largely governed the dating of the sources in the Documentary Hypothesis ever since.

It is not my purpose here to narrate the development of the Documentary Hypothesis in historical order, but instead to identify a series of particular issues and problems that arose within source criticism. Following the publication of Wellhausen's works, there was a broad acceptance of the Documentary Hypothesis and the method of source criticism as applied to the Pentateuch, and it remained for various scholars to put forward their refinements and modifications within the context of this critical method. These can be dealt with by looking at the discussions surrounding each of the individual sources.

2. The problems of the sources

a. The unity, nature and extent of J

It was not long before scholars began to suggest that within J there were two sources independent from each other and to distinguish them as J[1] and J[2] or by using similar rubrics. This fifth source could also be given a quite new name to signify some distinctive aspect or origin, such as Otto Eissfeldt's L for lay source,[8] Georg Fohrer's N for nomadic source,[9] or Robert Pfeiffer's S for Seir or Edomite source.[10] Most of these were rather similar and focused heavily upon the distinctive characteristic of the source in Genesis. Eissfeldt's L and Fohrer's N were very similar in content and extended to Numbers and beyond, while Pfeiffer's S was rather limited to special material related to Edom in Genesis.

The nature and extent of J were subjects of much debate. On the one hand, one could consider J as merely a compiler of old traditions[11] or the person who set down in written form a rather fixed Pentateuchal tradition with little addition,[12] which was therefore limited to the Tetrateuch. On the other hand, Gerhard von Rad[13] argued for J as a historian whose work extended to include a basic stratum of Joshua as well. For von Rad J was also a theologian of some sophistication and he associated him with the time of the 'Solomonic Enlightenment', as one who gave both historical and theological legitimation to the new state created by David and consolidated by Solomon. This view stood in rather marked contrast to the notions about a primitive J religion in Wellhausen, but the contradition was not viewed as a problem for the Documentary Hypothesis as such and von Rad strongly supported it. There was, in fact, an increasing tendency to date J to the early monarchy and to see it as a historical work that was not restricted to the Pentateuch or even to the Hexateuch but extended through Samuel into Kings to the time of the writer in the early monarchy.[14]

b. Was there an E document?

Some of the same issues that we noted concerning J also apply to E, that is, whether the source should be divided into two or more sources and whether the source extends beyond the Pentateuch into the later historical books. However, a more important issue that arose was whether there was sufficient evidence to justify the positing of a separate E source at all. Many scholars freely acknowledged that of all the sources it was the most fragmentary, that it hardly began before the patriarchal narratives and that it was difficult to trace in much of Exodus and Numbers. A rather full-scale attack on the separate existence of E was made by Paul Volz and Wilhelm Rudolph.[15] Volz argued that within Genesis 15–36 there is only one major narrative work by J, who made use of both Elohim and Yahweh in his work. Thus, texts that had previously been split between two sources (e.g. Gen. 22; 27; 28.10-22) should be attributed to J. In the cases where there are parallel texts, such as those in chs. 20 and 21.8-21, attributed by others to E, these were additions included in a later edition. Similarly, Rudolph argued that the Joseph story in Genesis 37, 39–50 could not be divided into two parallel versions on the basis of the designation for deity.[16] It is best to consider the parallel elements as interpolations. This perspective received support from a number of scholars, such as Sigmund Mowinckel[17] and F. V. Winnett.[18] Even when scholars were not yet prepared to give up the notion of a separate E source, they were willing to concede that it was not present in a number of texts and more fragmentary than previously thought. The E document still has its advocates, but even among documentarians there is considerable difference of opinion as to the usefulness of the designation.

c. The nature and unity of P and its relationship to D

Even before Wellhausen the unity of P had been questioned but in a way that was different from J as discussed above. If there were different strata within P they were still recognized as belonging to the same Priestly school. Thus, early on, the block of legislation in Leviticus 17–26, called the Holiness Code because of its emphasis on the people's 'holiness', was recognized as a distinct, early P corpus of laws. In addition to this, there was some carry-over from the pre-Wellhausen era, when P was viewed as the *Grundschrift* of the Pentateuch and the laws as secondary, such that scholars still continued to view P as divided between Pg and Ps, signifying the basic narrative strand and the legal supplement respectively. Of those who accept this division, there is still a difference of opinion as to what belongs to Pg and what belongs to Ps, because at a number of points the priestly legal material is closely connected to the narrative. Other scholars dispute that there is any division within P, with the possible exception of some late additional material. This dispute about the unity of P also leads to the discussion of the nature of the basic P work. Is it a historical work similar to that of J or a legal corpus with a brief historical prologue? Is it limited to the Tetrateuch or does it extend into Joshua and the settlement of the land?

Another major area of concern is the relationship of P to the other sources. Volz[19] raised the question of whether P ought to be considered as an independent source and not simply a supplement to J. To admit this would be to dissolve the Documentary Hypothesis and few were willing to follow him in this. (To this issue we will return below.) The other major issue of the relationship of P to D was raised from two different directions: the Scandinavians and the Jewish/Israeli scholars. The Uppsala school, under the leadership of Ivan Engnell,[20] rejected the European 'bookish' mentality of the Documentary Hypothesis in favor of a notion that the Pentateuch had been preserved in two circles of oral tradition until the exilic period, at which time they had been put into written form, the Tetrateuch by a Priestly school of editors and Deuteronomy by the Deuteronomists.[21] They also dated the P material as earlier than D.

The Jewish/Israeli scholars were strongly inclined to reject Wellhausen's Documentary Hypothesis because it implied a rather derogatory view of Second Temple Judaism, which was considered a decline from the ethical monotheism of eighth-century prophetic religion. One Israeli scholar, Y. Kaufmann,[22] although accepting the literary principles of the Documentary Hypothesis, rejected Wellhausen's understanding of Judaism as biased by Protestant liberalism and proposed the view that P is pre-exilic and much older than D. In this he was followed by a number of other Israeli and American Jewish scholars.[23] However, the effort to find a substantial body of ancient Priestly tradition, especially within the legal corpus, seems as confessionally biased as the position that it condemns.

Within the P corpus the Holiness Code has been viewed by the classical Documentary Hypothesis as the earliest part of this legal corpus. On the one hand, it stands in close proximity to Ezekiel; on the other hand, it shows close similarity in some of its laws and in its closing parenesis in Leviticus 26 to Deuteronomy. It is therefore regarded as exilic, with the rest of the P corpus as postexilic. However, those who would date P earlier than D consider the Holiness Code as the latest part of P for the same reasons.

d. Deuteronomy and the Deuteronomistic history

A major new development in the study of Deuteronomy came about with the publication of Martin Noth's *Traditio-historical Studies* of 1943. This suggested that Deuteronomy did not develop as part of the Pentateuchal tradition, but as an independent corpus of laws with parenesis that was soon incorporated into a history that extended from Deuteronomy to 2 Kings. This historical work was strongly influenced by the ideology and language of Deuteronomy and was given the name of Deuteronomistic History (DtrH). In Noth's view, the study of the Pentateuchal tradition should be restricted to the Tetrateuch with the eventual separation of Deuteronomy from the history and its place in the Law as a very late development.

This position had some similarity to the Uppsala school, which also considered the development of the Tetrateuch and Deuteronomy as distinct. Nevertheless, in contrast to the Uppsala school, Noth retained the other elements of the Documentary Hypothesis, using the same division of sources, J, E and P, for the Tetrateuch and the same relative order and dating. There were those, however, like G. von Rad, who questioned this thesis on the grounds that the earliest pre-D sources, with its scheme of divine promises of land and their fulfillment in the conquest, presuppose a continuation into Joshua and, therefore, a Hexateuch. One could always posit a lost J account of the conquest and settlement of the land west of the Jordan, but that does not offer a very satisfactory solution. There is, in Num. 21.21-35, a report of the conquest of the eastern Transjordan region and in Numbers 32 a distribution of this land to the eastern tribes, so why not a similar account for the west? If one accepts, as many have, Noth's thesis of a DtrH that includes Deuteronomy, then some explanation for the relationship of the Tetrateuch to this corpus is essential to the Pentateuchal problem as a whole.

e. The Documentary Hypothesis and the problem of redactors

The proliferation of sources by the splitting up of J, E and P into multiple strata and the documentarian conviction that the sources are independent of each other as separate literary works creates the need for multiple 'redactors'. These are the literary agents responsible for the combination of sources in such a way that the wording of the original sources remained intact. However, since some of the sources are found to contain serious gaps, and since E is admittedly very fragmentary, it is necessary to view the redactor as sometimes including parallel versions, while at other times leaving one version out in preference to another. Thus, it is the redactors who are responsible for any lack of unity, coherence and cohesion in the extant sources and for permitting contradictions to stand without exercising their editorial skills to get rid of them.

Furthermore, since the broad acceptance of Noth's theory of a Deuteronomistic corpus (Deuteronomy–2 Kings) that was distinct from the Tetrateuch, the problem has arisen of how to account for those Deuteronomistic elements that are still observed to be present in the Tetrateuch. The solution is to identify one or more Deuteronomistic redactors of the Tetrateuch, probably also responsible for the combination of JE(P) with D.[24]

In this case, however, the redactor's own additions begin to rival those of the other sources. In a similar fashion one discovers in the recent literature a P redactor (Rp) who also supplements the older corpus 'in the style of P'.

The greatest weakness of the Documentary Hypothesis is its lack of clarity about the literary role and function of the 'redactor' and how one can identify redactional activity in a text. The redactor seems merely to serve the literary critic as a *deus ex machina*, solving problems that arise in the Documentary Hypothesis that cannot be explained any other way. The supplementation model of composition does not need redactors for its literary explanation of literary development so that it is encumbent upon the documentarians to demonstrate that the theory of multiple redactors is a more cogent and economic way of explaining the same literary process.

3. The rise of form-criticism and the tradition-history of the Pentateuch

Before considering form-criticism and tradition-history as methods of literary analysis, one must consider the background of this discussion within the larger context of *Religionswissenschaft* of the late nineteenth and early twentieth centuries.[25] There were two important, and at times conflicting, tendencies within the study of the history of religions. The one was to look for vestiges of early religious rituals and beliefs among the remnant of 'primitive peoples', and among the Semitic peoples this was considered to be the nomads.[26] It was widely believed that the nomadic way of life preceded and evolved into the sedentary and from there into urban life and statehood. This same form of evolution was generally viewed as relevant to the evolution of Israel and its religion.[27]

The other approach to religious origins was to focus on the rise of major centers of civilization, such as those in the Tigris-Euphrates basin and to view this civilization as having established, from hoary antiquity, a basic and pervasive system or pattern of religious beliefs and rituals. This theory of origins went under the rubric of 'Pan-Babylonianism'.[28] From this major center there flowed a general diffusion of the pattern to the more peripheral regions, such as the Levantine coast, and to the later inhabitants of this region, such as the Israelites. Once scholars had uncovered the basic pattern of belief, the myth and its corresponding ritual, it was not difficult to piece together from the Old Testament the vestiges and clues to the same basic pattern of myth and ritual.[29]

Alongside this interest in the origins of religion was the fascination for the origins and distinctive traditions of the various European states, the basis of the scholars' own identity.[30] While it was recognized that a major component of European civilization was based upon the diffusion of classical civilization through the Roman conquest and then through Christianity, the distinctiveness of the individual peoples and nations was preserved in their folk traditions. With the rise of modernity these were under threat so that there was great concern to recover these traditions, many existing only in oral form, and to preserve them for posterity. The anthropological study of the basic forms of oral tradition (myths, legends, folktales, and their social and ritualistic settings) began to flourish at the beginning of the twentieth century.

Hermann Gunkel, a student of Wellhausen who was schooled in the method of the Documentary Hypothesis, broke new ground in the study of the Pentateuch in two respects.[31]

1. He was a founding member and the leader of a new movement among biblical scholars and other theologians known as the 'history of religions school', whose primary interest was to trace the origins of Judaism and Christianity back through the religion of ancient Israel and then back to its earliest foundations. With the recovery of many ancient texts from Babylon and the decipherment of the cuneiform script and the Sumerian and Akkadian languages in which they were written, the Babylonian myths of creation and the flood gave support to the notion of cultural and religious diffusion from Babylon to ancient Israel and ultimately to Christianity.[32] Gunkel's earliest work, *Chaos and Creation in Primeval Time and the End of Time* (1895), was a study of the notions of final judgment in Christian apocalyptic and its origins through ancient Israel back to the Babylonian myth of creation. Within the history-of-religions school great interest was taken in ancient Near Eastern texts and their biblical parallels, something that was completely lacking in Wellhausen's approach to the Old Testament.[33]

2. At the same time Gunkel was also interested in the vestiges of Israel's primitive past, before its rise as a state, and these he found in the 'simple forms' of Genesis, the small units of myth, legends (German: *Sagen*[34]), and folktales.[35] Gunkel believed that each individual unit originally had a life of its own before it became part of a source in the Pentateuch, similar to the fragmentary hypothesis. However, this approach was only applied to the earliest stage of Pentateuchal growth, when these units were handed down by oral tradition from the time of Israel's nomadism or earliest transition to a settled culture. This was its particular 'setting in life' (*Sitz im Leben*), from which it was detached when it became part of a written collection in a particular 'source', such as J or E.[36]

This shift by Gunkel had several important consequences for the study of the Pentateuch. For Wellhausen, the evolution of Israelite religion was to be found in a comparison of the written sources from the ninth or early eighth centuries onwards. For Gunkel this was much too late. His interest was in the pre-state development of Israel, the evidence for which he saw in the traditions embedded in the small forms, particularly the Pentateuchal legends. One could unfold the history of these traditions along with the evolution of the forms from simple legends to more elaborate ones, to extended hero-legends and finally to the rise of historiography, which coincided with the rise of the state. This method of tradition-history tended at the same time to push back the date of the earliest source, J, to the time of the rise of the state in the tenth century and to view it as the culmination of a long earlier evolution and something much more sophisticated than the mere beginning of Israelite religion in Wellhausen's sense.

Gunkel's principal work on the Pentateuch was his commentary on *Genesis*, published in 1901, which went through many editions. In Genesis there are many short stories that have little connection with each other. They usually center on an ancestor in a remote time. These are not history, an account of political events within a fixed chronology, but have all the marks of legend (*Sagen*). One common type of legend in Genesis that is found among many 'primitives' is etiology. An etiology is an explanation, in story form, of the origin or cause of something. It may explain the sacredness of a particular place (e.g. Bethel in the story of Jacob's dream), a striking geological formation (e.g. the Dead Sea and salt pillars in the Sodom and Gomorrah story), the origin of tribes and peoples (e.g. Ishmael, the father of the Arabs), or the origin of languages (e.g. the Tower of Babel story). Since these stories have parallels in the folklore of other peoples, Gunkel argued that in order to understand the biblical material one must grasp the nature of folklore, the role it plays in primitive, pre-literate societies, and how it is transmitted by oral tradition.

In addition to Gunkel, Hugo Gressmann and Albrecht Alt also took up his form-critical and traditio-historical methods and applied them to the Pentateuch. Gressmann, in *Moses and his Time* (1913), attempted to explore the traditions about Moses in the legends that lay behind J and E in a way similar to Gunkel's treatment of Genesis. Alt, in 'The Origin of Israelite Laws' (1934),[37] was concerned to uncover the oldest forms of Hebrew law, which he saw as a fusion of nomadic traditions of the pre-state period with the more advanced civil codes of the settled Canaanites. This approach combined notions about primitive nomadic origins and what was distinctive in Israelite law with the concept of the diffusion of the advanced system of Babylonian law to the pre-Israelite Canaanites and from them to Israel. Alt, in 'The God of the Fathers' (1929),[38] also developed a thesis about the patriarchal religion in which the god of the forefather is a nomadic form of religion belonging to the earliest tribes of Israel, and, as they began to settle down, they identified the nomadic god with the high god El of the Canaanite sedentary communities. It was this thesis in particular that laid the foundation for the future discussion of the tradition-history of the patriarchs.

4. Tradition-history: Gerhard von Rad and Martin Noth

Tradition-history may refer either to the development of the *content* of a tradition through various stages over time or to the *process* of transmission from the past. Gunkel, Gressmann and Alt believed that each small unit or individual story of the patriarchs or the Moses tradition was connected with a particular locality, such as the sanctuary at Bethel or the region of Kadesh, and was the special preserve of a particular tribe or clan. Each story or piece of tradition was handed down *orally* from one generation to another during their primitive period of existence. As the tribes or clans of Israel came together to form larger political entities—a twelve-tribe league in the time of the judges or the state of the United Monarchy—the individual traditions of the various tribes merged to become the possession of the entire nation. Two students of Alt, Gerhard von Rad and Martin Noth, dominated the discussion of the tradition-history of the

Pentateuch from the time of World War II onwards, and it is hard to overestimate their influence.

Von Rad's concern in his study 'The Form-Critical Problem of the Hexateuch' (1938) was to try to explain why the Pentateuch took the particular form it did, that is, why the units of tradition were not put together in a random collection but in the historical sequence as we now have it. This could not be accidental, and one may view von Rad as critical of Gunkel's notion that the sources J and E represented only schools of storytellers. Von Rad found his answer to the form-critical problem in a form of liturgy that made use of a historical summary as a *credo*. The best example is Deut. 26.5-9, which tells of the forefather (Jacob?) who descended into Egypt with his family and sojourned there. The Egyptians treated them harshly so that they appealed to Yahweh and he rescued them, led them through the desert and brought them into the promised land. This was the Hexateuch (Genesis to Joshua) in miniature. Von Rad found a number of other examples of this credo form in the Bible and concluded that early in Israel's history religious festivals were used to celebrate the 'saving acts' of Yahweh that were recited in the credos. In time the historical credo (salvation-history) formed the basis for the expanded history of the J source (adding the account of creation and the life of the patriarchs). Von Rad further noted that the earliest form of the creeds made no mention of Sinai and the giving of the law, but that the deliverance from Egypt was followed directly by conquest and settlement of the land. He concluded, therefore, that the tradition of the giving of the law was celebrated in a separate festival and was combined with the exodus-conquest theme only at a later stage. In the same way, the patriarchal traditions were added as a new theme at the beginning of the saving events. For von Rad, all of this took place before J wrote the first version of the Hexateuch in the time of Solomon.

Noth, in *Überlieferungsgeschichte des Pentateuch* (1948; ET *A History of Pentateuchal Traditions*, 1972), developed this approach of von Rad a little differently. He suggested that the Pentateuch consists of five originally separate blocks of tradition: (1) exodus out of Egypt, (2) entrance into the land of Canaan, (3) promise to the patriarchs, (4) guidance in the wilderness, and (5) Sinai. (In this way von Rad's three blocks become five.) This combination of traditions took place in the time of the Judges and the twelve-tribe league before any written version was made. Writers of the Pentateuch like J were collectors and recorders of the traditions handed down to them. Each of these traditions had its own complex development. For example, Noth suggests that the stories of Abraham, Isaac and Jacob originally belonged to separate regions: Jacob traditions in the north and central Palestine (Shechem and Bethel), the Abraham ones in the Judean hill country of Hebron, and the Isaac stories in the south around Beersheba. When all these groups came together to form a tribal league, the separate traditions were combined by a genealogical scheme. Abraham became the father of Isaac, who became the father of Jacob. Similar developments apply to the other major blocks of the Pentateuchal traditions. This explanation of how the individual stories eventually came together to become part of one long written composition epitomizes the method of tradition-history.

Noth's views of the Pentateuch's (Tetrateuch's) development led to considerable differences with von Rad over the nature of the sources, particularly J. For Noth, the essential blocks of Pentateuchal tradition, with the exception of the primeval history in Genesis 1–11, had come together in a *Grundlage* (G), whether in written or oral form is not clear, prior to the first source J. It is this G that accounts for the similarity of both J and E. It also means that, as an author, J added little of his own except the non-P material in the primeval history; thus, he merits little special attention in Noth apart from a discussion of source division that follows closely that of Wellhausen. Von Rad, by contrast, treats J as a historian and theologian and a creative genius who left a major imprint upon the traditions that he took up.

5. A critique of form-criticism: Oral tradition

While Gunkel's treatment of the stories of Genesis was very influential in suggesting that behind the writers of the Pentateuch was a large body of folk tradition, the exact form and character of that folk tradition continues to be discussed. Gunkel, in the third edition of his *Genesis* commentary (1910), endeavored to use a set of 'epic laws of folk narrative' as enunciated by Axil Olrik to identify the oral character of the Genesis stories.[39] However, Gunkel's application of these laws was not very thorough and many scholars since Gunkel have emphasized the difficulty in distinguishing too sharply between oral forms of narrative and the earliest forms of written compositions.[40] Furthermore, the idea of restricting oral tradition and folklore to the pre-state period is also problematic. Even by the end of the monarchy, the level of literacy was not very high, so that oral tradition persisted alongside a very restricted literacy throughout the biblical period.[41] Whether or not there are ways of identifying orality behind any of the narratives in the Pentateuch is still a matter of debate.[42]

For form and tradition critics from Gunkel to Noth, etiology was a standard way of recognizing early forms of tradition. But does etiology provide an adequate criterion for identifying the legends (*Sagen*) and their social setting in primitive Israelite society? A number of scholars have found fault with this evaluation of etiology in biblical narrative.[43] In light of this critique Claus Westermann[44] has put forward the notion that the stories of the patriarchs of Genesis are more akin to Icelandic 'family sagas' than what the Germans mean by *Sagen*. However, the similarities are superficial and the question of whether these medieval literary compositions have any basis in oral tradition is itself a matter of controversy.[45] The form-critical study of the small units of Genesis in the Gunkel tradition has not succeeded in arriving at a broadly accepted classification of the genres of Genesis nor in uncovering a primitive social setting for these units within the history of Israelite culture.

6. A critique of the tradition-history method

Tracing the development of a theme or tradition from its oral origins to its earliest fixed written form is fine in *principle*, but it becomes too speculative in *practice*. The problem with reconstructing the oral tradition behind the written text is that one can only guess at its content. There is no control over the original shape of the tradition and its development through various stages is conjectural. Modern study of oral tradition involves folklorists with tape recorders going to places and cultures where oral tradition is alive in order to collect their stories, songs and other lore. When this has been done over a period of years or among related peoples one can talk about the history or transformation of certain traditions based upon actual transcribed records. But we do not have the oral stage of the biblical tradition so no two scholars ever propose the same tradition-history for the stories of the Pentateuch.[46]

The traditio-historical schemes of von Rad and Noth, discussed above, are not limited to individual units of tradition but go on to propose reconstructions for the development of the Pentateuch (Hexateuch) as a whole. These larger schemes, however, have also come in for much criticism. The problem with von Rad's thesis is that all his examples of 'little credos' occur in Deuteronomy or literary material influenced by Deuteronomy, which is late monarchic or exilic in date, and not at the beginning of Israelite history. There is no evidence that they were ever part of a primitive liturgy. Consequently, his proposal can no longer be used to explain how a body of seemingly old and disparate traditions came together in the form of a history as we have it in J, at the very beginning of Israel's unified existence as a state. Von Rad seems to have been too strongly influenced by the analogy of early Christian confessional creeds as a model (e.g. the Apostles' Creed).

Noth's theory of Pentateuchal growth depends very much on his ideas about a pre-monarchical twelve-tribe league having a certain religious structure in which the Pentateuchal confessional themes played an important role similar to von Rad's credo. But lately there has been much criticism of his notions of such a sacred twelve-tribe league, based on Greek analogies, and few scholars now support this position.[47] There is little evidence for such a league in the book of Judges, which at any rate is a late composition, so there is no contemporary information about such a pre-state society. There is also little agreement on whether the blocks of tradition Noth has identified are so distinct from each other and on how they came together.

In actuality little can be done with the oral level of the material, except to recognize that there are, in the stories of the Pentateuch, certain folkloristic features that may reflect the fact that popular stories about early times were in circulation in ancient Israel. The basic weakness with both von Rad and Noth is that they restricted the use of oral tradition to the earliest period of Israel's history, but Israel and Judah continued to be predominantly oral throughout its history to the end of the monarchy and beyond. We may therefore assume that the biblical writers could draw upon a body of oral tradition throughout this time period. Nevertheless, our primary concern is an analysis of the *written* text.

7. The Pentateuch and the Albright school

What we have been describing above is the development of biblical studies, primarily in Germany, with its impact on the rest of Europe and America, although with a certain lag and breakdown in communication during World War II and its aftermath. At this same time, in the mid-twentieth century there was a movement in biblical studies in America that began to rival and counterbalance German biblical scholarship with a quite different perspective. The impetus for this new direction was the archaeological recovery of large quantities of cuneiform texts from the ancient sites of Mari, Ugarit, Nuzi, Boghazkoy, and many other places. All of this was regarded as providing a historical context into which the patriarchal stories of Genesis could be fitted, giving some degree of historicity to the figures in these stories and providing confirmation for the antiquity of the traditions in the early to mid-second millennium BCE. In a similar fashion, the historical texts from Egypt for the time of the Egyptian empire in the 18th and 19th Dynasties were being exploited to recover the historical background for the Israelite sojourn and exodus from Egypt.

While a number of major figures in American biblical and Near Eastern studies could be mentioned, the leading personage was undoubtedly that of W. F. Albright[48] and the school or movement that he created. Like the German scholars mentioned above, the Albright school also emphasized the importance of cultural diffusion from Mesopotamia and the 'semi-nomadic' character of the early Israelites represented by the patriarchs. But for the American scholars the cultural influence was much more direct because they believed that the patriarchs actually came from Mesopotamia, bringing the eastern heritage with them. At the same time, they were semi-nomads who were not so different in religious beliefs and cultural practices from the settled culture of Mesopotamia; like the semi-nomads of Mari, they were related to the 'Amorites' who dominated the urban centers of the whole fertile crescent. It was the texts of these urban centers that provided abundant parallels to the stories of the patriarchs. Thus the god of the fathers among the patriarchs was not distinct from, but identical with, the high god El of the urban population in Canaan.

It is important to understand the relationship of the Albright school to German biblical scholarship. Albright and his students largely accepted the literary method of the Documentary Hypothesis, while at the same time rejecting Wellhausen's notions about Israel's religious evolution as unduly influenced by Hegelian philosophy and Wellhausen's skepticism that there was any history in the Pentateuch. Albright answered the form-critical question of the Pentateuch in a way quite different from Gunkel by proposing that behind the early sources of J (tenth century) and E (ninth century) were national epics similar to the great epics of Babylon and Ugarit. Indeed, for Albright in his later work,[49] and particularly for Frank M. Cross,[50] the emphasis came to rest more and more on the Ugaritic (= Canaanite) myths and epic poems as the most important sources for understanding the evolution of Israelite religion.

From the viewpoint of form-criticism the genre of 'epic' could explain how the traditions could be transmitted in a relatively fixed form by epic poems, similar to those of Homer, over long periods of time and in oral form, as well as accounting for the whole extent of the Pentateuchal themes from creation to the conquest of the land. Albright adopted an old theory of nineteenth-century classical scholars that early prose narratives composed by 'logographers' were always preceded by their poetic epic counterparts, and he applied this to the sources J and E. He even pointed to bits of ancient poetry that still remained in the Pentateuch as remnants of this poetic epic tradition. The notion of J and E as prose epic sources, therefore, became a dogma within the Albright school and the whole German form-critical and traditio-historical discussion was simply dismissed with little debate.[51]

Cross and his students carried this thesis about epic sources a step further. The classical scholars Millman Perry and Albert Lord had developed a system of identifying certain features of formulaic language and their use in epic by studying modern oral poems among the Serbo-Croatian peoples of the Balkans and then applying these observations to the Homeric poems. Their intent was to establish that the Homeric poems had these same qualities of formulaic language and therefore belonged to a similar tradition of oral poetic composition. Cross and his students applied this same method of identifying formulaic language in the Pentateuch, especially Genesis, in order to confirm their belief that the Pentateuchal tradition rested upon an oral epic base.[52]

The tradition-history of the Albright school, especially as reflected in Cross and the Harvard school, was altogether different from the approach of Noth and von Rad. Cross adopted from the myth-ritual school of the UK and Scandinavia the notion that there was a mythological *pattern* common to Israel's Near Eastern environment that constituted the basic structure for its religion, whether in the Pentateuch, the Prophets or the Psalms. While the myth-ritual school emphasized the Babylonian center of this cultural influence, Cross was more concerned with the derivative Canaanite one that can be discerned most clearly in the Ugaritic myths. Thus the title of his book: *Canaanite Myth and Hebrew Epic*. Furthermore, Cross rejected the form-critical approach of small units of tradition with separate *Sitz im Leben* developing into a series of separate confessional blocks (Noth) in favor of myth-ritual's notion of a comprehensive 'pattern' and the tradition's *Sitz im Kultleben*. Briefly stated, this mythic pattern consists of the weather and warrior god Baal, who appears in theophany of the storm and defeats his enemies; whereupon he ascends his mountain dwelling to be enthroned and take up his abode in his new temple on Mount Saphon. Cross believes that the pattern became the basis of Israelite religion in a special historicized transformation at the beginning of Israel's history as a people. Cross accepted from Albright the conviction that the Pentateuchal tradition actually reflects historical events of the exodus from Egypt, the Sinai theophany and covenant-making at the sacred mountain, and the conquest. These events were understood and interpreted by the mythological pattern to form a new symbiosis. However, the pattern, once established, becomes frozen and therefore applies both to the earliest poetry and to the latest apocalyptic.

In a manner similar to von Rad and Noth, Cross believes that the great saving events were celebrated and remembered in early Israelite cult liturgies of covenant renewal and in the context of the sacred tribal league of the pre-state period. For Cross, however, this set of events (exodus, Sinai/covenant, conquest) represents the actual sequence of historical events and not merely a combination of separate traditions. The interpretation of these events as directed and controlled by Yahweh rests entirely upon the pattern of the god as divine warrior.

8. A critique of the Albright school

While there were a few dissenting voices raised against the mania for finding second millennium parallels to the patriarchal stories and the early dating of these traditions, the full-scale attack came from Thomas L. Thompson (*The Historicity of the Patriarchal Narratives*, 1974) and John Van Seters (*Abraham in History and Tradition*, 1975), that called into question the whole range of such parallels for the patriarchal stories of Genesis. In the case of similarities in social customs, sometimes the cuneiform texts were misconstrued to make them seem parallel with the biblical texts. In other cases, the biblical texts were interpreted in a very forced fashion to create the desired parallel. Thus, in one of Albright's most celebrated examples,[53] Abraham is represented as a great donkey caravaneer, trading between Mesopotamia and Egypt, when there is scarcely anything in Genesis that would suggest such a picture of the patriarch's life. In many cases where examples of parallels in customs and place names could be demonstrated between second millennium texts and the biblical account, these parallels were just as valid for the first millennium. Furthermore, there are features within the patriarchal stories that only make sense within the context of the first millennium and not the second millennium BCE.

The result of this critique of the Albright school was the abandonment by most scholars of any attempt to date the patriarchal narratives early in this way and to concede that the stories about them are much later in time than previously held. At the same time, as a result of continued archaeological activity, serious questions were raised about the historicity of the exodus and conquest narratives such that radically new proposals for the origins and early history of Israel were presented in the histories. This is not the place to review all of the suggestions and the vigorous debate that followed and still continues. What is important is that all of this discussion produced a major shift away from the search for the historical background and context of the traditions within the political events of the second millennium to a quite different set of literary issues.

While the Albright school has largely conceded to the validity of the historical critique, it has continued to advocate through Cross and the Harvard school many of the other dogmas outlined above. In particular, Cross took over and continued to support Albright's notion of a national epic behind the prose 'epic sources' J and E, together with the early dating of most of the Pentateuchal poetry. However, the idea that an epic poem or series of epic poems lies behind the sources J and E is speculation for which there is no support. The analogy to classical sources that Albright used has long been rejected in classical studies.[54] Likewise, the early dating of poetry in the Pentateuch is strongly disputed and cannot be used as evidence for an original epic poem. While there are Mesopotamian epic poems that deal with the themes of creation and the flood, there are no Near Eastern epic poems that present the national origins of any peoples comparable to that of the J source in the Pentateuch.

Furthermore, the efforts of the Harvard school to use the methods of Perry and Lord to find evidence for oral epic poetry behind the Pentateuch are also problematic on two accounts.[55] First, the method has encountered some criticism within classical studies itself as not entirely reliable as a gauge of orality in a particular composition.[56] Secondly, the presence of formulaic language in a wide range of biblical texts as well as various literary genres of the ancient Near East make it a poor indicator both of orality in general and of epic forms in particular. One may reasonably conclude from this that the Albright school has not answered the form-critical question of the Pentateuch.

As indicated above, Cross combined his commitment to the positions of the Albright school with his adoption of the myth-ritual school's explanation of religious origins and a pervasive Near Eastern/Canaanite patternism. However, the demise of the myth-ritual school in all but the most qualified form makes Cross's 'patternism' problematic.[57] Furthermore, the critique by L. Perlitt[58] (1969) and many others of any early covenant ritual or theology and the demise of von Rad's liturgical credo and Noth's sacred tribal league with its confessional base leave Cross's scheme in chaos.

It may be helpful to illustrate this critique of Cross by looking at his treatment of a particular example, namely his approach to the exodus-Sinai tradition, especially as it is found in Exodus 14–15 and 19–24.[59] For Cross, the sources for the present form of the tradition are twofold: (1) the Canaanite myth of the Divine Warrior who overcomes his enemy, the sea, and who marches to his abode on the sacred mountain to take up his kingship as manifest through the theophany, and (2) the Hebrew memory of the saving events in historical time. The Canaanite mythological pattern Cross derives from a few disconnected fragments of Ugaritic texts having to do with Baal's conflict with Prince Yam (Sea), a separate reference to his abode on Mount Saphon and various isolated references to storm theophany in connection with his attributes as rain god. To these are added numerous biblical texts from Psalms and Prophets that are thought to reflect Canaanite mythology, out of which is then constructed the mythological pattern. The whole scheme is completely circular and reminiscent of the myth-ritual school's patterns of divine kingship, cosmic battle, annual enthronement of the god.

Cross regards the oldest witness to the exodus event to be the Song of the Sea (Exod. 15), which reveals the power of the mythic pattern in shaping the historical memories,[60] that is, the cosmic battle of Baal/Yahweh against the sea. Although the J version in Exodus 14 is later, it is still quite early and more nearly reflects the historical epic tradition; therefore, it is less mythological. The correlation between the sea event and Cross's mythic pattern is suspect for many reasons:

1. The early dating of the Song of the Sea is strongly disputed. In a recent monograph it is shown to be a very late and highly eclectic composition.[61]
2. The psalms that mention the sea event are dated by Cross as early but by most other specialists as late.
3. The earliest prophetic reference to the sea event is Second Isaiah and it is likely that he is responsible for making the cosmic connection with the sea monster.
4. There is no sea event mentioned in Dtn/Dtr, only in very late additions to Dtn and DtrH (Josh. 24 is not early as Cross suggests).
5. J does not represent the sea event in any way that resembles Yahweh's victory over the sea, only victory over the Egyptians. It is the late source P that introduces the splitting of the sea motif under the influence of Second Isaiah. All such 'cosmic' language is very late in its association with the sea event.
6. If there are any non-biblical parallels to the sea event in J it is in connection with holy war, and this in turn points to Mesopotamian parallels, especially the Neo-Assyrian royal inscriptions. There is no holy war ideology, in which a god fights against an enemy on behalf of his people, in Ugaritic texts or any other 'Canaanite' material.

Cross's attempt to impose his Canaanite mythic pattern upon the Sinai/Horeb tradition is equally problematic. It is true that the Ugaritic texts associate Baal with storm phenomena, especially his thundering voice and lightning bolts and their effects on nature. Cross therefore wants to restrict all theophanic elements in the

Sinai episode to storm phenomena in order to fit his pattern. But there are others, such as fire and smoke, that do not fit his pattern. Yet these and all the storm and volcanic features of the story are well attested in Mesopotamian texts that Cross easily brushes aside. Outside the Pentateuch, the only early poetic texts that mention theophany in connection with Sinai speak of Yahweh *coming from* a region in Edom/Seir and do not consider the theophany as associated with a particular mountain as the deity's abode. In recent studies of Deuteronomy, it would appear that both Horeb theophany units in Deuteronomy 4–5 belong to a rather late development of the book. Exodus 19–20, as I have tried to show,[62] is even later than the two. Furthermore, the Psalms that associate theophanic elements with the Zion tradition know nothing of Sinai, nor are they related to any particular cultic occasion.[63] It was, in fact, the Zion tradition that influenced the development of the Sinai tradition and not the reverse, as Cross, Clifford[64] and Levenson[65] claim.

I have taken up considerable space with my discussion of the Albright school, its successor, the Cross-Harvard school, and my critique of both, because of their pervasive impact on American biblical scholarship in the latter half of the twentieth century. It now also represents the major American defendent of the Documentary Hypothesis and the early dating of the non-P (J) source of the Pentateuch as the most compatible with its overall scheme of interpretation and consequently the most resistant to any change in the source-critical study of the Pentateuch.

Notes

1 Rogerson, *Old Testament Criticism*; Blenkinsopp, *The Pentateuch*; Houtman, *Der Pentateuch*; Nicholson, *The Pentateuch in the Twentieth Century*; Whybray, *The Making of the Pentateuch*.

2 For convenience, I have rendered the foreign titles in English translation.

3 See Rogerson (*Old Testament Criticism*, pp. 28–49) for more detailed treatment of de Wette.

4 His views are known from his unpublished lectures that began in Strasbourg in 1834.

5 See the full discussion of this issue in L. Perlitt, *Vatke und Wellhausen* (BZAW, 94; Berlin: W. de Gruyter, 1965); also the excellent review of Wellhausen by John Barton in R. Morgan and J. Barton, *Biblical Interpretation* (Oxford: Oxford University Press, 1988), pp. 76–88.

6 See the preface to the English edition of *Prolegomena* by Robertson Smith, pp. v–x.

7 It must be emphasized against Wellhausen's detractors, that his approach was not philosophical, which he rejected, but 'social scientific' albeit within the limitations of those disciplines in the nineteenth century.

8 Eissfeldt, *The Old Testament, an Introduction*.

9 Fohrer, *Introduction to the Old Testament*.

10 Pfeiffer, *Introduction to the Old Testament*.

11 So Hermann Gunkel, *Genesis*.

12 Noth, *Überlieferungsgeschichte des Pentateuch*.

13 Von Rad, *Das formgeschichtliche Problem des Hexateuchs*.

14 Eissfeldt, *The Old Testament, an Introduction*, pp. 244–48; H. Schulte, *Die Entstehung der Geschichtsschreibung im alten Israel* (BZAW, 128; Berlin: W. de Gruyter, 1972).

15 Volz and Rudolph, *Der Elohist als Erzähler*; Rudolph, *Der 'Elohist' von Exodus bis Joshua*.

16 See also R. N. Whybray, 'The Joseph Story and Pentateuchal Criticism', *VT* 18 (1968), pp. 522–28.

17 Mowinckel, *Erwägungen zur Pentateuch Quellenfrage*.

18 Winnett, *The Mosaic Tradition; idem*, 'Reexamining the Foundations', pp. 1–19.

19 Volz and Rudolph, *Der Elohist als Erzähler*, pp. 135–42.

20 Engnell, *A Rigid Scrutiny*, pp. 50–67.

21 For a thorough discussion of Scandinavian scholarship on the Pentateuch see D. A. Knight, *Rediscovering the Traditions of Israel* (Missoula, MT: Scholars Press, 1973).

22 Kaufmann, *The Religion of Israel*.

23 For a recent review, see especially J. Blenkinsopp, 'An Assessment of the Alleged Pre-Exilic Date of the Priestly Material in the Pentateuch', *ZAW* 108 (1996), pp. 495–518.

24 See the recent review of the problem and a survey of the literature in M. Vervenne, 'The Question of "Deuteronomistic" Elements in Genesis to Numbers', in F. G. Martinez *et al.* (eds.), *Studies in Deuteronomy in Honor of C. J. Labuschagne on the Occasion of his 65th Birthday* (VTSup, 53; Leiden: E.J. Brill, 1994), pp. 243–68.

25 Some standard works on the history of comparative religion are: E. J. Sharpe, *Comparative Religion: A History* (New York: Charles Scribner's Sons, 2nd edn, 1975); J. S. Preus, *Explaining Religion: Criticism and Theory from Bodin to Freud* (New Haven: Yale University Press, 1987); Jan De Vries, *Perspectives in the History of Religions* (Berkeley: University of California Press, 1977); and for more recent developments, F. Whaling (ed.), *Theory and Method in Religious Studies* (Berlin: W. de Gruyter, 1995). The *Encyclopaedia of Religion* (*EncRel*) is a valuable reference resource for biblical scholars.

26 W. Robertson Smith, *The Religion of the Semites* (New York: Meridian, 1956 [1889]).

27 See article on W. Robertson Smith by T. O. Beidelman, *EncRel*, XIII, pp. 366–67.

28 See J. Z. Smith, 'In Comparison a Magic Dwells', in *idem, Imaging Religion* (Chicago: University of Chicago Press, 1982), pp. 19–35 (26–29).

29 See W. Harrelson, 'Myth and Ritual School', *EncRel*, X, pp. 282–85. See also J. Z. Smith, 'When the Bough Breaks', in *idem, Map Is Not Territory* (Chicago: University of Chicago Press, 1978), pp. 208–39.

30 E. Hobsbawm and T. Ranger (eds.), *The Invention of Tradition* (Cambridge: Cambridge University Press, 1983).

31 See W. Klatt, *Hermann Gunkel: Zu seiner Theologie der Religionsgeschichte und zur Entstehung der formgeschichtliche Methode* (FRLANT, 100; Göttingen: Vandenhoeck & Ruprecht, 1969).

32 See the article on 'Religionsgeschichtliche Schule' by K. Rudolph, *EncRel*, XII, pp. 293–96.

33 Wellhausen dismissed Gunkel's book as merely antiquarianism. On this see Klatt, *Herrmann Gunkel*, p. 71.

34 There is a dispute among scholars as to how best to render this German term in English. I resist the common tendency to use the term 'saga' for *Sagen* as highly misleading and retain the English term 'legend' as the best equivalent.

35 Gunkel, *Genesis* (1910); see also *idem, The Folktale in the Old Testament* (Sheffield: Sheffield Academic Press, 1987 [1917]).

36 See J. Van Seters, *In Search of History; Historiography in the Ancient World and the Origins of Biblical History* (New Haven: Yale University Press, 1983), pp. 209–12.

37 Published in translation in *idem, Essays*, pp. 79–132.

38 Translated in *idem, Essays*, pp. 1–66.

39 A translation of Olrik's essay may be found in A. Dundes (ed.), *The Study of Folklore* (Englewood Cliffs, NJ: Prentice-Hall, 1965), pp. 129–41.

40 See Kirkpatrick, *The Old Testament and Folklore Study*, pp. 51–65; and Whybray, *The Making of the Pentateuch*, pp. 144–45.

41 See S. Niditch, *Oral World and Written Word: Ancient Israelite Literature* (Louisville, KY: Westminster/John Knox Press, 1996).

42 Compare the approaches of Kirkpatrick and Niditch in *The Old Testament and Folklore Study* and *Oral World* respectively. See also Wahl, *Die Jakob Erzählungen*, pp. 113–90.

43 B. S. Childs, 'A Study of the Formula, "Until This Day"', *JBL* 82 (1963), pp. 279–92; B. O. Long, *The Problem of Etiological Narrative in the Old Testament* (BZAW, 108; Berlin; W. de Gruyter, 1968).

44 C. Westermann, 'Arten der Erzählung in der Genesis', *in idem, Forschung am Alten Testament* (TBü, 24; Munich: Chr. Kaiser Verlag, 1964), pp. 9–91; ET *The Promises to the Fathers* (Philadelphia: Fortress Press, 1980), pp. 1–94.

45 Van Seters, *Abraham in History and Tradition*, pp. 133–38; Kirkpatrick, *The Old Testament and Folklore Study*, pp. 81–85; Whybray, *The Making of the Pentateuch*, pp. 152–58; Wahl, *Die Jakob Erzählungen*, pp. 182–87.

46 Van Seters, *Abraham in History and Tradition*, pp. 139–48.

47 See C. H. J. de Geus, *The Tribes of Israel: An Investigation into Some of the Presuppositions of Martin Noth's Amphictyony Hypothesis* (Assen: Van Gorcum, 1976).

48 Albright, *From the Stone Age to Christianity; idem, Yahweh and the Gods of Canaan*.

49 *Yahweh and the Gods of Canaan*.

50 Cross, *Canaanite Myth and Hebrew Epic*.

51 See Van Seters, *In Search of History*, pp. 18–31, 224–27.

52 H. N. Wallace, *The Eden Narrative* (HSM, 32; Atlanta: Scholars Press, 1985); R. S. Hendel, *The Epic of the Patriarch* (HSM, 42; Atlanta: Scholars Press, 1987).

53 'Abram the Hebrew: A New Archaeological Interpretation', *BASOR* 163 (October 1961), pp. 36–54.

54 Van Seters, *In Search of History*, pp. 18–20, 224–27.

55 This is still done by Niditch, *Oral World*, pp. 8–24.

56 See R. Thomas, *Oral Tradition and Written Record in Classical Athens* (Cambridge: Cambridge University Press, 1989), pp. 283–86; *idem, Literacy and Orality in Ancient Greece* (Cambridge: Cambridge University Press, 1992), pp. 29–51.

57 See Harrelson, 'Myth and Ritual School', and Smith, 'When the Bough Breaks'.

58 Perlitt, *Bundestheologie im Alten Testament*.

59 For the more detailed discussion see my *The Life of Moses: The Yahwist as Historian in Exodus–Numbers* (Louisville, KY: Westminster/John Knox Press; Kampen: Kok, 1994), pp. 128–49, 247–70, 286–89.

60 *Canaanite Myth and Hebrew Epic*, pp. 143–44.

61 See M. Brenner, *The Song of the Sea: Ex. 15.1-21* (BZAW, 195; Berlin: W. de Gruyter, 1991); also Van Seters, *The Life of Moses*, pp. 147–48.

62 *The Life of Moses*, pp. 270–80.

63 See J. Jeremias, *Theophanie: Die Geschichte einer alttestamentlichen Gattung* (WMANT, 10; Neukirchen-Vluyn: Neukirchener Verlag, 1965).

64 R. J. Clifford, *The Cosmic Mountain in Canaan and the Old Testament* (HSM, 4; Cambridge, MA: Harvard University Press, 1972).

65 J. Levenson, *Sinai and Zion: An Entry into the Jewish Bible* (San Francisco: Harper & Row, 1985).

4

New Currents in Pentateuchal Studies from 1975 to the Present

Bibliography

Albertz, R., 'Der Beginn der vorpriesterlichen Exodus-komposition (K^Ex): Eine Kompositions- und Redaktionsgeschichte von Ex 1–5,' *TZ* 67 (2011), pp. 223–62.

Alt, A., 'The God of the Fathers' (1929).

Baden, J. S., *J, E, and the Redaction of the Pentateuch* (Tübingen: Mohr Siebeck, 2009).

Blenkinsopp, J., *The Pentateuch* (1992).

—— 'Priestly Material in the Pentateuch' (1996).

Blum, E., *Die Komposition der Vätergeschichte* (WMANT, 57; Neukirchen-Vluyn: Neukirchener Verlag, 1984).

—— *Studien zur Komposition des Pentateuch* (BZAW, 189; Berlin: W. de Gruyter, 1990).

—— 'Gibt es die Endgestalt des Pentateuch?', in J. A. Emerton (ed.), *Congress Volume: Leuven, 1989* (VTSup, 43; Leiden: E.J. Brill, 1992), pp. 46–57.

Coats, G.W., *Genesis with an Introduction to Narrative Literature* (FOTL, 1; Grand Rapids: Eerdmans, 1983).

—— *Moses: Heroic Man, Man of God* (JSOTSup, 57; Sheffield: JSOT Press, 1988).

Cross, F. M., *Canaanite Myth and Hebrew Epic* (1973).

Dozaman, T. B. and K. Schmid (eds.), *A Farewell to the Yahwist? The Composition of the Pentateuch in Recent European Interpretation* (Atlanta: SBL, 2006).

Galling, K., *Die Erwählungstraditionen Israels* (BZAW, 48; Berlin: W. de Gruyter, 1928).

Gertz, J. C., K. Schmid, and M. Witt (eds.), *Abschied vom Jehwisten: Die Komposition des Hexateuchin der jüngsten Diskusion* (BZAW, 315; Berlin: de Gruyter, 2002).

Gressmann, H., *Mose und seine Zeit* (1913).

Gunkel, H., *Genesis* (1910).

Haran, M., *Temple and Temple Service in Ancient Israel* (Oxford: Clarendon Press, 1978).

Hiebert, T., *The Yahwist's Landscape: Nature and Religion in Early Israel* (Oxford: Oxford University Press, 1996).

Hoftijzer, J., *Die Verheissungen an der drei Ertzväter* (Leiden: E. J. Brill, 1956).

Jackson, B. S., 'Revolution in Biblical Law: Some Reflections on the Role of Theory and Methodology,' *JSS* 50 (2005), 83–115.

Levinson, B. M., 'Is the Covenant Code an Exilic Composition? A Response to John Van Seters,' in J. Day (ed.), *In Search of Pre-exilic Israel* (JSOTS, 406; London: T & T Clark, 2004), 272–325.

Niditch, S., *Oral World* (1996).

Noth, M., *The Deuteronomistic History* ([1981] 1943).
—— *A History of Pentateuchal Traditions* ([1972] 1948).
Otto, E., a review of J. Van Seters, *A Law Book for the Diaspora*, in RBL, published on its website July 2004 and with a German version in *Biblica* 85 (2004), pp. 273–77.
Rad, G. von, *Das formgeschichtliche Problem des Hexateuchs* (1938).
Rendtorff, R., *Das überlieferungsgeschichtliche Problem des Pentateuch* (BZAW, 147; Berlin: W. de Gruyter, 1977).
Römer, T., *Israels Väter: Untersuchungen zur Väterthematik im Deuteronomium und in der deuteronomistischen Tradition* (OBO, 99; Freiburg: University Press; Göttingen: Vandenhoeck & Ruprecht, 1990).
Rose, M., *Deuteronomist und Jahwist* (ATANT, 67; Zürich: Theologischer Verlag, 1981).
Schmid, H. H., *Der sogenannte Jahwist* (Zürich: Theologischer Verlag, 1976).
Schmid, K., *Erzväter und Exodus: Untersuchungen zur doppelten Begründung der Ursprünge Israels innnerhalb der Geschichtsbücher des Alten Testaments* (WMANT, 81; Neukirchen-Vluyn: Neukirchener Verlag, 1999).
Schmitt, H-C., *Arbeitsbuch zum Alten Testament*, 3rd edn (Göttingen: Vandenhoeck and Ruprecht, 2011).
Thompson, T.L., *The Historicity of the Patriarchal Narratives* (1974).
Van Seters, J., *Abraham in History and Tradition* (1975).
—— 'The Yahwist as Theologian? A Response', *JSOT* 3 (1977), pp. 15–20.
—— *In Search of History* (1983).
—— *Prologue to History: The Yahwist as Hstorian in Genesis* (Louisville, KY: Westminster/ John Knox Press; Zürich: Theologischer Verlag, 1992).
—— *The Life of Moses* (1994).
—— *A Law Book for the Diaspora: Revision in the Study of the Covenant Code* (Oxford: Oxford University Press, 2003).
—— 'The Patriarchs and the Exodus: Bridging the gap between two origin traditions', in R. Roukema (ed.), *The Interpretation of Exodus: Studies in Honour of Cornelis Houtman* (Leuven: Peeters, 2006), pp. 1–15.
—— 'The Report of the Yahwist's Demise Has Been Greatly Exaggerated!', in Dozaman and Schmid (eds.), *A Farewell to the Yahwist?* (2006), pp. 143–57.
—— *The Edited Bible: The Curious History of the 'Editor' in Biblical Criticism* (Winona Lake, IN: Eisenbrauns, 2006).
—— 'Revision in the Study of the Covenant Code and a Response to my Critics', *SJOT* 21 (2007), pp. 5–28.
—— *The Yahwist: A Historian of Israelite Origins* (Winona Lake, IN: Eisenbrauns, 2013).
—— 'The Israelites in Egypt (Exodus 1–5) within the Larger Context of the Yahwist's History', in *idem*, *The Yahwist* (2013), pp. 267–89.
—— 'Dating the Yahwist's History: Principles and Perspectives', *Biblica* (forthcoming).
—— "The Tent of Meeting in the Yahwist and the Origin of the Synagogue', *SJOT* (forthcoming).
Vink, J. G., *The Date and Origin of the Priestly Code in the Old Testament* (Leiden: E. J. Brill, 1969).
Wellhausen, J., *Prolegomena* (1885).
Westermann, C., *The Promises to the Fathers* (1980).
Whybray, R. N., *The Making of the Pentateuch* (1987).
—— *Introduction to the Pentateuch* (1995).
Zenger, E., et al., *Einleitung in das Alte Testament* (1995).

1. The source-critical problem of the Pentateuch

In the mid-1970s three books appeared that can be said to have significantly changed the direction of Pentateuchal studies. These are John Van Seters, *Abraham in History and Tradition* (1975), Hans Heinrich Schmid, *Der sogenannte Jahwist* (1976) and Rolf Rendtorff, *Das überlieferungsgeschichtliche Problem des Pentateuch* (1977). There had been a number of important precursors by earlier scholars as well as some preliminary forays in articles by these authors, but with the appearance of these works the debate about the continuing adequacy of the Documentary Hypothesis came to a head. The question for the primarily European discussion was whether the Documentary Hypothesis could be salvaged in a drastically revised form or whether it needed to be scrapped in favor of a different approach. These three 'revisionists', as they are often labeled, while working out their views largely independent from each other, shared many of the same criticisms of the Documentary Hypothesis, but were not entirely in agreement about the method or the specific form of analysis that was to replace it.

a. J. Van Seters

I took up the challenge offered by Fredrick V. Winnett in his 1964 Society of Biblical Literature presidential address, 'Re-examining the Foundations', in which he raised a number of questions about some of the tenets of the Documentary Hypothesis.[1] Winnett, following the lead of Volz and in agreement with Mowinckel, could not accept the source E as an independent document. At most it was merely a morally and theologically motivated revision of the older patriarchal tradition, and it was not to be found at all in Exodus to Numbers. Indeed, the literary development of Genesis was separate from Exodus to Numbers until the final stage of composition, when they were combined by P. Within the J material of Genesis, Winnett found two different sources, but, unlike others who had divided J, only one of these was early; the other was quite late and exilic in date. Furthermore, these sources are not related to each other as independent documents but as documents that were added to, or which supplemented earlier ones. The same could be said to be the case for P (as Volz also held). It, too, was a supplement to the preceding corpus and not an independent document. Winnett's published address did not receive much attention at the time.

I endeavored to test the proposed scheme of Winnett within the limits of the Abraham tradition. This could be done because within the corpus of Genesis 12–26 there is a rich body of narrative parallels. Thus, it was discovered that of the three episodes in which the ancestress is represented to foreigners as a sister and not a wife, Gen. 12.10-20 corresponds to Winnett's early J, Genesis 20 to his 'E' supplement and Gen. 26.1-11 to his late J. In these and all other cases of story parallels I argue that the relationship is that of supplementation and not a set of independent documents put together by redactors. The latter are a quite unnecessary invention by literary critics. The same could be said for P's relationship to J, as in the case of the two Abrahamic covenants, Genesis 15 (late J) and Genesis 17 (P).

Within the scope of the Abraham tradition it was found that the oldest 'pre-J' material was quite modest in extent[2] and even 'E' consists of only one story in 20.1-17; 21.25-26, 28-31a. The rest of the non-P material all belongs to the 'late' Yahwist. Since the earlier material does not constitute sources that are found in the rest of the Pentateuch, they should be viewed as the sources of tradition used by the Yahwist and nothing more. With respect to dating the Yahwist, I found that the closest affinities were with Second Isaiah and the latter's appeal to Abraham and the theme of divine blessing of the patriarch. Furthermore, in a previous article,[3] as well as in subsequent studies,[4] I argued that the form of land promise in J was a later development than that found in Deuteronomy and the Dtr tradition. The Yahwist therefore had to be viewed as a post-D author and the order of the documents in the classical Documentary Hypothesis had to be revised accordingly.

In my subsequent publications (*Prologue to History*, 1992 and *The Life of Moses*, 1994) I have extended my study of J to the whole of the Tetrateuch. In this analysis I departed rather substantially from Winnett's work on the Moses Tradition,[5] in that I view virtually all of the non-P texts of Exodus–Numbers as the work of the 'late' Yahwist and the unity between Genesis and Exodus–Numbers as the work of J not P. Thus, within the patriarchal stories the Jacob story manifests the presence of pre-J materials[6] similar to that of the Abraham materials, but without any 'E' component. Likewise, the story of Judah in Genesis 38 and the story of Joseph in Genesis 37, 39–50 were originally self-contained narratives prior to their incorporation into J's larger narrative. It was J who used the Joseph story as a bridge between the patriarchal traditions and the exodus tradition. In the primeval history of Genesis 1–11, J combined eastern Mediterranean and Mesopotamian origin traditions to create a prologue for the stories of the ancestors. To these P added still further parallel materials.

In Exodus–Numbers J has structured the traditions of the Egyptian oppression, the exodus and the wilderness trek to the promised land by means of the life of Moses.[7] Within this body of J material I do not feel that it is possible to isolate an earlier Moses tradition with a specific set of episodes, as was the case with Abraham and Jacob. The only body of specifically Israelite source material about Moses that can be found in J is the parallel accounts in Deuteronomy, and comparisons with these all demonstrate that the D versions are the earlier ones.[8] This means that the J corpus as a whole must be understood as a prologue and supplement to Deuteronomy and to the larger Dtr history. In this way I seek to resolve the problem between Noth's arguments for a Tetrateuch separate from D/DtrH and von Rad's insistence upon a Hexateuch, with Joshua as the goal of the patriarchal promises. Since J was post-D/DtrH, he tied the two larger works together and added his own final conclusion to the Hexateuch by means of a second Joshua speech in Joshua 24.[9]

b. H. H. Schmid

His primary contribution to the Pentateuchal debate (*Der sogenannte Jahwist*, 1976) was to call into question the early dating of the Yahwist in the Solomonic period. He disputed von Rad's notion of a 'Solomonic Enlightenment' as the appropriate background for understanding the Yahwist. Instead, in a series of chapters that dealt with broadly accepted J materials: the call of Moses, the Egyptian plagues, the passage through the Red Sea, examples from the wilderness wandering, the Sinai pericope and the promises to the forefathers, Schmid tried to show that J was heavily dependent upon both the prophetic tradition and the Deuteronomic school. The conclusion to be drawn from this was that the Pentateuch was as much a product of the prophetic movement as was the book of Deuteronomy and that J must be viewed in close association with the Deuteronomic school of the late monarchy or exilic period.

Unlike me, Schmid did not commit himself to the question of which source, J or D, was the earlier and their precise relationship. However, in a study that compared parallels between J and Deuteronomy–Joshua, his student, Martin Rose (*Deuteronomist und Jahwist*, 1981), argued in agreement with me that D/DtrH was prior to J and Schmid has subsequently adopted that position as well. My later studies on J in the Moses tradition are heavily indebted to this work of Schmid.

c. R. Rendtorff

The point of departure for his critique of the Documentary Hypothesis is his view that such a method is incompatible with the method of tradition-history as set forth by Noth and von Rad, and it was their mistake not to carry forward their program to its logical conclusion that would entail rejecting the Documentary Hypothesis.[10] Building upon Noth's block model of Pentateuchal development (more on this below), Rendtorff points to the lack of a close connection between Genesis and Exodus–Numbers. He considers any connections that do exist as rather late and 'Deuteronomistic', so that one should give up the idea of sources such as J and focus on the development of the traditions instead. His primary example of the way in which this process works is the divine promises to the patriarchs in Genesis and their relationship to the development of the whole patriarchal block separate from the other Pentateuchal blocks.

Rendtorff's view must be considered primarily in the context of a review and critique of tradition-history, which will ensue below, as will the subsequent development of this position by E. Blum. Rendtorff's rejection of J does not really address my late J or the Yahwist of Schmid. While he speaks of the combination of the blocks of tradition as being the work of a Dtr editor, he does not address the relationship of this corpus in the Tetrateuch to Deuteronomy and DtrH.[11] P is viewed as a later supplement and not a source. Thus, the method is a combination of the fragmentary and the supplemental models.

2. The traditio-historical problem of the Pentateuch

Tradition-historical method, as it has developed within German biblical scholarship, has three aspects that need to be considered. First, it has to do primarily with tradition as it evolved during the preliterate stage of Israelite society, transmitted orally over a long period of time. As indicated above, the degree to which orality can be identified within a written text and the possibility of tracing different oral stages within the present literary corpus is highly problematic. Secondly, tradition-history attempts to associate various reconstructed oral forms of the tradition with hypothetical social settings in early Israel. Again, we have seen above that such conjectured settings as an amphictyonic tribal league (Noth) have been strongly disputed and scholars are becoming increasingly wary of saying very much about a preliterate, pre-state form of Israelite society. Thirdly, the theme that has become fundamental to the whole current discussion of tradition-history in the Pentateuch is that of the divine promises to the patriarchs and the way that it relates to the other major tradition, namely the exodus from Egypt and the conquest of the land. At what point does the latter become the fulfillment of the former? These three aspects of tradition-history have become so closely associated in the study of the Pentateuch that any basic shift in the first two must result in a major reconsideration in understanding the third. It is to this last aspect that we now turn our attention.

a. The promises to the patriarchs

There are two fundamentally different approaches to the theme of the patriarchal promises. The one stresses the basic unity of the theme within the source J and the impact that the theme has on the shaping of the Pentateuch as a whole. The other looks for the origin and growth of the promises theme by dividing it into small units and then relating their evolution into more complex forms to successive stages in the growth of the patriarchal tradition as a whole. In the first approach, the role of the author J (or its equivalent) is paramount. In the second, the literary activity of an author is of little consequence. In my view, there is little room for compatibility between these two positions. Yet the discussion of the promises theme continues to fluctuate between these two poles.

The current discussion of this subject began with K. Galling's study, *Die Erwählungstraditionen Israels* (1928), in which he identified two major traditions of the divine election of Israel: the exodus-settlement tradition and the promises to the patriarchs tradition. He viewed the exodus-settlement tradition as originally independent and self-contained, whereas the patriarchal tradition was secondary and dependent upon the other. Galling further observed that the exodus tradition, but not that of the patriarchal promises, was to be found in the pre-exilic prophets. However, since he accepted the Documentary Hypothesis and its early dating of J and E, he was hard pressed to explain why the patriarchal promises were missing from pre-exilic sources.

Even though Galling describes his approach as tradition-history, he is only concerned with the literary presentation of the election traditions by authors. With A. Alt's study, 'The God of the Fathers' (1929), there was a shift to a completely different method of tradition-history. For him the literary sources of the patriarchal stories reflected older oral traditions that still contained vestiges of a nomadic presettlement religion of a 'god of the fathers'. Essential to this religion were the promises of land made by the personal deity to the forefather and founder of the cult. Alt's presentation set the stage for the subsequent attempts to recover this preliterary promises tradition and to account for the various literary forms that arose from them.

Von Rad combined these two approaches by acknowledging the origins of the land promise theme in the preliterary traditions. At the same time, however, he laid most of the emphasis upon the Yahwist's 'free treatment' of the tradition by making the settlement tradition the fulfillment of the patriarchal promises.[12] For von Rad, it is this author who has made the promise theme basic to the structure of the Pentateuch. By contrast, Noth (*A History of Pentateuchal Traditions*, 1972 [1948]) sees the patriarchal tradition with the promises developing as an independent block that combined with the other exodus-settlement traditions by a vague process at the preliterary level and through several stages, although he never identifies these layers or explains how they come together.[13]

The whole basis for the traditio-historical treatment of the patriarchal promises theme by Alt and Noth was challenged by J. Hoftijzer (*Die Verheissungen an der drei Ertzväter*, 1956), who called into question the evidence for Alt's 'god of the fathers' thesis. This meant that there was no warrant for regarding the promise theme as early and preliterary. Hoftijzer then identified all of the promise texts as belonging to only two groups, those associated with Genesis 15 (= non-P or J) and those associated with Genesis 17 (= P). Of those in the Genesis 15 group, he considered all of them, except Genesis 15 itself, as belonging to a stratum of late redactional additions to their literary context.

Claus Westermann (*The Promises to the Fathers*, 1976) conceded to Hoftijzer the secondary character of many of the promise references, but he still believed that the promise theme derived from the 'patriarchal age' and looked for the origin of the promise theme, not in the land promise but in the promise of offspring, and in particular in the stories about childbirth in Genesis 16 and 18.1-15. In my view, the inclusion of such childbirth stories, which are similar to others in Genesis and elsewhere in the Old Testament, completely muddles the issue and does not address the problem raised by Hoftijzer's analysis of the promise texts.

Schmid and I build directly upon Hoftijzer's work and consider the promise theme to be the development of J, as did von Rad, but in the late monarchic or exilic period. Rendtorff, however, continues to build upon Alt, Noth and Westermann in his traditio-historical study of the promise theme. He rejects the Documentary Hypothesis and, therefore, von Rad's emphasis upon the author J as the one responsible for the development of the promise theme. Instead, he adopts Noth's block model of the tradition's growth and sees in the variety of formulas that Genesis uses to express the various promises the clue to tracing the history of the forefathers' tradition. In his view one can construct a 'relative chronology' of the formulas and use them to understand the growth of the traditions in which they were imbedded.

There are two fundamental problems with Rendtorff's approach. First, he does not address the major critiques of the whole traditio-historical method of Alt and Noth, but if this is invalid then his own method is in jeopardy. Secondly, the scheme for the chronology of the formulas that Rendtorff works out cannot be applied to the same formulas in Exodus–Numbers or Deuteronomy. Thus it seems entirely arbitrary.

E. Blum, a student of Rendtorff, followed his lead in two massive studies on the Pentateuch. The first of these, *Die Komposition der Vätergeschichte* (1984), seeks to reconstruct the whole history of the composition of the patriarchal tradition. It traces the basic units of the individual forefathers through multiple stages of growth by supplementation within the Jacob and Abraham traditions to their combination as a *Vätergeschichte* and their final integration into the Pentateuch as a whole by both a Deuteronomistic and a Priestly composer. Basic to Blum's analysis is Rendtorff's notion that the promises reflect several layers of composition. Where Blum seems to modify the older traditio-historical search for primitive oral tradition (in response to Van Seters?) is in construing the development as a history of literary composition within the monarchic and exilic periods. What was previously viewed as reflecting the activity of oral composition and transmission is now regarded as the work of authors and editors/redactors.

In Blum's second volume (*Studien zur Komposition des Pentateuch* [1990]), the elaborate system worked out in the earlier volume has become greatly simplified. Blum recognizes a body of older traditions within the corpus from Exodus to Numbers without attempting to identify the traditions precisely or to assign them to specific blocks. They remain vague 'fragments' used by the two major compositions of the Pentateuch. These are designated as a D composition (KD) in the Deuteronomic tradition and a Priestly composition (KP). The former, KD, corresponds to what we have called the non-P corpus (= Van Seters J) and is later than Deuteronomy or DtrH and postexilic. It is this author who is responsible for the integration of the patriarchal stories into the Pentateuch. KP corresponds to the P corpus of the older Documentary Hypothesis except that it is viewed sometimes as a supplement (so also Rendtorff) and sometimes as a work based upon an independent body of priestly material.

With Blum's work the whole discussion of tradition-history has come full circle to the question of whether the Pentateuchal tradition's development is not essentially literary rather than oral. This can be seen in my work, especially the recent books, *Prologue to History* and *The Life of Moses*. Blum and I are in agreement that there are some individual units of tradition within the patriarchal stories that were taken up by a later literary composition. Where we disagree is that I ascribe virtually all of the non-P promises texts to one compositional layer (as did Hoftijzer) in place of Blum's multiple layers. I also dispute that one can separate a body of pre-J (= pre-KD) texts from J (= KD) in Exodus–Numbers since signs of lateness are quite uniform throughout the whole non-P corpus.

In my own study of the literary tradition history of the patriarchal promises,[14] I return to the work of Galling and the problem of the late integration of the promises theme with that of the exodus-conquest tradition. The difference is that I am no longer committed to an early date for J. First, I confirm Galling's observation that the promises theme does not come to the fore in the prophets before Ezekiel and is only integrated into the exodus theme by the time of Second Isaiah. This strongly argues for the Pentateuchal combination also being late and exilic. Yet it cannot be as late as P, as Winnett and some recent scholars have proposed, which must be at least a century later. Secondly, the promise to the fathers of land in Deuteronomy and the Dtr corpus did not originally include the forefathers. The 'fathers' of D originally meant the exodus generation, and the promise to these fathers was only modified to apply to the patriarchs when they became part of the Pentateuchal tradition in the late exilic period. This thesis was also defended in an exhaustive study by Thomas Römer (*Israels Väter*, 1990).

One question that is left open by Blum is the relationship of KD and the pre-KD traditions it contains to Deuteronomy and DtrH. This is important, especially in the study of Exodus–Numbers, because of the substantial overlap in the parallel materials. My extensive study of these parallels suggests that the accounts in Deuteronomy/DtrH are all earlier and that the Moses tradition in Exodus–Numbers is an expansion and modification of that tradition. Since the patriarchal promises theme of Genesis likewise points to a post-D/DtrH development of the Pentateuch, it means that the Pentateuchal tradition is an exilic (or postexilic) literary development. Tradition-history following the methodology of Alt and Noth is no longer possible.

3. The form-critical problem of the Pentateuch

The problem of the Pentateuch's form is directly related to whether the object of form-critical inquiry is the small unit, the 'fragment', or is the shape of the larger composition. It is also related to the part of the Pentateuch to which it is applied, whether the primeval history (Gen. 1–11), the patriarchal stories (Gen. 12–50), the exodus-wilderness stories (Exodus–Numbers), or the law-giving at Sinai (Exod. 19–Num. 10). The task is to find a form or genre that will adequately encompass the whole of the Pentateuchal tradition. Let us review the options.

a. Folkloristic forms: Gunkel to Westermann on Genesis

As indicated above in the historical survey, Gunkel understood Genesis primarily in terms of the small units of folklore genres, namely, myths in the primeval history and legends (*Sagen*) in the patriarchal stories, with the Joseph story as a more advanced novella. The larger units, the sources such as J and E, were merely collections of folklore, 'schools of storytellers', and were not historical in form or content. Gunkel's identification of such forms depended heavily upon the presence of etiology (= an explanation of origin) within the individual units. Such legends were of many different types and from many different ethnic or national origins, the result of a long period of cultural diffusion throughout the whole of the Near East long before Israel came on the scene. It was typical in Gunkel's day to interpret the patriarchal stories as a form of tribal history, but Gunkel found very few legends that related directly to the Israelite tribes and did not find in these a nucleus for the development of the whole. There does not appear to be in Gunkel's treatment of Genesis any form or genre that accounts for the larger units of Genesis or the Pentateuch as a whole.

What Gunkel did form-critically for Genesis, Hugo Gressmann (*Mose und seine Zeit*, 1913) did for Exodus–Numbers. Gressmann adopted the same folkloristic genres for analysis as Gunkel, especially the legend (*Sage*) as the basic unit in larger 'legend cycles', which, however, do not correspond with the legend collections of J and E. The most important of these legend cycles are the episodes that make up the hero legend (*Heldensage*) of Moses. Apart from the secondary law-giving of Sinai, this hero legend is able to give a comprehensive form to much of the material in Exodus–Numbers. Nevertheless, Gressmann does not account for the form of the Pentateuch as a whole any better than Gunkel.

This lack of a formative nucleus within the Pentateuch changes with Alt and Noth. Alt accepts Gunkel's understanding of the small units of tradition as *Sagen* (legends) but identifies those that have to do with divine revelations to the patriarchs as the decisive and distinctive kernel of tradition belonging to those sheep-breeding nomads who were penetrating and settling in the land, who later became Israel.[15] Noth (1948) adopted from Alt both the historical context for the earliest patriarchal traditions and the traditio-historical implications for a formative nucleus from which the whole body of later traditions can be explained.[16] The decisive form of the nucleus was a cultic history of patriarchal religion whose 'confessional theme' was the promise of land by the deity. Furthermore, Noth, in his treatment of the non-P material in Exodus–Numbers, seems to turn the legend cycles of Gressmann into confessional themes and greatly minimizes, if not obliterates, the hero legend of Moses as a primary form.

Von Rad's form-critical solution to the Hexateuch (*Das formgeschichtliche Problem des Hexateuchs*, 1938) is quite different from Noth's. He begins with an implicit criticism of Gunkel's understanding of J, not as a random collection of folktales but as a carefully constructed history. This historiographic form calls for an explanation in the prior tradition-history of the Pentateuch. For von Rad the formative nucleus of the Pentateuch as a whole is the ancient liturgy as found in Deut. 26.5-9, which encompasses the whole sacred history from the patriarch Jacob to the conquest of the land. From this cultic history von Rad derives the form of J's historiography for the whole of the Hexateuch, including all of its major components. While von Rad accepts both Gunkel's understanding of the smaller units of Genesis as legends (*Sagen*) and Alt's thesis of the god of the fathers and an old tradition of land promise, he attributes to J the elaboration and extension of the promise theme throughout Genesis and to the Pentateuch as a whole.

While Noth takes over from von Rad the origins of the Pentateuch in Israel's early cultic history, Noth's block model of separate themes means there is not one but several cultic histories, of which the patriarchal promises theme is only one. The coalescence of these larger units (without the primeval history) takes place prior to J in a *Grundlage*. In place of Gunkel's collection of folklore, we now have a collection of confessional themes by a community of tribes in premonarchic Israel. It is no wonder that Rendtorff, in following Noth, could so easily dispense with the documentary source J as unnecessary.

Gunkel, Alt and Noth all placed a great deal of importance upon the etiological character of the basic units of tradition and their close attachment to specific places as evidence of their primitive character. However, it is on this point that their form-critical analysis of early tradition (Genesis to Joshua) has been strongly criticized, because the etiological formulas often have a rather loose association with the stories to which they are connected.[17] Etiology may be prescientific but it occurs in literary works of great sophistication and complexity and is no clear witness to a preliterate society.

As we saw in the last chapter, Westermann addresses this critique of etiological legends by redefining what was usually meant in German by *Sagen* to make it correspond to the Scandinavian term *sagn* (saga), especially as it is used in the so-called 'family sagas' of medieval Iceland. This revised usage was then applied to the 'family' stories of the patriarchs. However, Whybray and I have strongly criticized this comparison as inappropriate. The saga, as in English, does not correspond to small units but to large comprehensive compositions, and the continued use of 'saga' to translate German *Sagen* in biblical studies is unfortunate and confusing. George Coats, in his form-critical study of Genesis,[18] continues to use Westermann's category of saga, but now applies it to the somewhat larger units, such as the primeval history and the larger blocks of patriarchal stories.[19] Furthermore, in his study of the Moses tradition, Coats returns to Gressmann's emphasis upon the hero legend and combines this with Noth's confessional themes as the two competing elements throughout the Moses tradition.[20] Coats continues to use the term 'saga' for the Moses tradition in a highly ambiguous way without clarifying how such a genre explains the combination of 'heroic saga' and the confessional themes. As a way of understanding the form of the Pentateuch the term 'saga' has become meaningless, and for Coats, like Rendtorff, the 'sources' have little significance for the whole.

b. National epic: the Albright-Cross school

As we have seen above, the Albright-Cross school solves the problem of the Pentateuch's form by positing a primitive national epic at the time of Israel's origins in the Late Bronze Age comparable to those epics of other Near Eastern civilizations. This is a comprehensive genre and is generally viewed as co-extensive with the 'epic sources', J and E. In this way the epic genre is closely integrated with the Documentary Hypothesis and little room is left for any tradition-history of the smaller units. It necessitates the earliest possible dating for J and an even earlier dating for the poetic vestiges of epic in the Pentateuch's poems. The critique in the previous chapter of any epic basis for the Pentateuch need not be repeated here.

c. Historiography: Van Seters

Within his study of the history of Israelite literature, Gunkel[21] advocated the social evolution of Israelite historiography from the earliest folkloristic forms of the Pentateuch dealing with the most distant past, through the hero legends of the judges and early monarchy (Saul), to the rise of full state self-consciousness and the record of the recent past in the narratives about David, especially in what is now called the Succession Narrative (2 Sam. 9–20; 1 Kgs 1–2). Gunkel dismissed the later histories as too ideological. Noth followed closely Gunkel's evolutionary scheme, except that he allowed for a more positive judgment of the work of the Dtr historian.[22] Yet he held strongly to the view that the Pentateuch could not be treated as a history in the same way as DtrH but must be approached by a quite different method (i.e. traditio-historically). Von Rad likewise accepted Gunkel's evolutionary scheme, with the important exception of J, which he regarded as a history contemporary with the Succession Narrative and therefore belonging to the high point of Israelite historiography in the time of Solomon.[23] This was in agreement with his idea of a 'Solomonic Enlightenment'.

In my work *In Search of History* (1983), I give an extensive critique of the Gunkel-Noth-von Rad evolution of Israelite historiography, which has no comparative control, and I offer a different proposal. Using a wide range of historiographic genres in the Near Eastern and early classical civilizations as a base for comparison,

I propose the rise of a national history in Israel (DtrH) in the early exilic period, about the same time that such histories first begin to appear in the Greek world. Likewise, the non-P (J) corpus of the Pentateuch is also a historical work (in agreement with von Rad and against Noth) corresponding to a type of history of national origins that was very popular in the classical world for several centuries. Such 'antiquarian' histories that trace national origins from the first ancestors contain a structure of genealogies in which are embedded narratives about each generation of ancestors, their migrations to new lands to found new cities and peoples, their establishment of cult places, the etiologies of new customs and institutions, and their conquests of the older inhabitants of new colonies. In short, in both content and form, J belongs closely to this form of antiquarian historiography. Such 'histories' contain much that belongs to the folklore genres of myth and legend but have, in varying degrees, been rationalized and historicized and fitted into a chronological and orderly presentation of the past.[24] More on this below.

d. Literacy and orality and the form-critical question

Both the rise of historiography (Gunkel-von Rad) and the earliest written sources of the Pentateuch have been viewed as the result of the beginnings of literacy in the Davidic-Solomonic period. Such literary works would have played an important role in the service of the new state. The suggestion is made plausible by the fact that literacy had already been an important part of the great states of Mesopotamia, Egypt, the Hittites and the cities of Syria-Palestine prior to the rise of the Israelite state. It is assumed that David inherited a complete bureaucracy of scribes with court archives and even a library when he took over Jerusalem.

The evidence for literacy in the tenth and ninth centuries BCE in Palestine (Israel and Judah), however, is very sparse and does not justify the notion that literacy was widespread or that many literary works were produced at this time.[25] Comparison with the Greek world suggests that the transition from an illiterate to a literate society was a slow process, and that for at least three centuries in Greece, from the eighth to the fifth centuries BCE, the amount of epigraphic materials and the range of use from brief inscriptions and commercial records to longer literary works took a long time.[26] During this period the transition from oral forms and modes of composition to those associated with more advanced levels of literacy is reflected in the literary materials produced. Early in this spectrum of literary works in Greece are the epic poems of Homer and Hesiod, followed in the sixth century by other poetic works and wisdom sayings, oracular collections and inscribed temple dedications. Only in the fifth century were works of narrative prose produced and this began the great period of classical literature.

The analogy between Greece and Israel is very suggestive. Current historical discussion about the Jerusalem of David and Solomon regards it as of rather modest size and a state bureaucracy of any size was not developed until the eighth century BCE.[27] There may have been some brief inscriptional material, but it is only in the late ninth or eighth centuries that one begins to find administrative ostraca that increase, along with royal seals and bullae attesting to documents, in the seventh century. From the eighth century also come the first collections of prophetic oracles. All of this points to a time no earlier than the sixth century as the most likely time for the beginning of extensive prose narrative.

If it could be decisively shown that the earliest Pentateuchal sources stand very close to older poetic epics, then one might be able to argue for an older date for their composition. But as we saw above that is very problematic. If epic poetry ever existed in Israel, then why was it not preserved as it was in Mesopotamia and Greece? The form of historiography evident in J corresponds to that of Greek historiography in the great age of narrative prose, long after the epics of Homer and Hesiod had become 'canonical' and authoritative for the Greek intellectual and religious tradition.

The question of whether one can gauge the degree of orality within the non-P (J) stratum of the Pentateuch has been a matter of discussion and debate since Gunkel. He addressed this issue from the perspectives of both form and the method of composition. He asserted that the folkloristic forms that he identified in Genesis pointed to a basis in oral tradition and these were composed according to Olrik's 'epic laws of folk narrative'. These critieria for orality, however, are of rather limited usefulness. First, the historian Herodotus makes use of a wide range of folkloristic materials within his history,[28] and his work is a masterpiece of literary narrative prose. Secondly, the 'epic laws' work not only for oral literature but can be applied to many written works to varying degrees. The fact is that there is no sharp line between oral and written composition.

The Albright-Cross school, which advocates an epic basis for the early sources (J and E) of the Pentateuch has combined this with the Perry and Lord method in order to demonstrate a high degree of orality in J and E. However, the study of oral tradition in classical studies has found fault with the Perry and Lord method as well,[29] and its application within biblical prose is even more dubious. Furthermore, since ancient Israel continued to be primarily an oral society, with only a rather elite group of literates down to the end of the monarchy and beyond, prose narrative of the Pentateuch could have been continuously influenced by this oral style of storytelling and by popular story motifs throughout its compositional history. Again, the example of Herodotus should make one cautious about viewing historiography as a form of narration distinct from oral tradition. Herodotus claimed that most of his sources were oral in nature and his use or imitation of oral tradition in his history is extensive.[30]

4. Current models of literary criticism

It should be clear from the foregoing discussion that there is no consensus, or even a majority viewpoint, concerning the literary criticism of the Pentateuch at the present time. So prolific have the various methods and datings of sources or strata become that it is difficult to classify them. Even the three basic methods of the fragmentary, supplementary and documentary hypotheses are being used in various combinations, thereby multiplying the possibilities. Nevertheless, I will attempt some general classification of method in spite of the hazards that this entails, in the belief that for the novice some order in the present chaos is better than none.

a. The documentarians

There are still a large number of scholars, including Europeans, Israelis, Jews and Americans, belonging to the Albright-Cross school, who adhere to some form of the Documentary Hypothesis.[31] Their commitment to it is often integral to a theological or history-of-religions orientation. There is a tendency, particularly among the European scholars, to lower the dating of the early sources, on the one hand, and, on the other hand, to admit to a large measure of Deuteronomistic redaction and supplementation of the JE corpus throughout the Tetrateuch. This is in response to the critique of Schmid, Rendtorff and myself, among others. For the most part, the American and Israeli documentarians have largely ignored this movement to a later dating of the sources and still advocate the tenth-century dating for J.[32]

There has also been an increasing disaffection with the separate existence of an E source, even among some documentarians, although others staunchly defend its existence.[33] Its abandonment, however, has sometimes led to a modified version of the Documentary Hypothesis. A good example is the case of Erich Zenger, who advocates a Jerusalemite History (*Jerusalemer Geschichtswerk* = JG) as the earliest literary source, dating to about 700 BCE and contemporary with the earliest collection of the Deuteronomic Code (Deut. 12–26). It was based upon collections of stories (the small units of Gunkel) shaped into a historical work by a Jerusalemite under the influence of eighth-century prophecy. This combines the fragmentary approach with the documentary. JG was then expanded by a Deuteronomistic author/redactor in the exilic period as a non-priestly history. This work remained independent from the separate development of Deuteronomy and the DtrH (Deuteronomy–2 Kings) and also separate from the Priestly *Grundschrift* (Pg). Only in the Persian period were JG and an expanded P combined and a little later integrated with Deuteronomy, which was then separated from the rest of DtrH to form the Torah. This view retains the documentarian view of separate sources (JG, D and P) while at the same time using a supplementary method for the development of each source individually.

The above example of documentarian accommodation to the critique of the 'revisionists' is purchased at the expense of simplicity and theoretical economy of literary explanation. So complex does the editorial and compositional process become and so speculative the reconstruction of its history that it loses credibility.

Indeed, every criticism or weakness of the Documentary Hypothesis concerning the dating of the sources or their dependence upon other earlier sources has been met by invoking the intervention into the text of a 'redactor' to account for the piece of evidence that goes against the theory. Ultimately, one must ask whether or not it is still worth retaining such a literary hypothesis.

b. The block-composition model: Rendtorff, Blum

It is difficult to describe this method because it has already gone through three phases from the time of its originator, Rendtorff,[34] to its development by Blum.[35] Yet it has gained a certain currency among German biblical scholars so that a few additional descriptive remarks are called for here. Rendtorff's initial study builds heavily upon Noth's contention that the basic compositional components of the Pentateuch are the blocks of the five confessional themes whose combination by G already constitute the Pentateuchal tradition. Given this view of tradition-history, Rendtorff regards the method as incompatible with documentary sources, which he eliminates. Using the theme of the patriarchal promises, he demonstrates the block-compositional method of literary development as an evolution of the promises formulas through a series of stages. Only in the latest stage of Deuteronomistic redaction is the promise theme integrated with the rest of the Tetrateuch and the other themes of this corpus. Rendtorff has replaced Noth's pre-state G with an exilic or postexilic Dtr redactor.

In Blum's first work, *Die Komposition der Vätergeschichte* (1984), the compositional levels of the patriarchal tradition are spelled out in detail in terms of a series of literary strata that supplement each other to build up the whole. This composition history resembles the older tradition-history only in its presupposition of a long multi-staged process. But literary composition has replaced oral tradition, and this is made much more explicit than was the case with Rendtorff. The final non-P composition is a Dtr redaction that belongs to the postexilic period and P is a supplement, as in Rendtorff.

In Blum's second work, *Studien zur Komposition des Pentateuch* (1990), he virtually abandons the method of block-composition within Exodus–Numbers along with any attempt to separate the earlier levels of tradition and composition from the final two phases. These he identifies as a D-Komposition (KD), corresponding to non-P and a P-Komposition (KP). Both of these are postexilic in date and both are quite distinct from Deuteronomy, which he does not discuss. Blum's KD is treated in Exodus–Numbers as an extensive literary composition by an author who has reworked his sources to such a degree that they cannot be separated from his own contribution. Yet this same KD stratum in Genesis is only a rather thin redactional layer. In comparison with KD, KP becomes more of a compositional work than a supplement, although Blum disputes that it can be reconstructed into a free-standing source.[36]

In this third stage of the block method it has lost all of its connection with its point of departure in Noth's confessional blocks and the traditio-historical foundation. We are left, in fact, with three literary sources or documents, KD = J or non-P, KP = P, and D. If one were to simplify Blum's analysis of the patriarchal stories of Genesis greatly and follow those scholars who see the promises theme as much more unified, thereby expanding KD/J's contribution in Genesis, there would be little difference between Blum's KD and my J. A mediating position may be seen in the work of David Carr (*Reading the Fractures of Genesis*, 1996). For the non-P material in Genesis, he adopts a less complex stratification of the tradition but still posits more levels than I am willing to accept.[37] For P he advocates the documentarian view of an independent P source. More on this below.

c. New supplementary model: Van Seters

The literary model that I have developed in my own work and that I propose to follow in this book shares some of the features of both the documentary model and the fragmentary or story-collections model, but places the greatest weight upon the supplementary or expansion model. I agree with those who identify three sources or literary strata within the Pentateuch, which I call J (= non-P) and P in the Tetrateuch, and D (Deuteronomy). I do not accept the existence of an extensive source E. My basic differences from the documentarians are twofold. First, I regard D as the earliest source, which makes the relative order of the sources D, J, P. Secondly, I do not view the later sources J and P as independent documents but as direct additions to the earlier corpus. Since there are no separate sources after the first one, there is no need for redactors. The elaborate system of multiple redactors used by current documentarians is unnecessary.

With the fragmentary model I share the view that the sources, and particularly J in Genesis, had a body of traditions, both local Israelite and also some foreign, which were used by the authors within their compositions. But I reject Noth's block-model of tradition-history in general and the resulting notion that the promises theme of Genesis developed in a series of successive stages, as Rendtorff and Blum have proposed. I agree with von Rad and others that the *development* of this theme is entirely the work of J,[38] who is also responsible for the first version of the primeval history and for the connection of the patriarchal traditions with the exodus-conquest tradition.

This combination of models results in the following scheme. The first Pentateuchal source was Deuteronomy (seventh century), which was then used as an introduction to a larger historical work, DtrH (early exilic period), extending from Joshua to 2 Kings. This was expanded in the late exilic period by a history of the people's origins (J) from creation to the death of Moses. This historian made use of a body of traditional 'fragments', some in literary form, others as popular motifs and stories, all of which he shaped and infused with his own ideological and theological concerns. This combined D+J work was then supplemented in the postexilic period by a Priestly writer with his own distinctive traditional material and his own ideological interests. This model has the advantage of the greatest economy of all the proposals. It arises out of a study of the parallels and doublets throughout the Pentateuch and the degree to which these can clarify both the separation of sources and the relationship of those sources to each other. This is primarily what my three books on the Pentateuch are about,[39] which may be consulted for the detailed arguments. Furthermore, this supplementary model also applies to other bodies of narrative in the Old Testament, notably the DtrH[40] as well as the books of Chronicles. Indeed, the historiographic genre that I have proposed for the Pentateuch agrees very well with the supplementary model. In Chapters 5, 6 and 7 some attempt will be made to apply this method to the contents of the Pentateuch in greater detail.

R. N. Whybray[41] has, likewise, taken up my use of the genre of early historiography to explain the literary nature of the Pentateuch, but he then uses this historiographic form to argue against any division of sources in Genesis to Numbers. The differences in style and repetition of accounts can all be accounted for, in his view, as the result of a historian's sources. He points to similar features in Herodotus and sees little need for the distinctions between J and P. This is not the place to respond in detail to Whybray's proposal, but a few observations may be made. First, Whybray[42] has not entirely done away with sources but merely reduced them to two, because he still treats D as separate and distinct. He even regards D as having a complex history of growth by supplementation. Secondly, if one compares the parallels in D with those in Numbers to distinguish differences in outlook and language, then the same kinds of difference can also be seen between J and P. In fact, the latter are even more marked than those between J and D. Thirdly, Herodotus's parallels and repetitions are not such that one set is permeated by one ideology and outlook and another set by a quite different perspective. Whybray simply avoids any serious discussion of this question. Finally, Whybray does not deal with how the Tetrateuch as a historical work is related to Deuteronomy and DtrH. If the Tetrateuch is a supplement to Deuteronomy-2 Kings, then within the larger corpus Genesis-2 Kings there must be multiple sources, even by his reckoning. Whybray, however, avoids any literary discussion of these issues.[43]

5. The problem with P

As we have seen thus far, most of the 'revisions' in the recent study of the Pentateuch have focused attention on the non-P (J, KD) corpus and formulated models and approaches that serve to deal with its characteristics and problems. By contrast, there is widespead agreement across all of the methods and models on the content of the P corpus, its characteristics, theology and extent. In spite of this, there is still substantial disagreement about a number of important issues, with no quick resolution in sight. These include such issues as: (1) the dating of P vis-à-vis D, (2) the unity of P or its division into narrative and legal components, (3) P's status as a separate source or a supplement to J, (4) the ending in P, and (5) the existence of a late priestly redactor (Rp) as the final redactor of the Pentateuch.

a. The dating of P

Since the work of Wellhausen, Pentateuchal studies have largely accepted the dating of P as the last of the sources, coming from the late exilic or postexilic period. As we have seen above, however, the Israeli scholar Kaufmann and his followers have dissented from this view on ideological grounds, claiming that Wellhausen and his contemporaries were motivated by a liberal Protestant negative judgment against Judaism of the Second Temple period, which they saw reflected in the P code. Thus, to refute this pejorative assessment of a 'devolution' of Israelite religion from the ethical monotheism of the eighth-century prophets to the ritualistic cult of the Second Temple, Kaufmann and his followers have argued for a greater antiquity for P and the priestly materials that it contains. In particular, they argue that P is older than D, which would completely undermine the line of development that Wellhausen proposed.

The problem with this kind of argument is that its primary motivation is ideological, no less so for the Israeli scholars than for those they accuse of anti-Judaism bias. However, the primary argument for the dating of P to the Second Temple period has nothing to do with any scheme about the evolution of Israelite religion. It has to do, instead, with the fact that neither the early prophetic texts before Ezekiel, nor Deuteronomy and the DtrH and all of the earlier material it contains seem to reflect the highly centralized and hierarchical priesthood, the elaborate festival calendar and the sacrificial cult of the P Code. By contrast, when one reads the biblical literature of the postexilic period this religion is present, and in the books of Chronicles the P cult has been restored to the time of the monarchy, where it was completely lacking, as in the books of Kings.[44]

While many of Kaufmann's original arguments justifying his position are no longer used, his position is still supported in a number of ways. M. Haran[45] accounts for the silence of P in pre-exilic writings by suggesting that the P code was an esoteric work of priests that was kept secret for three centuries until the time of Ezra, when it was combined with the other sources to form the Pentateuch. There are many problems with this view, the most obvious of which is the fact that it is D that seems to be a document discovered in the temple and brought forward by the priests in the late seventh century and it shows no familiarity with the P code. Furthermore, there is much in the P Code that presupposes centralization of worship as an established fact.

Very much in vogue with supporters of the early date for P are the linguistic and philological comparisons of terminology in P and other biblical texts with special emphasis in trying to establish its priority to Ezekiel. The case has been thoroughly examined by Blenkinsopp, who finds it seriously flawed, and I would concur with this judgment.[46] Furthermore, none of these scholars would regard P as earlier than J (non-P), and if in our view J is late exilic, then P could not be pre-exilic but must belong to the Second Temple period.

b. Unity or diversity in P

There have long been certain questions about the unity of P, because some kinds of material within P have the appearance of being secondary additions. Thus, early on, the distinction was made in German biblical scholarship between a P *Grundschrift* (Pg) and the P supplements (Ps). This suggests a kind of supplementary model for the development of P, even among strict documentarians. Within Genesis little such Ps material has been identified, except perhaps for the genealogy of the sons of Jacob in Gen. 46.8-27, but in Exodus–Numbers the Ps additions are often identified with some of the laws, lists, genealogies and other material that does not fit easily into the larger narrative structure of Pg. This distinction means that a large part of the P Code of Leviticus and most of the P material in Numbers 28–36 belong to this supplement, as well as many other shorter texts. The result of this division is that the original Pg resembles much more a narrative source than a law code with only a narrative framework. Even Pg was regarded by some scholars in the past as a combination of two documents, but this has not had much of a following. Nevertheless, it is still a matter of considerable discussion as to what belongs to Pg and what is secondary expansion by Ps.

One block of legal material in Leviticus 17–26 stands apart from the rest of the Ps legislation, and has long been viewed as a separate code of laws, called the Holiness Code because of its repeated concern for the people's 'holiness'. This is usually considered an early priestly collection because it shares in language and in some of its ethical and legal concerns many similarities with Deuteronomy and Ezekiel. For this reason it is dated to the early exilic period and viewed as an early priestly source that was secondarily combined with the rest of the P work. Those scholars, however, who view P as earlier than D regard it as the latest part of P.

c. P as a separate source or a supplement

In the last few years this issue of P's independent status has become a major topic of discussion. This is obviously an important issue between the strict documentarians, on the one hand, and the supplemental approach on the other.[47] The principal reason for viewing P as the *Grundschrift* of the Pentateuch and the source to which the others were added (long before Wellhausen reversed this order) was the fact that P contained a clear framework of chronology and genealogical sequence that seemed to provide a structure for the whole. While this P framework proved deceptive for the dating of P, scholars have not abandoned this notion of P as a basis for the redactional combination of the sources. It still influences the attribution to this source of some texts that could otherwise be viewed as belonging to non-P.

The primary reason for not regarding P as an independent source is the simple fact that in large parts of the narrative there are such obvious lacunae or the barest thread of narrative connection between one part of the history and the next. Thus, in the patriarchal stories, when one puts all of the texts ascribed to P together, one ends with a few scattered episodes, such as God's covenant with Abraham (Gen. 17), the death and burial of Sarah (23), no story of Isaac but his blessing of Jacob (28.1-9), no story of Jacob except the divine appearance at Bethel (35.9-13) and some birth, death-burial and chronological notices and incidental additions to the other J narratives. Most of the P pieces are parallel to those in J, as they are throughout the primeval history. To say that this is not appropriate content for an independent narrative may be dismissed by documentarians as 'subjective judgment', but it is persuasive nonetheless.

The other kind of argument against P's independence is that in many cases the P texts do not make any sense without the larger J context. This is certainly the case with many of the short notices and introductory formula 'these are the generations [*toledot*] of . . .' in Genesis. In Exodus there is in P no explanation for the oppression of the people by the Egyptians (Exod. 1.13-14), no introduction to Moses' sudden appearance (6.2), no account of the death of the first-born of the Egyptians in spite of the elaborate preparations to anticipate the event (12.1-27). The list could be greatly extended. Two types of explanation are used to account for this lack. The one is to say that a redactor has left out the P account in favor of the J version, but this contradicts the position that P has been used as the base text with J used as filler material. The second explanation is to attribute many of the short notices and remarks to a P redactor. Such proposals are special pleading, that go against the economy of the theory and greatly weaken the whole position. There are still too many instances where invoking a redactor will not work.

Another major argument against P as a supplement is to say that the contradictions between P and J are often so great that only the conflation of two independent sources could account for their presence. P would not directly supplement an older account by an obvious contradiction. This assumes that it is easier for a redactor to do so than an author, but if this redactor is also at liberty to omit material from either source as is claimed, then one would expect the redactor to harmonize the text and avoid contradictions. It is assumed by most documentarians that P was quite familiar with J and wrote his version in conscious contradiction to it. Now it seems to me that there are a number of similar instances of contradiction in the national history (Joshua–2 Kings), for example, the radically different presentation of David as a good or bad king.[48] Yet by far the most common way of treating the literary analysis of DtrH is either as an author directly appropriating source material that he feels free to contradict or as later additions that have been made to the earlier history that deliberately contradict it for ideological reasons.

One problem that has to do with the separation of J and P in Genesis is that the only criterion used in some mixed texts may be the difference in the divine name. But this criterion may be misleading in some cases. One can be reasonably sure that all texts that use Yahweh will be J, but there are instances where J does use Elohim, so that not in all texts in which J and P occur together, as in the flood story (Gen. 6–9), does the term Elohim indicate a P text. In all cases of this kind there must be some other reason for making such judgments. The fact is that it is sometimes in just such texts that by assigning some passages to P instead of J the argument is made for P's greater coherence and, therefore, its independence.

In my view, and the one that will be used later in the discussion of P, the preponderance of the evidence points to P's dependence upon, and supplement of, J. What the novice of Pentateuchal studies must ultimately do, however, is to look at the texts in question and weigh both possibilities carefully. A few generalizations cannot replace an examination of the text.

d. Where does P end?

The question of where P (Pg) ends has had some discussion. The issue is important because it bears to a considerable extent on the ideology of P and its 'program' for the Second Temple period. Since Noth[49] there has been a strong tendency to see it ending in Numbers 27, followed by the brief note in Deut. 34.7-9 of Moses' death.[50] This means that all of the material in Numbers 28–36, much of which anticipates the conquest and division of the land beyond the Jordan, is secondary. But Noth wants to keep the development of the Tetrateuch quite separate from DtrH and therefore regards the interconnection as secondary. Others have argued in favor of seeing P present in Joshua as well and particularly in the account of the division of the land.[51] The priestly language and outlook has long been recognized, so it is a matter of deciding if this is part of a priestly supplement or the scope and goal of the original narrative. From the perspective of the supplementary approach, since both J and P are part of a major supplementation of DtrH, and since both emphasize the theme of the promise of land, its fulfillment in the final land division would make a most fitting conclusion to the whole.

There are some who take a more radical position in the other direction and view the end of P in Leviticus 9 with the dedication of the priesthood at Sinai. This is in keeping with a style of analysis that generally attributes a minimum of texts to the various sources and a very large portion to multiple redactions. The redactional analysis invariably becomes so complex as to tax credulity. The issues are credulity and cannot be debated here.

e. The existence of a final redactor of the Pentateuch

It is often suggested or assumed that there was a 'final redactor' of the Pentateuch. In the older documentary approach this is usually identified with Rp, but with the recent variety of proposals for literary analysis, terms like 'Pentateuchal Redactor' have become common. Such a figure is viewed increasingly as one who could tie up all the loose ends and could use different styles and language, both priestly and Deuteronomistic. The advantage to certain literary theories was that whatever could not be easily accounted for in the assignment of texts to one source or another could always be attributed to this final redactor. For those who did not wish to trouble themselves with any diachronic analysis, it was convenient to attribute to a final redactor a grand design for the whole of the Pentateuch or any particular book within it and then engage in synchronic analysis of the 'final form' that such a redactor must have produced.

The problem with this approach is that it assumes one particular literary model out of many, for which there is very little hard evidence and much that speaks against it. In particular, the degree to which any method of analysis accepts the notion that the Pentateuch may have received additions and expansions, some large and others small, to that extent any final form is problematic.[52] Unless all contributors were working under the discipline of a grand design, it is very unlikely that all the additions will produce the kinds of ingenious structures and intricately balanced patterns that scholars seem to find. If redactors are combining the works of quite different authors whose works have quite different forms and structures, the resulting combination is going to manifest less pattern and design than either work individually. It is possible that an author like P could supplement J and at the same time impose his own pattern on the whole, as his chronology seems to do. But small additions to particular parts of the Pentateuch are not likely to have such an effect.

6. New developments since 1999

Since the first publication of this book, there have been new developments that call for some additional comment in this edition. These have to do with the trend in European scholarship to separate the non-P (J) sources in Genesis from those in Exodus to Numbers and to regard P as the source that first made the connection between these two blocks of tradition. At the same time the advocates of this new approach regard the collection and combination of these two bodies of non-P tradition in Genesis and Exodus–Numbers, not as the work of an author (J), but as the activity of multiple editors or redactors. What follows is a review of this new development in Pentateuchal studies.

a. The patriarchs and the exodus

Konrad Schmid, in 1999, published his University of Zurich *Habilitationsschrift* (a second dissertation) under the title *Ancestors and Exodus: an Investigation into the Double Foundation and Origins of Israel within the Historical Books of the Old Testament.*[53] This work, which follows the lead of Rendtorff in playing down the role of J or any other pre-P as author, represents a radically new movement in European scholarship, and for this reason deserves some detailed comment. Schmid begins by examining the biblical history of Genesis to 2 Kings for narrative breaks and transitions as evidence of separate blocks of tradition, and among the most significant for his study is the one between the time of the patriarchs in Genesis and the story of Moses and the exodus from Egypt in Exodus. This obvious break between the two and the problem of their relationship to each other, long recognized in biblical scholarship, leads him to call into question a continuous 'J' source connecting the two and to re-examine the nature of the connections between Genesis and Exodus. Of course there are many different breaks between the different biblical eras, such as the primeval history of Gen. 1–11, or the transition between the time of Moses in Deuteronomy and Joshua in the book of Joshua, and from the time of the Judges to the rise of the monarchy. These transitions are easily recognized and reflect a great variety of sources and traditions about these eras, so that fact is not in dispute. The various differences among scholars are how to account for the literary connections that were made between these epochs.

As indicated earlier, in my view the one responsible for compiling the sources about the patriarchs and combining them with the exodus story was J, an author writing in the exilic period, but this is flatly rejected by Schmid. Instead, he regards the non-P corpus as a body of traditions compiled by 'redactors' over a long period of time, and it was P who made the connection between the patriarchal traditions in Genesis and the exodus story in Exodus. The heart of his thesis lies in demonstrating that those texts that make such connections, such as Gen. 15, 46.3, 50, Exod. 1 and Exod. 3–4, or parts thereof, are all post-P additions, and therefore it was P who was the first to connect the patriarchs with the exodus. I will select a few examples from his work that, in my view, will illustrate the weakness of his position.[54]

The first of these texts to refer to a connection between the patriarchs and the exodus is Gen. 15.12-15, in which Yahweh tells Abraham about their descent into a foreign land (Egypt) where they will be slaves, and after many years they will come back to this land. This text was formerly assigned to J and earlier than its counterpart in Genesis 17 (P), but now re-dated to post-P and therefore late in the

Persian period. However, this quite arbitrary re-dating will not work because the reference to Ur of the Chaldeans in v. 7 clearly places it in the time of Nabonidus, the king of Babylonia, when Ur was in its heyday (the date that I assign to J). This city was in decline and no longer of any importance in the later Persian period.

A second non-P text that makes the connection between the patriarchs and the exodus story is in the divine appearance to Jacob in the Joseph story in Gen. 46.1-4 in which the deity appears to Jacob, and identifies himself to him as 'the God of your father', and then tells him, 'do not be afraid to go down to Egypt for I will make of you a great nation there. I will go down with you to Egypt and I will also bring you up again; and Joseph's hand shall close your eyes'. Now the obvious way of interpreting this text is to understand the first part as a promise to make of Jacob's descendants a great nation in Egypt and then to predict that after he dies in Egypt, Joseph will bring him back to be buried in Canaan. The first of these promises is reflected in Exod. 1.7 and the second in Gen. 50.1-12. However, Schmid wants to interpret the remarks about becoming a great nation in Gen. 46.3 as limited to the time of Jacob's life, and points to the statement in 47.27-28, which refers to the people being fruitful and multiplying greatly in the land of Goshen, followed by a remark about Jacob living in Egypt for seventeen years. However, this text is not by the same author in Gen. 46.3, but is a remark made by P and the reference to the people greatly multiplying is typical of P and clearly refers to their whole time in Egypt, and not just to the seventeen years of Jacob's time there. In a similar fashion, Joseph and his brothers bury their father in Canaan (Gen. 50.1-12) in agreement with Gen. 46.3, but then return to Egypt. However, Schmid, by eliminating the references to their return in Gen. 50.5b and 8b as late additions, then suggests that in the original story at the time of Jacob's death all of his family returned to their homeland and had no connection with the exodus story. This is a very forced interpretation of events, because Joseph as a high Egyptian official is given a large Egyptian escort to accompany him and this only makes sense if they all return together after the burial. The elimination of the references to their return is quite arbitrary.

The non-P connections between the patriarchs and the exodus story in Exod. 1.6, 8 create a problem for Schmid because these non-P texts refer back to Joseph, so he simply rejects the whole chapter as either P or post-P, even though it is very hard to see how vv. 13-14 (P) makes much sense without the preceding vv. 8-12 (post-P?) as an explanation. Schmid regards Exod. 2 as the beginning of the pre-P Moses story but without Exod. 1.22, the order of Pharaoh to throw all of the Hebrew newborn children into the Nile, he must come up with another explanation for the behavior of Moses' mother. His explanation is so far-fetched that it has left others following his lead into trying to find other ways of dealing with Exod. 1.6, 8, with dubious results.[55] This still leaves the reference to the patriarchs in Exod. 3–4, in which the god who appears to Moses is declared to be the God of Abraham, Isaac and Jacob. This language is very similar to that used in the patriarchal promise in Genesis, and particularly in Gen. 46.1-4. These references in Exodus 3, however, are simply dismissed as late 'redactional' additions. One can prove anything by so easily eliminating any evidence against this thesis advocated by Schmid.

I have taken the liberty of dealing with this thesis by Schmid at length because the same perspective appears in additional studies and articles along the same lines as set forth by Schmid. These European scholars published a collection of some of these papers in German in a volume entitled *Farewell to the Yahwist*, as if to announce the end of an era in Pentateuchal studies.[56] This collection was criticized as being too one-sided and so it was followed by a second volume in English, *Farewell to the Yahwist?* (note the question mark), which included not only the Europeans in support of this 'farewell' but also other scholars who rejected their views.[57] This so-called demise of the Yahwist has put in its place the notion of a large collection of stories and traditions, whether oral or written is not clear, which are not the work of authors. Instead of an author we are introduced to a large body of editors or redactors, belonging to many different periods of time, who collected and strung together these pieces of tradition. This process now comes under the rubric of 'redaction criticism', *Redaktionsgeschichte*. The status of P, whether author or editor, remains unclear.[58]

b. The use and abuse of the redactor in Pentateuchal studies

In response to this serious abuse of the so-called 'redactor' I did an extensive and detailed study on the history and use of the notion of editor or redactor.[59] The editing or redaction of biblical text is understood in two senses, the one having to do with the creation of a written text out of an older body of traditions, and a second sense that deals with the standardization of the text by the critical examination of textual variants. At the beginning of the nineteenth century it was proposed that the epics of Homer, the *Iliad* and the *Odyssey*, were put together from a large body of old tradition by a group of editors, brought together for this purpose in Athens by the tyrant Peisistratus in the mid-sixth century BCE. Over the course of time, so it was thought, this text became corrupted by the existence of many variant copies so that the great scholars of the Alexandrian library during the early Ptolemaic period in Egypt, by collecting and comparing texts of Homer's epics, were able to produce a standard critical text of these works. These two senses of the editing of Homer, the original creation of the text out of older traditions by editors, and the recovery of the original text by a group of scholarly 'text critics', dominated classical studies for at least a century and a half, from the early nineteenth to mid-twentieth centuries. Furthermore, due to the close association of classical studies with biblical criticism, the critical study of the Pentateuch adopted the same two-fold approach in the forms of higher and lower criticism, with *higher criticism* concerned with how a succession of ancient editors combined the various sources of the Pentateuch into a single corpus and *lower criticism* concerned with how in early Roman times the *sopherim*, understood as editors, created a standardized text of the Hebrew Bible.

With respect to *lower criticism* (also called 'textual criticism'), in my historical study of the editor I attempted to show that the role of the editor as the one who created a standard text out of variant versions of the Hebrew Bible and the Greek New Testament did not exist before the rise of the printing press in the early Renaissance period. In contrast to these modern editors, the scholars of Alexandria in the Hellenistic period merely compiled commentaries of Homer, which sought to identify those parts of the epics that were 'Homeric' and those that were later additions to the text, but they never produced a standard text for the market-place and had little influence on the so-called 'medium' text that became the choice of the Greco-Roman book market. Nor is there any evidence that the *sopherim* created a standard text of the Hebrew Bible that was used as the basis for the later Masoretic text, or that Origen's objective, in his very elaborate comparison of Hebrew and Greek Old Testament texts, was to produce a definitive standard text, as the later scholars did in the Renaissance.

Likewise, with respect to *higher criticism*, the editor as the collector and publisher of folk traditions, such as the Brothers Grimm, only came into existence in the Romantic period of the eighteenth and nineteenth centuries. It was a serious anachronism, therefore, to use this model of an editor of traditions for the understanding of classical or biblical texts. After a long period of vigorous debate, classical scholars in the mid-twentieth century gave up the idea that editors created the Homeric epics in the time of Peisistratus out of a collection of independent stories. This would mean that textual additions that are not the work of the original author, whether small or great and for whatever purpose, would have to be viewed as deliberate modifications or textual corruptions. Biblical scholars, however, who had for so long relied on the model of Homeric studies as support for their use of ancient editors, were reluctant to give up their redactors and continued to rely on the myth of the ancient editors of tradition (*Redaktionsgeschichte*) against all evidence to the contrary.

In order to defend their extensive use of redactors in Pentateuchal studies, biblical scholars simply made the role of authors in the composition of the Pentateuch as non-existent. Against this objection that authors did not exist in antiquity, only the collectors of traditions who remained anonymous, i.e. redactors, the classical world of Greece and Rome contains abundant evidence to the contrary. The term 'author' is derived from the Latin *auctor* and was applied in antiquity to historians, such as Herodotus, who often claimed to gather their information from oral tradition as the sources for their histories. One very popular form of history was the 'antiquities', which began with the earliest generations of mankind and traced the generations of national ancestors and heroes down to the establishment of cities, states and nations. There is good reason to believe that this form of Greek antiquarian historiography was derived from the Phoenicians (Canaanites) along with their alphabet, and it is most likely that this was the case for the Israelites as well. Consequently, my book, *The Edited Bible*, set out to justify the complete legitimacy of attributing the antiquarian history of the Yahwist to an author and the quite erroneous application of the terms editor or redactor to the content of the Pentateuch, with the intent of stimulating serious dialogue on this issue. Instead, those strong advocates of 'redactional criticism' simply chose to ignore this critique and continue with their proliferation of redactors and the fragmentation of the Yahwistic history. It should come as no surprise that so many biblical scholars and students have deemed this kind of critical study as pointless and have turned to some meaningful way of dealing with the text in its present form.

c. An attempt to revive the Documentary Hypothesis

In America, where there was a reluctance to give up the Documentary Hypothesis, especially among those of the Harvard school of Frank Cross, a young scholar of this group, Joel Baden, attempted to address in his dissertation some recent criticism of the use of the term 'editor' in Pentateuchal criticism, a term which he strongly defends.[60] It is not appropriate in this book to carry out a detained review of Baden's thesis so I will limit my remarks to a few comments.

First. Baden, in his historical review of prior scholarship on this subject, begins his review of the upheaval in the mid-seventies with the statement: 'The most important challenge to the Documentary Hypothesis has come from Rolf Rendtorff ... and those who followed him. As it was Rendtorff who laid the methodological foundations for the challenge, it is his work on which we will focus here,' and then makes reference to his *Das überlieferungsgeschichtliche Problem des Pentateuch*.[61] Actually, there were two previous works, my book, *Abraham in History and Tradition* (1975), and that of H. H. Schmid, *Der sogenannte Jahwist: Beobachtungen und Fragen zur Pentateuchforschung* (1976), and all three were written from somewhat different perspectives.[62] It was this threefold attack on the Documentary Hypothesis that made the 'revolution' so effective. In addition to my critique of the Documentary Hypothesis, in the same book I also raised serious questions against the 'Albright school', as did Thomas Thompson,[63] as well as the early dating of the Pentateuch, J and E. It was this attack on the foundations of Pentateuchal studies, more than what the Europeans had to say, which had the greatest impact in America.

Second. This lack of any references to my earlier work and its place in the development of current Pentateuchal studies is troubling, especially when Baden begins his comments on my recent work, *The Edited Bible* (2006), with the statement: 'John Van Seters has long been a vocal opponent of the Documentary Hypothesis, and his views are well known and well published, to the point that they do not bear repeating or rebutting here, except as they directly concern the combination of J and E.'[64] On the contrary, since my views on the weakness of the

Documentary Hypothesis are quite different from those of 'Rendtorff *et al.*' I think they are quite worthy of discussion because they bear directly on Baden's own position. However, to make matters worse, he later makes the statement: 'Indeed, if one could successfully defend a theory of pentateuchal composition which did not include originally independent documents, then the figure of the redactor would be rendered superfluous. The difficulty, of course, is defending such a theory. But that is not what Van Seters is doing here; he is trying to undermine the theory by attacking the redactor, which is methodologically backward.'[65] The problem with this statement is that I have spent most of my career doing exactly what he says is a priority, by publishing over a thousand pages and identifying literary works, such as D, J, and P, and their direct connection with each other by successive supplementation without the need of 'redactors', and only then did I undertake to discuss at length the complete fiction of ancient editors. However, as indicated by the earlier quote, he has deliberately chosen not to discuss these earlier works because they are presumably so well known.

Third. As indicated above, in my own study in *The Edited Bible* I took great pains to show that the biblical scholars depended on the nineteenth-century classical scholars' use of redactors as an explanation for the origin of the Homeric epics, in order to justify the notion that redactors were responsible for the creation of the Pentateuch. Yet when classicists were forced to admit, by the mid-twentieth century that this was a serious mistake, they abandoned all references to such editors. In spite of this, however, biblical scholars still persisted in their belief in such redactors to explain how the various components came together, but they no longer had any evidence to support their notion that redactors ever existed in antiquity. Baden takes exception to this, and states: 'Van Seters thereby claims that since biblical studies borrowed the idea of the redactor from a field that has since rejected it, biblical scholars should reject it as well. This reasoning is flawed: just because an idea doesn't work in the field that invented it, it does not mean that it cannot work in a field that borrows it. The idea is to be judged on its own merits within each independent field.' This statement is quite misleading. It was not primarily a case of adopting a method of literary analysis but what they regarded as firm evidence that ancient editors actually existed in the creation of Homer's epics, evidence that was quite independent from the analysis of the text itself. And this evidence was limited to Homer and to no other literary work. Biblical scholars argued that if it was true for Homer it could also be true for the Pentateuch. It was only when the evidence for Homer proved false that the notion of editors in Homeric studies was abandoned and the focus shifted to what one could characterize as a supplementary hypothesis of textual expansion and corruption. Consequently, what happened to the redactor in classical studies is directly relevant to the literary criticism of the Pentateuch.

Baden continues with his critique of my position: 'Furthermore, it is fundamentally incorrect to state that the idea of the redactor is borrowed from classical studies. Though the understanding of how an editor works may have been taken over by analogy with Homeric scholarship, the existence of the redactor in some form is derived by necessity from the Documentary Hypothesis; it is not imposed on source criticism from without.' This statement is quite false because it is precisely the reverse that is true. One could not have separate documents, J, E, D, P (to use Baden's terms), without a series of redactors to put them together. But European scholarship, which completely rejects the Documentary Hypothesis, also makes an abundant use of redactors. One may reject their understanding of redactors, as Baden must, but the same can be said for Baden's use of the redactor as equally arbitrary, as I believe they all are. However, the point is that quite apart from the Pentateuch as we now have it, where there is a great deal of strong evidence for large and small additions made directly to biblical and non-biblical texts without any intervention of an editor, and after the demise of the Homeric editors, there has never been one clear example of an editor making any such additions or combinations of texts as that suggested by the Documentary Hypothesis.

d. Recent developments in the studies of biblical law

Since the end of the twentieth century and for the following decade the primary focus in the study of biblical law in the Pentateuch was on the 'Book of the Covenant' in Exod. 20.22–23.33, also known in scholarship as the Covenant Code. The reason for the lively discussion regarding the origin, nature and dating of this code was the upheaval in Pentateuchal studies in general, as indicated above, and how this corpus of laws was to be related to its present setting in the non-P (J) source. In my monograph, *A Law Book for the Diaspora* (2003)[66] I attempted to address these issues, and to defend my view that the whole of this corpus was the work of a single author, the Yahwist, written in the late exilic period as part of his larger history. Needless to say, this book evoked a vigorous response, most of it negative, by those who held long-established views to the contrary. My purpose in the remarks that follow is not to lay out in summary fashion all of the conclusions in my book. Instead, I will indicate briefly what I call the four 'pillars of priority' that scholars have long used to support a date for the Covenant Code as the earliest biblical law code and their understanding of the relationship that it has with both the laws of Deuteronomy and those within that part of the Priestly law code, known as the 'Holiness Code'. Any student of biblical law must be aware of these four 'pillars' that are used to support the priority of the Covenant Code, and if they cannot stand up to close scrutiny, then one must be prepared to consider alternatives.

The first of these pillars is the Documentary Hypothesis, in which the Covenant Code is associated with one of the pre-Deuteronomic sources, usually E, or if one excludes E from consideration, then J. If one calls into question the Documentary

Hypothesis then it lays open the whole question of dating the Covenant Code as well, which must be established on entirely new grounds. The second pillar has to do with the remarkable correspondence between casuistic laws in the first half of the Covenant Code with similar laws in the Hammurabi Code. It is suggested that it was the Canaanites who first received this law code from the Babylonians in the second millennium BCE and at a later stage the Israelites inherited it from them. Such a suggestion has become increasingly discredited, and the only viable alternative seems to be the close contact that the Judean exiles had with Babylonian culture in the exilic period. Consequently, this similarity actually supports a date for the Covenant Code that is later than the Deuteronomic Code and suggests it was composed by an author who lived among the Babylonian exiles.[67]

The third pillar supporting an early date for the Covenant Code has to do with attempts to identify its content with the particular social evolution of Israelite society that is reflected in the code. While Wellhausen and others were able to point out the rather simple level of social life with its lack of royalty or any highly developed aspects of society, this argument has become problematic because the level of literacy reflected in the code certainly requires a society that includes a scribal class and a legal tradition that demands a rather late stage in Israelite and Judean development. Instead, it is the semi-autonomous community of Judeans in exile that would best account for the kind of social laws that are included and the reason why other laws that one might have expected in a major urban center, such as Jerusalem in the late monarchy period, are absent.

The fourth pillar supporting the Covenant Code's early date arises out of the application of the doctrines of form-criticism in which each particular form is thought to have its own particular social setting and hence its distinctive forms of law, separate from the others. This approach to the analysis of biblical laws and the Covenant Code in particular has led to the curious development of an elaborate discussion about which laws were developed early and which arose later, and a complex history of how they all came together. All of this however amounts to sheer speculation. There is nothing in the identification of different forms of law appropriate to different settings that would prevent a single learned individual from constructing a code that contained examples of all of these types of law appropriate to the particular community for which it was intended.

Let us suppose, for the sake of argument, that there was in the late Neo-Babylonian period a gifted scribe living among the Judeans in Babylonia, such as I have suggested above was the case with the Yahwist. This scribe had at his disposal such earlier legal traditions as those reflected in the Book of Deuteronomy and some within the Priestly tradition as contained in the Holiness Code, as well as those passed on to successive generations of scribes. Such laws were of varying forms, both social and religious, and in addition there were also the legal traditions of the Babylonians, including the Hammurabi Code. This code was almost certainly available in Aramaic translation and script, the official language of the empire.

Within such an environment where the creation of law codes for the society of the day had long been practiced, it is entirely reasonable to believe that our gifted scribe could also put together a modest, but comparable, law code for his own community, and following the example of Deuteronomy place its origin in the time of Moses, the great law-giver.

My book begins in Chapter 1 with a detailed history of research on the Covenant Code leading up to my assigning it to the Yahwist as its author and its place within his larger account of the story of Moses in the wilderness. Chapter 2 discusses the larger narrative context of the Covenant Code as part of the Sinai story and its conclusion in the ceremonial enactment of the covenant at the conclusion of its reception. Chapter 3 deals with the civil laws in the first half of the code and Chapter 4 covers a wide range of social, ethical and religious laws. In all of this study, careful attention is given to similar or parallel versions of those laws that have their counterpart in the other Pentateuchal codes and the debate about which version of the law is dependent on which. This is an area of considerable difference of opinion and debate.

Needless to say, after the publication of this book on the Covenant Code, discussion on biblical law at conferences debated the thesis of my book. Three leading scholars on biblical law, Bernard Jackson, Bernard Levinson and Eckart Otto, wrote extensive critical reviews of the book, each reflecting somewhat different perspectives but all of them defending an early date for the Covenant Code and its priority over Deuteronomy.[68] To all of these I responded in the *Scandinavian Journal of the Old Testament*.[69] I will not attempt to repeat that defense of my position here, but what is particularly significant is how these critics attempted to offer support for one or more of the 'pillars' mentioned above, particularly that of the similarities with the Hammurabi Code as supporting an early date. One of the more thoughtful and helpful issues raised by Jackson has to do with the social and institutional location of such a law code in the exile. How did it actually function in such an environment? What sort of judiciary and communal institution could make this code work? In contrast to Deuteronomy, the Covenant Code appears to make one vague reference to a group of 'judges' in setting damages in a particular case, but says little about the legal context in which such judgments are made. The community of Judeans living in exile would certainly have a much simpler social structure that was the case during the time of the monarchy. Beyond saying that, however, I did not have an answer to Jackson's question at that time.

e. The case for the Yahwist as historian

My most recent study on the Pentateuch is *The Yahwist: A Historian of Israelite Origins* (2013). Part 1 contains 'An Outline of the Yahwist's Antiquities of Israel', which includes the creation story, the history of the patriarchs, the Israelites' sojourn in Egypt, the exodus under Moses, their wilderness journey, and their conquest of those nations living east of the Jordan River. This brief 140-page survey gives an overview of how the whole J narrative fits together as a composition in the style of an ancient historical work, similar to those known from ancient Greece. It also includes remarks, where necessary, about how the Yahwist is to be distinguished from the later additions of the P writer. Part 2 includes a series of 'studies in defense of the Yahwist' that deal in greater detail with current points of controversy as they have to do with the present debate in Pentateuchal studies.[70] These studies also provide a fairly broad spectrum of European, British and North American scholarship as it pertains to the historical-critical study of the Pentateuch at the present time.

In addition to these articles I have recently addressed in two further studies the issues related to the social and historical context in which the Yahwist's narrative came into being. The first has to do with the evidence for dating the Yahwist in the late Neo-Babylonian period and the implications this has for an understanding of this literary work.[71] This study gives special attention to the social and historical context of the Yahwist in the late Neo-Babylonian period. Of primary importance for dating the Yahwist is the close similarity with Second Isaiah in the prophet's emphasis on creation and the Garden of Eden, the patriarchs and the exodus, and the same use of distinctive terminology for the deity. Also significant is J's use of Babylonian literature and culture as reflected in the Flood Story, the Tower of Babel, and the use of the Hammurabi Code, as well as the references to the cities of Ur of the Chaldeans and Harran in the account of Abraham's migration to Palestine, which make sense only in the time of Nabonidus in the late Neo-Babylonian period.

The second article has to do with the nature of the Judean community in exile and the way in which they were able to sustain their identity in this period.[72] To whom was such a work of the Yahwist directed and within what social and religious context? The prophet Ezekiel, while in exile in Babylonia, makes frequent reference to the elders of Israel as if they played a significant role in the leadership of the people. Likewise in J the elders receive mention as representatives of the people, and in Num. 11.16-17, 24-25 the elders are especially consecrated to assist Moses in the 'burden' of governing the people. This special consecration of the seventy elders takes place at the 'Tent of Meeting'. In this study I argue that these references to the elders in J and their close association with the Tent of Meeting reflect the origin of the synagogue in Babylonia during the period of the exile. The synagogue served as both a 'meeting place' and as a 'place of prayer' in the diaspora and the elders of the people had an important role in its function. The synagogue throughout its history was a lay institution, with no priests involved in its leadership. Likewise in Exod. 33.7-9 the Tent of Meeting is also characterized as a place of prayer and Joshua was in charge of it with no priest associated with it. Furthermore, it was the elders of the synagogue (Tent of Meeting) who could serve as judges (Exod. 21.22) to adjudicate matters of guilt and punishment on behalf of the community of Judeans in exile. Thus the synagogue could provide just the necessary communal context for the survival of the Judeans' identity and the Covenant Code would obviously serve an important role in the governance of Judeans in their local communities in Babylonia. This solves the social and religious context of the Yahwist better than any other explanation of which I am aware. The Yahwist did not invent the synagogue; he merely provided a legitimation for its existence by placing its origin in the time of Moses and a 'history' that supported the Judeans' traditions and identity in a foreign environment.

If this reconstruction of the synagogue's origin is correct, then there is one important group of Judeans that is left out of the picture, and that is the whole priestly establishment. The Yahwist simply eliminates them from any future role and gives no place for them in his narrative. Not even Aaron, the Levite, functions as a priest in J. A large part of the P document is intended to make up for this lack by substituting for J's simple Tent of Meeting the elaborate Tabernacle as a grand portable temple, to which he then refers 150 times as the 'Tent of Meeting'. Now in P the priesthood is supreme and entirely in charge of this institution and the lay community, including the elders of the people, are completely excluded. Furthermore, this text was superimposed on the older J text with the intention of overwhelming the brief remarks about J's Tent of Meeting, i.e. the synagogue, to give the Temple and its priesthood the priority. Nevertheless, the lay synagogue survived and thrived in the diaspora and eventually replaced the Temple and its priesthood after the demise of the Second Temple in the Roman period.

Notes

1 Winnett, 'Reexamining the Foundations', pp. 1–19.
2 Gen. 12.1, 4a*, 6a, 7, 10-20; 13.1*, 2; 16.1-3a, 4-9, 11ab, 12; 13.18; 18.1a, 10-14; 21.2, 6-7.
3 'Confessional Reformulation in the Exilic Period', *VT* 22 (1972), pp. 448–59.
4 'The So-called Deuteronomistic Redaction of the Pentateuch', in J. A. Emerton (ed.), *Congress Volume: Leuven, 1989* (VTSup 43; Leiden: E.J. Brill, 1992), pp. 58–77.
5 *The Mosaic Tradition.*
6 Gen. 25.21-27, 29-34; 28.11-12, 16aα, 17-19; 29.31-30.34; 32.2-3 [1-2], 23-33* [22-32*]. These texts can be identified as pre-J. Within chs. 29–31 there is also a substantial portion of pre-J material but also a number of J additions.
7 J's account of Moses actually ends in Deut. 34 with his death.
8 J. Van Seters, 'The Conquest of Sihon's Kingdom: A Literary Examination', *JBL* 91 (1972), pp. 182–97; *idem*, 'Etiology in the Moses Tradition: The Case of Exodus 18', *HAR* 9 (1985), pp. 355–61; *idem*, ' "Comparing Scripture with Scripture": Some Observations on the Sinai Pericope of Exodus 19–24', in G. M. Tucker, D. L. Petersen and R. R. Wilson (eds.), *Canon, Theology, and Old Testament Interpretation: Essays in Honor of Brevard S. Childs* (Philadelphia: Fortress Press, 1988), pp. 111–30; *idem*, *The Life of Moses.*

9 J. Van Seters, 'Joshua 24 and the Problem of Tradition in the Old Testament', in
   W. B. Barrick and J. R. Spencer (eds.), *In the Shelter of Elyon: Essays in Honor of
   G. W. Ahlström* (JSOTSup, 31; Sheffield: JSOT Press, 1984), pp. 139–58.

10 I strongly dispute that such a rejection is implicit in von Rad and regard Rendtorff's
    position as based primarily upon Noth. See Van Seters, 'The Yahwist as Theologian?',
    pp. 15–20.

11 See J. Van Seters, 'Recent Studies on the Pentateuch: A Crisis in Method', *JAOS* 99
    (1979), pp. 663–73, for my review of Rendtorff's book.

12 Von Rad, *Das formgeschichtliche Problem des Hexateuchs*.

13 Noth, *A History of Pentateuchal Traditions*.

14 See nn. 3 and 4 above.

15 Alt, 'The God of the Fathers'.

16 Noth, *A History of Pentateuchal Traditions*.

17 Long, *The Problem of Etiological Narrative*.

18 Coats, *Genesis*.

19 Coats, *Genesis*, p. 319.

20 Coats, *Moses: Heroic Man, Man of God*.

21 H. Gunkel, 'Geschichtsschreibung im A.T.', *RGG*, II, pp. 1348–54; 2nd edn, II,
    pp. 1112–15.

22 M. Noth, 'Geschichtsschreibung im A.T.', *RGG*, 3rd edn, II, pp. 1498–504.

23 G. von Rad, 'The Beginning of Historical Writing in Ancient Israel' (1944), in *idem,
    The Problem of the Hexateuch and Other Essays* (Edinburgh: Oliver & Boyd, 1966),
    pp. 166–204.

24 See Van Seters, *Prologue to History*, pp. 86–99.

25 Van Seters, *Prologue to History*, pp. 38–42; Niditch, *Oral World*.

26 W. V. Harris, *Ancient Literacy* (Cambridge, MA: Harvard University Press, 1989);
    Thomas, *Oral Tradition; idem, Literacy and Orality*. Comparison with the Greek world
    seems more appropriate than with the Mesopotamian world in the case of Israelite
    literacy, because the Hebrews, like the Greeks, were indebted to the Canaanite/
    Phoenecian form of alphabetic literacy and not the cuneiform system of Mesopotamia.
    It is within the context of the rise of literacy in the Levant and the eastern Aegean that
    Israel's own literacy is to be understood.

27 See N. Na'aman, 'Sources and Composition in the History of Solomon', in L. K. Handy
    (ed.), *The Age of Solomon* (Leiden: E.J. Brill, 1997), pp. 57–80; H. M. Niemann, 'The
    Socio-Political Shadow Cast by the Biblical Solomon', in Handy (ed.), *The Age of
    Solomon*, pp. 252–99.

28 W. Aly, *Volksmärchen, Sage und Novelle bei Herodot und seinen Zeitgenossen*
    (Göttingen: Vandenhoeck & Ruprecht, 1921).

29 See Thomas, *Literacy and Orality in Ancient Greece*, pp. 29–51.

30 Contrary to the criticism of Niditch (*Oral World*, pp. 114–16) that the genre of
    historiography is inappropriate for the biblical material in Genesis–2 Kings,
    and her rejection of any comparison with Herodotus, it may be pointed out
    that scholarship on Herodotus has long emphasized the close proximity of
    Herodotus and his contemporaries to oral tradition and folklore. Indeed, the
    major work of Aly (*Volksmärchen*) was inspired by the work of Gunkel on
    Genesis. See also Thomas, *Oral Tradition*, pp. 283–86; *idem, Literacy and Orality*,
    pp. 101–108.

31 R. E. Friedman, *Who Wrote the Bible?* (Englewood Cliffs, NJ: Prentice-Hall, 1987; *idem,
    'Torah (Pentateuch)', ABD*, VI, pp. 605–22; Nicholson, *The Pentateuch in the Twentieth*

Century; A. F. Campbell and M. A. O'Brien, *Sources of the Pentateuch: Texts, Introduction, Annotations* (Philadelphia: Fortress Press, 1993).

32 See most recently Hiebert, *The Yahwist's Landscape*. This is a work of the Albright-Cross school and advocates a date for J in the early monarchy (p. 25).

33 See Friedman, *Who Wrote the Bible?*; idem, 'Torah (Pentateuch)'.

34 Rendtorff, *Das überlieferungsgeschichtliche Problem des Pentateuch*.

35 Blum, *Die Komposition der Vätergeschichte; idem, Studien zur Komposition des Pentateuch*.

36 Blum, 'Gibt es die Endgestalt des Pentateuch?', pp. 46–57.

37 See my recent discussion of his work in 'Divine Encounter at Bethel (Gen. 28,10–22) in Recent Literary-Critical Study of Genesis', *ZAW* 110 (1998), pp. 503–13.

38 J did not invent the promises theme which appears as a land promise to Abraham in the pre-J material, as is also evident in Ezek. 33.24.

39 Van Seters, *Abraham in History and Tradition; idem, Prologue to History; idem, The Life of Moses*.

40 Van Seters, *In Search of History*.

41 *The Making of the Pentateuch*.

42 *Introduction to the Pentateuch*.

43 Blenkinsopp (*The Pentateuch*, pp. 37–39) lumps my view and Whybray's view together and does not do justice to the distinction between them. Many of his reservations do not apply to me.

44 Wellhausen, *Prolegomena*, pp. 1–13.

45 *Temple and Temple Service*.

46 Blenkinsopp, 'Priestly Material in the Pentateuch', pp. 495–518.

47 See J. A. Emerton, 'The Priestly Writer in Genesis', *JTS* 39 (1988), pp. 381–400; K. Koch, 'P-Kein Redaktor: Erinnerung an zwei Eckdaten der Quellenscheidung', *VT* 37 (1987), pp. 446–67; J. L. Ska, 'De la relative indépendence de l'écrit sacerdotal', *Bib* 75 (1994), pp. 396–415. However, the Cross school views P as a supplement. See Cross, *Canaanite Myth and Hebrew Epic*, pp. 293–325.

48 On this contradiction in the assessment of David see Van Seters, *In Search of History*, pp. 277–91; also 'The Court History and DtrH: Conflicting Perspectives on the House of David', in A. de Pury and T. Römer (eds). *Die sogenannte Thronfolgegeschichte Davids: Neue Einsichten und Anfragen* (Freiburg: Universitätsverlag and Göttingen: Vandehoeck & Rupprecht, 2000), pp. 70–93.

49 *A History of Pentateuchal Traditions*.

50 See also Blenkinsopp, *The Pentateuch*, pp. 229–32.

51 N. Lohfink, 'The Priestly Narrative of History', in *idem, The Theology of the Pentateuch* (trans. L. M. Maloney; Philadelphia: Fortress Press, 1994), pp. 136–72; Van Seters, *In Search of History*, pp. 324–37; Vink, *The Date and Origin of the Priestly Code*.

52 Blum, 'Gibt es die Endgestalt des Pentateuch?', pp. 46–57; also S. Boorer, 'The Importance of a Diachronic Approach: The Case of Genesis-Kings', *CBQ* 51 (1989), pp. 195–208.

53 K. Schmid, *Erzväter und Exodus: Untersuchungen zur doppelten Begründung der Ursprünge Israels innnerhalb der Geschichtsbücher des Alten Testaments*, (1999).

54 For a more detailed review see J. Van Seters, 'The Patriarchs and the Exodus' (2006), pp. 1–15.

55 See most recently, R. Albertz, 'Der Beginn der vorpriesterlichen Exodus-komposition (K^{ex}) (2011), pp. 223–62, and my response in Van Seters, 'The Israelites in Egypt (Exodus 1–5) within the Larger Context of the Yahwist's History', in *The Yahwist*, pp. 267–89.

56 J.C. Gertz, K. Schmid, and M. Witt, eds., *Abschied vom Jahwisten* (2002).

57 T.B. Dozaman and K. Schmid eds., *A Farewell to the Yahwist?* (2006). This contains my own critique of this position in much greater detail that can be included here, Van Seters, 'The Report of the Yahwist's Demise Has Been Greatly Exaggerated', in Dozaman and Schmid (eds.), *A Farewell to the Yahwist?* (2006), 143–57.

58 A useful recent survey of European scholarship on the Pentateuch may be found in H-C Schmitt, *Arbeitsbuch zum Alten Testament*, 3rd edn (2011).

59 Van Seters, *The Edited Bible* (2006).

60 J. S. Baden, *J, E, and the Redaction of the Pentateuch*, (2009), pp. 85–94.

61 R. Rendtorff, *Das überlieferungsgeschichtliche Problem des Pentateuch* (1977).

62 J. Van Seters, *Abraham in History and Tradition*, (1975); H. H. Schmid, *Der sogenannte Jahwist: Beobachtungen und Fragen zur Pentateuchforschung* (1976).

63 T. L. Thompson, *The Historicity of the Patriarchal Narratives* (1974).

64 Baden, *Redaction of the Pentateuch*, p. 85.

65 Baden, *Redaction of the Pentateuch*, p. 88.

66 J. Van Seters, *A Law Book for the Diaspora: Revision in the Study of the Covenant Code* (2003).

67 The same applies to the Yahwist in general with his use of the Babylonian Flood story, the Tower of Babel and the migration of Abraham from Ur of the Chaldeans.

68 B. S. Jackson, 'Revolution in Biblical Law: Some Reflections on the Role of Theory and Methodology', *JSS* 50 (2005), pp. 83–115; B.M. Levinson, 'Is the Covenant Code an Exilic Composition? A Response to John Van Seters', in J. Day (ed.), *In Search of Pre-exilic Israel* (2004), pp. 272–325; E. Otto, a review of *A Law Book for the Diaspora*, in RBL published on its website July 2004 and with a German version in *Biblica* 85 (2004), pp. 273–77.

69 'Revision in the Study of the Covenant Code and a Response to my Critics', *SJOT* 21 (2007), pp. 5–28.

70 Of the twelve studies that are included in part 2, six have appeared in previous publications, and half of these are not easily accessible; the other six are published here for the first time.

71 'Dating the Yahwist's History: Principles and Perspectives,' *Biblica* (forthcoming).

72 'The Tent of Meeting in the Yahwist and the Origin of the Synagogue,' *SJOT* (forthcoming).

5

Deuteronomy

Bibliography

Baltzer, K., *Das Bundesformular* (WMANT, 4; Neukirchen-Vluyn: Neukirchener Verlag, 1964); *ET The Covenant Formulary* (trans. D. E. Green; Oxford: Basil Blackwell, 1971).

Braulik, G., 'Deuteronomy and the Birth of Monotheism', in *idem, The Theology of Deuteronomy* (trans. U. Lindblad; N. Richland Hills, TX: BIBAL Press, 1994), pp. 99–130.

Driver, S. R., *Deuteronomy* (ICC; New York: Charles Scribner's Sons, 1895).

Lohfink, N., *Das Hauptgebot: Eine Untersuchung literarischer Einleitungsfragen zu Dtn 5-11* (AnBib, 20; Rome: Pontifical Biblical Institute, 1963).

—— 'Deuteronomy', in *IDBSup*, pp. 229–32.

—— 'The Cult Reform of Josiah of Judah: 2 Kings 22–23 as a Source for the History of Israelite Religion', in P. D. Miller *et al.* (eds.), *Ancient Israelite Religion* (Philadelphia: Fortress Press, 1987), pp. 459–75.

—— 'Deuteronomium und Pentateuch', in *idem* (ed.), *Studien zum Deuteronomium, III* (Stuttgart: Katholisches Bibelwerk, 1990), pp. 13–38.

Lohfink, N. (ed.), *Das Deuteronomium Entstehumg, Gestalt und Botschaft* (BETL, 68; Leuven: Peeters, 1985).

Mayes, A. D. H., *Deuteronomy* (NCBC; Grand Rapids: Eerdmans, 1979).

McCarthy, D. J., *Old Testament Covenant: A Survey of Current Opinions* (Richmond, VA: John Knox Press, 1972).

Minette de Tillesse, G., 'Section "tu" et sections "vous" dans le Deutéronome', *VT* 12 (1962), pp. 29–87.

Nicholson, E. W., *Deuteronomy and Tradition* (Oxford: Basil Blackwell, 1967).

—— *God and his People* (Oxford: Oxford University Press, 1986).

Perlitt, L., *Bundestheologie im Alten Testament* (1969).

Preuss, H. D., *Deuteronomium* (ErFor, 164; Darmstadt: Wissenschaftliche Buchgesellschaft, 1982).

—— 'Zum deuteronomistische Geschichtswerk', *TRu* 58 (1993), pp. 229–45.

Rad, G. von, *Studies in Deuteronomy* (trans. D. Stalker; SBT, 9; London: SCM Press, 1953).

—— *Deuteronomy* (OTL; Philadelphia: Westminster Press, 1966).

Römer, T., *Israels Väter (1990)*.

Seitz, G., *Redaktionsgeschichtliche Studien zum Deuteronomium* (BWANT, 5.13; Stuttgart: W. Kohlhammer, 1971).

Van Seters, J., 'Confessional Reformulation in the Exilic Period' (1972).

—— 'The So-called Deuteronomistic Redaction' (1992).

—— *Prologue to History* (1992).

Weinfeld, M., *Deuteronomy and the Deuteronomic School* (Oxford: Oxford University Press, 1972).
—— *Deuteronomy 1–11* (AB, 5; New York: Doubleday, 1991).

1. Basic features

As the fifth and last book of the Pentateuch, Deuteronomy takes the form of *retelling* some of the events having to do with the wilderness journey (chs. 1–3) and the giving of the Ten Commandments at Horeb/Sinai (chs. 4–5) that were covered more fully in the earlier books. This constitutes a prelude for the full code of laws given to the Israelites at the end of the journey before they enter the promised land. For this reason, the Greek translators of the Septuagint gave it the name Deuteronomion, which means 'second law'. The setting of the book is the region east of the Jordan river opposite Jericho where Moses is addressing the people. Moses will not lead them into the new land but will die on Mount Nebo overlooking the northern end of the Dead Sea. It is Joshua who will be their new leader, and the story of the conquest will follow in the book of Joshua.

It may seem strange to begin a literary analysis of the Pentateuch with the last book and the end of the story. But Deuteronomy is the key to understanding both the Pentateuch (Torah) and the historical books that follow in Joshua–2 Kings, as well as the relationship between them. This is true for at least three reasons:

1. As noted above, Deuteronomy is a separate source in the Pentateuch whose 'first edition' can be dated to a particular period in Israel's history, namely, the time of Josiah's reform. The other 'sources' must be dated and placed in relationship to Deuteronomy.

2. Whenever the 'book of the Law of Moses' is mentioned in the history of Joshua–2 Kings, it is always Deuteronomy that is intended, not the law in the rest of the Pentateuch. This can be seen by the language used to describe the law and the implied, or explicitly stated, content of the law and its correspondence with the language and content of Deuteronomy. Deuteronomy, therefore, has the closest relationship to this history. While we cannot explore this relationship in depth in this study of the Pentateuch, we cannot completely ignore it either.

3. If one adopts the supplementary model for Pentateuchal study whereby the Tetrateuch (Genesis–Numbers) is a later addition to the Deuteronomistic History (Deuteronomy–2 Kings), then the reason for starting here is all the more apparent. There is even a broad recognition in the current discussion of the Pentateuch that the way Deuteronomy is viewed as related to the Tetrateuch and to the 'Deuteronomic' elements within it determines the approach that one takes to the rest of the Pentateuch.

2. Form and structure of Deuteronomy

a. Form

Deuteronomy in its present form is one long farewell address by Moses in the first person to the Israelites east of the Jordan. Underneath this simple surface form the work has a more complex structure and history of development. But in its present form, it is strikingly different from the other sources in the Pentateuch, and what makes it so different is its predominant sermonic, hortatory style. There is almost none of this in the rest of the Pentateuch. Yet the same style of language and form shows up in the later historical books in speeches by leaders and prophets and it is given the designation 'Deuteronomistic'. Even the form of a farewell address just before Moses' death is imitated in the later history by Joshua (Josh. 23), Samuel (1 Sam. 12) and David (1 Kgs 2.1-4) in the same sermonic style.

This style of farewell address and admonitory speech has some similarity to two foreign models. The one, associated with the wisdom tradition, is that of instructions given by a king to his successor (often using the fiction of posthumous advice) and these usually have a high moral tone of admonition. The other is that of a testament of loyalty on the occasion of the designation of the royal successor.[1] While there are some elements of similarity with both of these models, the element of 'succession' by Joshua is limited to only a few texts in the prologue and epilogue (3.21-22; 31.7-8, 14-15, 23) and these have a quite separate short admonition. The speech of Moses is directed primarily at the people as a whole and not the successor. Nevertheless, the notion of speeches by leaders is a widespread convention used in many contexts in historiography and is employed by Deuteronomy as the basic form for the work.

The occasion of Moses' final speech is also the point at which he gives to the people the laws that are to govern their behavior when they enter the promised land. Deuteronomy 5 suggests that at Horeb (= Sinai) God gave the people the Ten Commandments by speaking to all of them directly. However, because the experience of the divine presence was so terrifying for them, they called upon Moses to deal with God directly on their behalf and to receive the rest of the laws in private. It is this 'whole law' that Moses passes on to the people in the land of Moab in the form of a book (i.e. Deuteronomy).

b. Structure

The core of Deuteronomy is the code of laws in chs. 12–26, which is framed by exhortation to obedience in chs. 5–11 and the promise of blessings for compliance and curses for disobedience in chs. 27–28. This in turn is enclosed in a second framework of historical prologue in chs. 1–4 and concluding exhortation and covenant making in chs. 29–30, followed by Joshua's installation as Moses' successor in ch. 31 and Moses' death in ch. 34. Into this ending have been fitted two poems in chs. 32–33. This may be represented as follows:

First prologue: a historical résumé (1–4).
    Second prologue: exhortation to keep the law (5–11).
        Laws: the Deuteronomic Code (12–26).
    Blessing and curses ([27] 28).
The epilogue: the Moab covenant and concluding exhortation (29–30),
    Joshua's installation (31) and Moses' death (34).
Two poems: Moses' song (32) and blessing (33).

This simple structure is often used as an initial point of departure for the literary history and interpretation of the book. This generally yields the following broad outline of development:

(a) Laws in 12–26 are the oldest.
(b) First framework of 5–11, 28 equals the second stage.
(c) Second framework, 1–4 plus 29–31, 34 equals the third stage.
(d) Later additions: the ceremony of curse, 27; the two poems, 32–33; some secondary expansions.

This scheme is generally considered to be an oversimplification of the book's literary history. Its development was, in fact, quite complex and calls for further internal scrutiny to determine whether there are additional signs of literary stratification within the larger units.

3. Additional literary observations

The structural analysis has already suggested that one way of identifying major divisions in the book is through *multiple superscriptions* (1.1; 4.44, 45; 12.1; 28.69 [= 29.1]; 33.1).[2] Yet 4.44 and 45 are doublets in which the latter goes most easily with what follows and with ch. 5. Some have identified a major division in 6:4 that would fit well with the introduction in 4.44. This suggests that the unit in 4.45–6.3, which includes the giving of the Ten Commandments, is a later expansion of the oldest prologue to the laws.

The narrative on the Decalogue in ch. 5 has a parallel in 4.1-40 that constitutes an elaborate commentary on the nature of the theophany and law-giving at Horeb with special emphasis on the first two commandments. It is generally recognized as a later addition to the prologue, and when it is bracketed the unit on the cities of refuge set aside by Moses east of the Jordan in 4.41-43 follows on from ch. 3, which recalls the conquest of the land east of the Jordan and its distribution to the eastern tribes. The transition in 4.45-46 further suggests that the narrative description of the giving of the Decalogue in ch. 5 belongs to the prologue of chs. 1–3. At the same time the narrative recounting of the molten calf episode in 9.7–10.11 presupposes the events of ch. 5 so that it must also belong to this later level of composition. It has also been suggested that the close affinities between 4.1-40 and 10.12–11.32 mark this latter as a late addition.[3] This would restrict the oldest prologue to chs. 6–8.

The presence of doublets or parallels, therefore, is an indication of literary stratification. In addition to the parallel accounts of the giving of the law at Horeb in chs. 4 and 5, there are two quite different presentations of life in the wilderness, one in ch. 8, emphasizing God's miraculous provision and protection, and one in ch. 9, narrating the people's constant disobedience and divine punishment. There are two versions of blessings and curses in chs. 27 and 28 and two versions of Joshua's installation as successor in 31.7-8 and 14-15, 23. There are two versions of the law of centralization in 12.2-12 and 13-19, with a supplement in vv. 20-29. At times there appears to be an interweaving of different materials in an awkward fashion. Thus in ch. 31 Moses makes a final (?) speech to the people and to Joshua, his successor (vv. 1-8), followed by the delivery of the written law to the Levites with instructions about periodic public instruction in the law (vv. 9-13). This is followed by a divine speech to Moses with instructions about Joshua's installation (vv. 14-15), interrupted by a second divine speech of warning about the people's future unfaithfulness and instructions to Moses to compose a song as a 'witness' against them, which Moses does (vv. 16-22). The installation of Joshua is then completed in v. 23. The next section (vv. 24-29) returns to the theme of Moses giving the law to the Levites, repetitious of the earlier unit in vv. 9-13, but more negative. Finally, in v. 30 Moses recites the song (following v. 22), which is given in ch. 32. There appear to be several levels in this text by quite different hands.

With the general form of direct speech by Moses to the people, the latter are addressed in the second person 'you', but this may be rendered in the Hebrew by either a singular or a plural pronoun. The vacillation between these two forms, which occurs within the various units, has often been taken to be an indication of literary stratification, with the singular regarded as the earlier and the plural later.[4] This distinction, however, has been disputed,[5] and at least in some instances can be shown to have other explanations. Thus, in the law of centralization in ch. 12, vv. 13-19 are in the second singular and taken to be the oldest version with vv. 2-12 in the second plural and more recent. But what looks to be an expansion on both versions in vv. 20-27 uses the second singular, perhaps because it continues on from the use of the singular 'you' in vv. 13-19. It may be that such a distinction between singular and plural forms of 'you' are useful at the earliest stages of development of Deuteronomy. But once both forms were present in the text side by side, any subsequent writer may have felt free to use whichever form suited them, or even a mixture of both (see Deut. 4). In my view, the later the literary stratum, the more doubtful its usefulness.

All of these literary phenomena, the doublets, the change of second person singular and plural address, the shifts from exhortation to historical narration, have led scholars to identify considerable literary stratification within the large sections of prologues, laws, blessing and curses, and epilogue that we identified at the outset. While there is a large measure of agreement about the general stratification among specialists who study the book of Deuteronomy, there are still considerable differences of opinion on the details. Nevertheless, it is agreed that throughout most of Deuteronomy there is a uniformity of language and style that persists in spite of the different literary strata that scholars have discerned in the book. This has led to the notion of a Deuteronomic 'school' in which the work was created and expanded from time to time. Scholars generally designate these strata as 'deuteronomic' (dt) for the material belonging to the core document of the Josiah reform and 'Deuteronomistic' (dtr) for one or more subsequent strata that belong to later redactions and to the larger Deuteronomistic History of Joshua–2 Kings. The literary model widely agree upon for the development of Deuteronomy is the supplementary model.[6] This is also the case among documentarians, even though Deuteronomy manifests some of the same characteristics of disunity that one finds in the rest of the Pentateuch. I would therefore argue that the supplementary approach to Deuteronomy is equally appropriate for the rest of the Pentateuch as well.

There are other factors in the study of Deuteronomy that have a significant bearing on the literary analysis and interpretation. First, there is the question of the relationship of Deuteronomy to the subsequent history that follows in the book of Joshua and with which it is so closely associated in its present form. Secondly, there is the question of the relationship of Deuteronomy to the Tetrateuch. Parallels between the two bodies of material include both historical narrative and laws. Thirdly, there is the question of the historical context. If Deuteronomy is dated to the time of the late Judean monarchy, then any text that suggests an exilic background is viewed as a later redactional addition. Fourthly, there is the extent to which Deuteronomy as a code of laws or a covenant document corresponds in form and content with Near Eastern law codes and treaty documents and can therefore account for the form and character of Deuteronomy. These topics deserve some further discussion here.

4. Deuteronomy, the Deuteronomistic History and the Tetrateuch

We have indicated above that Deuteronomy was incorporated into a much larger history extending from Deuteronomy to 2 Kings. This was the thesis advocated by M. Noth[7] and is now widely accepted. I will not deal with this larger history here but only treat the question of the relationship of Deuteronomy to it. I will henceforth refer to this larger history as the Deuteronomistic History (DtrH). The connection between Deuteronomy and what follows in this history is most obvious at the end of Deuteronomy, where Moses encourages the people before their conquest west of the Jordan, installs Joshua in his place for this task (31.1-8) and then goes to his death on Mount Nebo (ch. 34). This is immediately followed in Josh. 1.1 with the statement:

> After the death of Moses, Yahweh's servant, Yahweh said to Joshua son of Nun, Moses' assistant, 'Moses, my servant is dead. Now arise, cross over the Jordan, you and all this people, to the land that I am giving to the Israelites.'

The words of divine encouragement that follow are very similar to the concluding speeches in Deuteronomy. Furthermore, the remarks of the eastern tribes in Josh. 1.12-18 relate back to the account of the eastern conquest described in Deuteronomy 2–3 and to Moses' instructions to these tribes in 3.18-20.

This means that the historical prologue of Deuteronomy 1–3 [4] and at least part of the epilogue in chs. 29–31 and 34 dealing with the final events in the land of Moab belong to DtrH. Within the second prologue section of Deuteronomy 5–11 there is a similar recapitulation of history in the account of the giving of the Ten Commandments at Horeb (5.1–6.3) and its sequel in the recounting of the molten calf episode (9.7–10.10), which I suggested above also belong to this same stratum and therefore to DtrH. The connection between this history (Joshua–2 Kings) and Deuteronomy is not a loose redactional one. While the rest of the DtrH is told in the third person narration in past tense, the events at Horeb, the wilderness journey and the eastern conquest are given as part of the speech of Moses, in keeping with the form and style of the work to which it was attached. The episodes of the giving of the Ten Commandments and the making of the molten calf, if they belong to DtrH, are even more closely tied into the larger parenetic context.

Within the first prologue of Deuteronomy 1–4, ch. 4.1-40 has been viewed as a later, second-stage Dtr addition that breaks the historical summary and uses the reminiscence of the Horeb theophany and law-giving for a discussion about the nature of Israel's deity and their appropriate response to him. Some other texts, in particular Deut. 10.12–11.32, are then associated with it as part of this late expansion.[8] This leads to a rather limited 'proto-Deuteronomy' within Deut. 6.4–9.6*; 12-26*; 28* (with several additions).[9] Within this more limited corpus there are also numerous references to the conquest of the land, and the question arises as to whether these presuppose DtrH's account of Joshua's conquest and should be added to the Dtr texts of Deuteronomy.[10] It is this more limited work that forms an ideological basis for DtrH. At the same time DtrH is an expansion of this core Deuteronomy into the early history of the people.

This raises the difficult question of the relationship of Deuteronomy to the Tetrateuch. Because Deuteronomy is in the literary form of a retelling of previous events, it has always been understood as dependent upon the narration of these events in the Tetrateuch. Where these presentations differ, the task of the exegete was to explain why Deuteronomy departed from his source in the way that he did.

Thus, Deuteronomy 1–3 has been explained as a way of relating Deuteronomy to the Tetrateuch by way of recapitulating the events from Sinai (Horeb) to Moab. But this goes against Noth's thesis that it stands at the beginning of an independent historical work. Other texts have also been identified as part of a broader Pentateuchal redaction.

In a similar fashion, the Deuteronomic laws that were parallel to those in the Pentateuch were understood as a conscious revision of the earlier code, especially that of Exodus 21-23, in terms of Deuteronomy's own time and outlook. This ordering of the sources or strata has a major impact on the way that Deuteronomy is interpreted. However, as I have suggested above, I propose a quite different relationship between Deuteronomy and the Tetrateuch. But further discussion about this must wait for our examination of the Yahwist (Chapter 6) and for a separate treatment of the laws (Chapter 8).

5. The origins of Deuteronomy

The question of Deuteronomy's origin cannot be answered in a simple statement. As I mentioned above, scholars long ago noted a similarity between Deuteronomy and the reforms of King Josiah of Judah (2 Kgs 22–23). During the process of renovations of the temple a 'Book of the Law' was found that inspired the king to carry out a series of cultic reforms. It has been suggested that Deuteronomy was written in order to create this reform program. In the older studies of the Pentateuch, the authors of Deuteronomy were often identified with the priests of Jerusalem, who stood to gain a great deal of power and wealth from the centralization of worship in Jerusalem and all the offerings to be brought to this one place. There are, however, some difficulties with this view. Nowhere does Deuteronomy give any special recognition to those priestly families that are particularly associated with Jerusalem. Only the Levites as a group are singled out for consideration and support, and Josiah's reform seems to deny them some of the privileges given them by Deuteronomy (see 2 Kgs 23.9). Furthermore, many of the offerings did not go to the priests but were shared by various groups, and only subsequently in the Priestly Code were these all diverted to temple income. The matter of Deuteronomy's origin, therefore, is a more complex problem. The following suggestions may be helpful.

It is clear that Deuteronomy contains a body of traditional material about Moses, the exodus, wilderness journey and conquest of the land and a body of laws, all of which were not invented in the seventh century. Furthermore, it is also doubtful that these traditions could have originated in Judah and Jerusalem. The prophecy of Isaiah of Jerusalem about a century before Josiah makes no mention of the exodus and covenant traditions. Also, in all of his criticism of temple worship and sacrifices and his catalogue of social sins, Isaiah says nothing about disobedience to a corpus of divine laws.[11]

By contrast, the prophet Hosea, Isaiah's contemporary in the northern kingdom of Israel, makes frequent reference to the exodus and wilderness traditions. He is also concerned about disobedience to God's laws, and he is the first to mention the idea of a covenant.[12] Furthermore, he is especially concerned about the worship of 'foreign' deities (Baal) and of singular loyalty to Yahweh. Indeed, much of the language and themes of Deuteronomy seem to grow out of the concerns expressed by this prophet. This has led scholars to the view that the traditions behind Deuteronomy have a northern origin.[13]

The northern kingdom of Israel came to an end in 722/721 BCE and was replaced by the Assyrian province of Samerina (Samaria). This resulted in a number of refugees from the north—some of the social and religious élite who had escaped deportation—moving to Judah.[14] 'Israel' came to have a religious meaning instead of a political one, becoming the name of the exclusive 'people of Yahweh'. As such, the term 'Israel' could be transferred to the people of Judah, where Yahweh was also worshiped. Some have suggested that the reform movement inspired by northern prophets like Hosea can already be seen in the attempt at religious reform attributed to the southern king, Hezekiah, in 2 Kgs 18.1-8, but this is doubtful for at least two reasons. First, there is no hint of it in the prophecy of Isaiah and Micah, the southern contemporaries of Hezekiah. Secondly, eleven years after the supposed reform Sennacherib, the Assyrian king, captured Lachish, and in honor of the achievement he illustrated his conquest on the walls of his royal palace. Among the booty pictured as taken from the city are cult objects (large bronze incense burners) that were obviously used in temple worship in that city.[15] This strongly suggests that there was still an important sanctuary in Lachish at that time, contrary to the statements about centralization of worship by Hezekiah as presented in DtrH (2 Kgs 18.4).

If we assume that the reform program came from the north in the late eighth century BCE, it did not immediately take hold in Judah. Under King Manasseh, Josiah's grandfather, who was pro-Assyrian, a diversity of cults and deities was permitted in the temple and elsewhere. Any concern for reform would have to wait for a more favorable occasion. Only with the decline of Assyrian power and the rise of a new king, Josiah, did this reform movement come into its own.

According to the account in 2 Kings 22–23, in the course of renovating the temple a 'book of the law' was found and taken to be read before King Josiah. His reaction was one of great distress because it contained very serious threats against those who did not obey its instructions. This led to further consultation with a prophetess, Huldah, who confirmed that the divine threats would indeed be carried out because of the religious apostasy of the people. But because the king was repentant, the judgment would be postponed. Yet the king immediately summoned the people to a solemn commitment to keep the laws of the covenant in the book. After this, there was a reform instituted to get rid of all forms of 'foreign' worship, Baal and Asherah and the astral cults, to destroy all the 'high places' and depose their priests, to remove cult prostitutes from the temple, to prohibit child sacrifice and to keep the passover in Jerusalem according to 'the book of the law'. Since all of these reform measures have their counterparts in Deuteronomy but not in the rest of the Pentateuch, the book of the law is identified with Deuteronomy. From the time of Josiah onwards it was the divine law of the land, at least in some circles. The impact of this reform can be seen in the prophetic works that come after this time and in histories that were written at the end of the monarchy (Joshua–Kings).[16]

There is still a great deal of debate as to whether the account of the book's discovery and the subsequent reform in 2 Kings 22–23 represents anything close to the historical course of events.[17] Those who see the 'book' as the cause of the reform focus on a religious movement prior to Josiah that was only able to come to fruition through particular circumstances at the time of the temple renovation. Those who see the reform as motivated by political and social causes tend to view the story of the book's discovery as the legitimation of the reform after the fact. In my view, however, as much as the Dtr has colored his presentation of the event, it is best explained as a religious reform that temporarily gained important royal and public support to effect significant change in Judah's religious life.

Josiah's 'book of the law' was not the whole book of Deuteronomy as we now have it. As we have seen, Deuteronomy in its present form consists of an older nucleus with later expansions. The book purportedly found in the temple included part of the laws in chs. 12–26,[18] the blessing and curses of ch. 28 and at least part of the prologue in chs. 6–8. Several additions were made to Deuteronomy in the exilic period at the time that it was made part of a larger national history that extended from the time of Moses to the end of the monarchy. Nevertheless, there seems to be little point to a story about the 'discovery' of an ancient document at a particular time in the past that was then used to legitimate a reform program unless someone made such a claim at that time.[19]

6. Treaty and covenant in Deuteronomy and the ancient Near East

The concept of covenant in Deuteronomy and its possible Near Eastern parallels has come in for much discussion in recent years;[20] the literature is too voluminous to be reviewed here. The primary focus has been on two competing Near Eastern models. The one model is the so-called Hittite suzerainty treaty model of the time of the Hittite empire in the latter half of the second millennium BCE. In such documents the imperial ruler lays down the terms under which the vassal kings are to rule within the empire. It is suggested that the biblical covenant conforms to the basic elements of the Hittite treaty, which includes a historical prologue giving the motivation for the vassal's loyalty, the stipulations of the treaty, a list of divine witnesses, blessings and curses, requirements for recital of the treaty and their deposit in the temple for safekeeping. It is suggested that various components of Deuteronomy correspond to this model and that for this reason the form and concept of covenant reflected in the book goes back to the beginnings of the people in the late second millennium.

There are serious weaknesses to this proposal. The most obvious is the fact that there is a huge time gap between the days of the Hittite empire and that of the composition of Deuteronomy, with little evidence of continuity in such a covenantal tradition between the two. Against the proposal it has been argued that the concept of a covenant between God and Israel is no older than the Deuteronomic tradition itself[21] or a little earlier with Hosea.[22] Secondly, many of the elements of this form are not restricted to Hittite treaties but belong to later treaty documents of the first millennium, so that the form has a very long history. Other genres, such as law codes, may contain such basic elements as prologue, laws, curses and epilogue, which would fit the basic earlier form of Deuteronomy. Thirdly, to make some of the elements fit, such as the historical prologue, provisions for covenant recital and deposit of the covenant document, one must include the last Dtr expansion of Deuteronomy in Deuteronomy 1-3, 29-31. Furthermore, the historical prologue is not recited as a motivation for keeping the covenant but as part of the larger historical narrative of DtrH.[23]

The second model is the vassal treaties of Esarhaddon.[24] These have to do with the demand for absolute loyalty, expressed as 'love', by the subject states for the great king of Assyria. Much of the language used to express this loyalty is similar to that of Deuteronomy. Such treaties also contain a series of curses, many of which are parallel to those in Deuteronomy and even given in the same order. What this suggests is that the basic framework of Deuteronomy in the prologue of Deuteronomy 6-8 and the blessings and curses of 28 were influenced by the Assyrian vassal treaty or loyalty oath tradition.

Furthermore, within the D code itself there are a set of injunctions in ch. 13 that call for absolute loyalty to Yahweh with severe penalties against any 'insurrection' by individuals or towns (local cults) who do not comply with this religious policy. Both in language and style of presentation this has its closest parallels to the Assyrian loyalty oaths and treaties of the seventh century BCE. This is not surprising, given the fact that Judah was a vassal state to Assyria for over a century prior to the appearance of Deuteronomy and that it was at the height of its impact upon Judah during the Manasseh era when the basic text was being composed. Some have therefore proposed that Deuteronomy was written as a loyalty oath to Yahweh and an alternative to that of the political loyalty to Assyria. It is still a matter of debate as to whether the concept of covenant is part of the older stratum of Deuteronomy or belongs only to the later Dtr additions.[25] Decisive for me, however, is the fact that the laws that are considered to be most characteristic of Deuteronomy and its reform are in the form of second person demand or prohibition, which is an important feature of Assyrian loyalty oaths.[26] The development of the covenantal concepts of Deuteronomy best fits the social and historical conditions of the late monarchy period and not those of the exile.

7. Themes in Deuteronomy and their social context

In this introduction we cannot consider all of the subjects and content of Deuteronomy. That is best left to the commentary volume in this series. What we will do is look at a selection of themes that are characteristic of Deuteronomy and the reform movement of which it was a part in the late monarchy. These reflect a social matrix out of which the book with its laws developed.

a. Centralization of worship (Deuteronomy 12)

The most distinctive theme of Deuteronomy and its reform is that of centralization of worship in one place ('the place that Yahweh will choose out of all your tribes as his habitation to put his name there', Deut. 12.5) and the elimination of all other places of worship. The centralization of worship had its basic motivation in a program of 'purification' of worship by those who advocated the exclusive worship of Yahweh. The law as set forth in ch. 12 and elsewhere recognizes a long-standing practice of worship in many local sanctuaries administered by Levitical priests of Yahweh, as was the case during the monarchy throughout Israel and Judah. The archaeological remains of temples contemporaneous with the Israelite and Judahite monarchies have been found at Lachish, Dan, Arad and Megiddo, with additional cultic paraphernalia and installations, such as altars and offering stands, iconographic images and symbols of deities and other objects of worship at many locations throughout the region of Palestine from the tenth to the seventh centuries BCE.[27] In addition, inscriptions have been found in two different locations that make reference to Yahweh and 'his Asherah', which strongly suggest that for many during the eighth and seventh centuries BCE in Judah Yahweh was closely associated with a female consort, the goddess Asherah, who is well attested in other Syro-Palestinian sources from the late second millennium BCE onwards. One of the Judahite inscriptions comes from a tomb at Khirbet el-Qôm, near Hebron, and the other from Kuntillet 'Ajrud in the eastern Sinai desert. The inscriptions in both places are in the form of blessing formulas. In Kuntillet 'Ajrud, the blessing 'by Yahweh of Samaria and his Asherah' is inscribed in ink on a pithos and accompanied by two figures together, who may be god and goddess, and a third background figure of a lyre player.[28] The interpretation of the figures and their association with the inscription is disputed, as is the interpretation of the location as a sanctuary.[29] Nevertheless, most scholars are now agreed that, until the late seventh century at least, there were multiple sanctuaries practicing the cult of the god Yahweh, who was often associated with a consort and who was very likely accompanied by cult objects and images of other deities as well.

The intention of the reform, therefore, was to eliminate all of these sanctuaries in the interest of one authorized place that could presumably be kept 'pure' by a central authority committed to the worship of a single male deity without consort. The scope of the intended reform must have been enormous, reaching into so many aspects of the life of local communities throughout Judah. Deuteronomy never says where the chosen place would be, but the book of Kings makes it clear that it was understood to be Jerusalem and the temple there. Therefore, placing this law in the time of Moses before the people even entered the land is an obvious anachronism.

Centralization also leads to unity of authority, in this case religious authority. One deity with one sanctuary and one priesthood and one religious law strongly points to the ideal of a theocratic state. Deuteronomy's view of ultimate authority is that the law was supreme over political and civil authority (the king and his appointees) and the Levitical priests were to be the guardians and interpreters of the law (16.18–17.20).[30] Deuteronomy therefore sets in motion a radical religious change, although it scarcely foresees the full implications of that process.

There are certain aspects of this law that are programmatic and utopian that were not immediately or only partially inaugurated. Deuteronomy recognizes only one level of priests; all are sons of Levi. It disenfranchises those of the local sanctuaries but allows them to serve as priests in the central sanctuary (18.1-8). It also makes provision for their support in their local communities. The account in 2 Kgs 23.9 makes explicit the fact that these local priests did not get the right to serve at the altar in Jerusalem. This led subsequently to the elevation of the Jerusalemite priesthood over the rest of the 'Levitical' priests.

The religious festivals were also centralized as pilgrimages to Jerusalem, with obvious consequences for their prior local character as agricultural festivals (16.1-17). If all of the males living some distance from Jerusalem had to travel there three times a year to fulfill their obligations, then the family character of such festivals would be seriously undermined. The description of the festivals holds these two aspects in uneasy tension. There is also the effect of making such festivals into national and 'historical' celebrations associated exclusively with Yahweh (see 26.1-11).

b. From monolatry to monotheism

The reform to centralize the worship of Yahweh in Jerusalem and to eliminate the cults of all other deities and all other rival cult places set in motion an important theological development in the understanding of the nature of the god Yahweh.[31] The oldest core document of Deuteronomy probably began with the declaration in Deut. 6.4-5, 'Yahweh, our God is only one Yahweh', meaning that there is to be only a single form of Yahweh worship and that the people, 'Israel', are to give absolute loyalty to this one deity. Such a declaration is made out of the context and recognition of polytheism, so that it is described as *monolatry*, the worship of a single deity. This deity is then characterized by a number of epithets, using the special term for deity, *ʾēl* with predicate qualifiers, in particular, the term 'jealous god', *ʾēl qannāʾ* (5.9; 6.15). This was a threatening attribute used to suggest that Yahweh would not tolerate any disloyalty and would bring dire consequences upon those who defected from his worship. In similar fashion, other epithets were used, such as 'a great and terrible god' (7.21; 10.17) with respect to Yahweh's role in holy war. In the exilic revisions of Deuteronomy, there was a shift away from the threatening aspects of the 'jealous god' to 'the faithful god' (7.9) with respect to Yahweh's commitment to the destiny of his own people and to the 'compassionate god' who is willing to forgive their waywardness.[32] At the same time there is increasing emphasis upon the incomparability of Yahweh as the greatest deity: 'What god is there in heaven or on earth who can do such works and mighty deeds as you?' (3.24).

The law regarding the centralization of worship of the one deity, Yahweh, also enforces the aniconic nature of that worship by suggesting that the temple is not a place where the deity's image is set up or dwells. Rather, Yahweh sets up his 'name' or causes his 'name' to reside, as a kind of divine hypostasis. Even the ark with its flanking cherubim, which was understood in the Jerusalem temple tradition as the throne of Yahweh of the heavenly hosts, was reduced to the status of container of the tables of the law (10.3-5). The divine presence becomes immanent among Yahweh's people by means of the invocation of his name in the temple liturgy and in the Law as symbolized in the Decalogue, the direct words of the deity and inscribed on the stone tablets, said to reside in the ark.

This theological development in the nature of the god Yahweh leads finally, in 4.1-40, to an extended discussion on the Horeb revelation. It is there argued that not only is Yahweh incomparable but, in fact, he is the only deity, and what other peoples worship as gods, whether heavenly bodies—the sun, moon and stars—or objects made from wood and stone, are no gods. It is in the nature of the great theophany at Horeb and in the giving of the law to the people, as well as in the events of their history, that the deity manifested himself and fixed their destiny as his people, that the one true deity is disclosed. Yahweh is the god and there is no other. This is now monotheism. At the same time, the nature of this disclosure was such that the people heard only a voice speaking the Law, they saw no form, so that the cult of this deity must be aniconic. Thus, the aniconic nature of the cult is used to reinforce the fact that those cults that use images do not worship the one true god.

This theological treatise lays down the groundwork for the understanding of the deity in later Judaism. The discussion is taken up and extended by Deutero-Isaiah, but Braulik is correct in seeing Deuteronomy, especially in the late exilic addition in 4.1-40, as the precursor to this rise of monotheism. There are three other aspects to this development that must be touched on here. First, in this exilic context there is no cult, so the presence of the deity among his people is manifest primarily in the Law, which may be recognized by all nations as the gift of this incomparable deity (vv. 6-10). Secondly, since the 'name' of the deity represents his presence and not some image, the deity is as close to his people as the invoking of the divine name, even if it no longer resides in the destroyed Jerusalem temple. Invoking the divine name and reading the Law do not need an elaborate cult. Nevertheless, both the name of the god and the Law become objects of veneration and sanctity. Thirdly, the events of the divine activity among the people of Israel, especially in the exodus, are viewed as the greatest since 'god created man [*'ādām*] upon the earth', that is, since the beginning of the world. However, this author has not yet taken up the theme of creation as an aspect of his discussion of the sole deity. That remains for a later development of this theme in J and Deutero-Isaiah.

c. The 'promised land'

The theme of the 'promised land' is basic to Deuteronomy and permeates all parts and levels of the book.[33] The 'promised' land means the land of Canaan that was promised to Israel by God before they settled in the land that was later Israel/Judah. In the D Code (chs. 12–26) it is often expressed as the basis for the laws and institutions: 'When Yahweh brings you into the land that he is giving you …'. This statement or one similar to it is made the basis for all the laws of the D Code (12.1) and accompanies the instructions about the institutions to be set up: the law courts (16.18-20; 17.8-13), the appointment of a king (17.14-20) and the cities of refuge (19.1-10). The remarks about these institutions suggest some rather radical changes in the nature and operation of the state and have often been referred to by scholars as a 'draft constitution' (more below in Chapter 8). In fact, the whole of the law code, with its regulation of religion, government, the courts, taxes and social welfare, is viewed as a 'constitution' given through Moses in anticipation of their inheriting the land.

In the prologues (Deut. 1–11) it is repeatedly suggested that the land belonged previously to unworthy peoples, the 'Amorites'. It was because of their evil ways that God eliminated them and replaced them with the Israelites. However, if the Israelites behave in the same way as the former inhabitants, then they, too, will forfeit their right to the land. So the gift of the land is conditioned upon obedience to the law (the covenant).

The land is regularly spoken of as 'promised by oath to the fathers'. Originally, this referred to the ancestors who came out of Egypt. The wilderness then became a test period for them, to test their obedience to God. Because they failed, all that generation died in the wilderness. But their children became the heirs of the promise and were permitted to enter the land under Joshua. Only at a later stage in the development of the land promise theme did the reference to the 'fathers' take on a new meaning and come to stand for the promise to the patriarchs—Abraham, Isaac and Jacob. Their names were added to some of the promise texts in Deuteronomy. To this development we will return below.[34]

The idea that the land belongs to Yahweh (not Baal or any other deity) and that continued possession and prosperity are conditional upon loyalty to Yahweh and doing what he demands are themes of Hosea in the eighth century BCE. The loss of the land with the fall of the Northern Kingdom seemed to underline both the need for absolute loyalty to Yahweh (Hosea) and for social justice to one's fellow Israelite (Amos) as the conditions for those who now lived in the Kingdom of Judah.

Prior to the coming of the Israelites, the land was thought to have belonged to seven mighty nations (Deut. 7.1-10), often simply referred to as the 'Amorites'. The historical prologue (Deut. 1–3) makes it clear that not only Israel but also its neighbors, the Edomites, Moabites and Ammonites, all gained possession of their land by defeating the aboriginal populations of their region. The notion of a greater 'land of the Amorites' whose extension reached all the way to the Euphrates (Deut. 11.23-25; cf. Josh. 1.4) comes from the terminology used for this western region by the Assyrians. The Israelites adopted this usage and applied the term 'Amorites' to the prior inhabitants of the land.[35] It is this borrowed terminology that creates the notion of an extended promised land that covers greater Syria.

d. Election and covenant (Deuteronomy 7.6-11; 9.1-5; 26.16-18)

Closely linked with the theme of the promised land is the notion of 'chosen people' and their covenant with God. God's choice of Israel as his special people, the gift of the land to them and their faithful commitment to exclusive worship of Yahweh is the way in which Deuteronomy sets out their sense of identity. The theme has several basic components. First, Israel is a people chosen by God through their deliverance in the exodus from Egypt. By means of this event the people were freed from slavery in Egypt and created as a *new* people. This is their shared 'history'. Secondly, election by God is not a matter of pride or special distinction. It was not something earned because of obedience or goodness; they were a stubborn people and no better than other nations (7.6-10; 9.4). They were chosen because God loved them. But, being the 'elect' confers upon Israel a responsibility to obey the laws of God (cf. Amos 3.1-2). Thirdly, this relationship between Yahweh and Israel is expressed in a *covenant*. This is an oath, a sworn commitment. It has two sides. On God's part, he promises to give them the land of Canaan and to make it prosperous. On the people's part, they must be completely loyal to him only and obedient to his law. The covenant includes the whole people, the nation, and does not admit individual exceptions (26.16-19). Fourthly, the 'promised' land, taken from the wicked 'Amorites' and given to Israel, is theirs on condition that everyone keeps the covenant. If the covenant is broken, even by a few, then they can lose the land. So they must be vigilant to safeguand against any such threat. Finally, under this covenant the king and all the local officials—elders and judges (chs. 16–17)—are under the authority of this Deuteronomic law. The guardians of this law are the Levitical priests.

The understanding of corporate identity articulated in the Deuteronomic notion of the chosen people is not simply political or geographic, the two most important critieria to mark social identity in the ancient Near East. The 'boundary marker' of who belongs to Israel is primarily religious, even though it still has a strong political and social component in the code's constitution. The people of Israel are those who are committed to complete loyalty to Yahweh. The rest, regardless of where they live in the land of Palestine or to what political power they owe allegiance, are 'Amorites'.[36] In so far as they are perceived as a threat to the constitution, they are to be eliminated. Closely related to the religious criterion of identity is that of a shared 'history', those events in the time of their origin by which their god created them as a people through his rescue from Egypt and his gift to them of the land.[37]

What is perhaps remarkable about this construction of identity is that it is not 'ethnic' in the strict sense of identity based on descent from the ancestors. There is no reference to the forefather Jacob in Deuteronomy outside of the two poems (chs. 32 and 33), except the vague allusion in 26.5. Nowhere is ethnic descent made a criterion for participation in the people of Israel. This is surprising because of the earlier references to Jacob, the ancestor, in Hosea 12, which certainly suggests that such a body of tradition was known. Perhaps because it is used somewhat pejoratively in Hosea it was not taken up in Deuteronomy.[38]

This ideological construction of identity stands in some tension with the political and geographical identity of Judah in the late monarchic period. Judah had its own traditions of ancestral origins (the Abraham traditions) and its own form of political identity in the divine election of the 'house of David' that was hardly compatible with Deuteronomy's view of kingship (17.14-20). How these tensions in identity were resolved will be discussed below.

e. Prophetism: Moses as model prophet

Alongside these basic themes are three others that play an important supporting role. The first of these, prophetism, answers the question, how could this reform movement be given the authority to carry through such drastic changes in Israelite/Judahite society? The answer is to view Deuteronomy as the special and supreme revelation given by the deity to the greatest of all the prophets, Moses: 'There has not arisen a prophet in Israel like Moses' (Deut. 34.10). At Mount Horeb, where Yahweh gave to the people the Ten Commandments directly during a terrifying theophany, the people asked that Moses be made their intermediary from that point on to receive all further instructions from the deity and communicate them to the people. This arrangement was accepted by Yahweh, so that all the rest of the laws in chs. 12–26 were the word of Yahweh through Moses to the people (5.22-31) and therefore prophecy. The implication in Deuteronomy is that this original revelation was the complete and sufficient revelation of the divine will for the whole life of the people.[39]

Moses is presented as a preacher of obedience to the law. Most of chs. 5–11 is exhortation to be loyal to Yahweh and obedient to his law expressed in chs. 12–26. In fact, Deuteronomy views the primary function of prophecy in general as urging obedience to the law. Thus, prophecy becomes instruction in the law as given through Moses. Nothing more is needed. Another prophetic role taken on by Moses is that of *intercessor*, representing the people before the deity, especially when they have sinned and are threatened by the divine wrath (9.7-29). As a prophet Moses can be expected to suffer on their behalf. Thus, it is because of the people's disobedience that Moses cannot enter the promised land (3.23-29). In all these ways Moses becomes the supreme religious charismatic, the servant of Yahweh, the founder and leader, the giver of the law that is to govern the people in perpetuity.

It has been suggested that the prophetism of Deuteronomy was a way of bringing the phenomenon of prophecy under some control in the late monarchic period. Prophets could be put to the test by the religious authorities. The most obvious test of the true prophet is his absolute loyalty to Yahweh. No forms of prophecy in support of other deities could be tolerated (13.1-5). In addition, the prophets would have to be like Moses (18.15-22), and the most obvious way to identify this likeness would be the degree to which his message conformed to that of Deuteronomy. The DtrH represents the function of the true prophets in just this way. Furthermore, the test of true prophecy that predicts the future is whether the prophecy comes to pass. Such a test is, of course, completely useless at the time that a prophecy is uttered and was no help to Jeremiah in his struggle with the prophets of salvation of his day. It is more likely that this relates to the development of an accepted body of prophetic tradition from the eighth-century prophets. If one had always to suspend judgment on the prophecy of the day, the only recourse was to use the written revelation of Moses and the confirmed words of the older prophets as guides for life. As we can see from the texts cited, most of the articulation of Moses' role as prophet, and therefore the redefinition of prophecy, belongs to the Dtr redaction of Deuteronomy that was undertaken in the exilic period.

f. Militarism: holy war—purity of the land (7.1-5; 20)

Deuteronomy is militaristic and preaches uncompromising 'holy war' against the aboriginal nations, whom it labels the 'Amorites', and against their cultural and religious practices, especially the worship of other gods. This viewpoint (ch. 7) strives for a type of utopian cultural and religious purity within the 'promised' land. This militaristic attitude is carried over into the following historical books, especially the book of Joshua. It reflects the concern for a distinct religious and social identity, and as such is reactionary and conservative. The rhetoric of holy war, with its language of extermination and 'ethnic cleansing' of the land (ch. 20), understandably makes modern readers uneasy. Here it is used as a 'religious' polemic to support a distinct religious identity (ch. 7).[40]

Wars fought in the name of a god or at his bidding and military extermination were not unknown in the ancient Near East. In an inscription of Mesha, king of Moab in the ninth century BCE, he speaks of fighting against Israel under the command and protection of his god and the extermination of the entire population of Gadites of Ataroth and the population of Nebo, using the same language that one finds in Deuteronomy.[41] Prominent in Assyrian royal inscriptions are the notions of divine instigation of military campaigns, the guidance of the deity in the conduct of the wars, divine intervention in battle that turns the tide of war and the dedication of the spoils of war to the god.[42] The whole conduct of the war by Joshua in Joshua 1–11 has numerous close parallels in the Assyrian royal inscriptions.[43] The close association of religion and war is the common attitude to military engagement in the ancient world.

g. The law code—a nation of 'brothers'

On a more positive note, the law code sets forth the view that one should treat all fellow-Israelites, one's neighbors, as 'brothers (and sisters)' (15.7-11; 22.1-4). This perspective is often described as the humanitarian concern of the code, an ideal that is beyond the limits of a set of laws that are typical of a civil code. It is a moral code, an ethic that is preached and reflects the passionate concern of the eighth-century prophets. If the reform movement of Deuteronomy arises from the religious concerns of Hosea, it also represents the social message of Amos. It may relate to those who are one's equals. But it has special concern for the poor, the widow and the 'fatherless'. There is complete equality 'under God' to whom all must answer for their actions to their fellows.[44] However, this brotherhood only includes those within the community of Israel. No such compassionate attitude holds for the foreigner who has another religion and way of life.

We will reserve for Chapter 8 any further discussion on the Deuteronomic Code, where we can deal with it in comparison with the other codes of the Pentateuch.

Notes

1 See Weinfeld, *Deuteronomy 1–11*, pp. 4–9.
2 See Seitz, *Redaktionsgeschichtliche Studien zum Deuteronomium*; Mayes, *Deuteronomy*, pp. 34–41.
3 So Mayes, *Deuteronomy*, pp. 207–9.

4 Minette de Tillesse, 'Section "tu" et sections "vous" dans le Deutéronome', pp. 29–87.
5 Lohfink, 'Deuteronomy', pp. 229–32; Mayes, *Deuteronomy*, pp. 35–36; Weinfeld, *Deuteronomy 1-11*, pp. 15–16.
6 In the history of the critical study of Deuteronomy, all three models of documentary (Wellhausen), block or fragmentary (Noth) and supplementary have been proposed. See Lohfink, 'Deuteronomium und Pentateuch', pp. 13–38.
7 *The Deuteronomistic History.*
8 See Mayes, *Deuteronomy*, p. 208.
9 I shall discuss the problem of the additions to the law code in Chapter 8.
10 Lohfink ('Deuteronomy', p. 230) considers all references to the future conquest and the giving of the law by Moses as part of the earliest version of DtrH, which leaves a very brief version of the document discovered in the time of Josiah.
11 This is in striking contrast to all the southern prophets (Jeremiah, Ezekiel and Second Isaiah), who belong to the period after the Josianic reform.
12 On this, see Nicholson, *God and his People*, pp. 179–88.
13 For a more detailed discussion of these issues, see Nicholson, *Deuteronomy and Tradition*.
14 See G. Ahlström, *The History of Ancient Palestine* (Philadelphia: Fortress Press, 1993), pp. 680–82.
15 See N. Na'aman, 'The Debated Historicity of Hezekiah's Reform in the Light of Historical and Archaeological Research', *ZAW* 107 (1995), pp. 179–95. There is no reason to believe that the depiction of booty in the Lachish reliefs of Sennacherib's palace did not represent part of the spoils of war of this very important campaign. A similar depiction of temple booty from the destruction of the Second Temple may be seen on the arch of Titus in Rome.
16 The notion of a lost manuscript being the basis for a religious reform is not entirely novel—see the Memphite theology of Egypt. See T. C. Römer, 'Transformations in Deuteronomistic and Biblical Historiography: On "Book-Finding" and Other Literary Strategies', *ZAW* 109 (1997), pp. 1–12.
17 See the discussions by Mayes, *Deuteronomy*, pp. 81–103; Lohfink, 'The Cult Reform of Josiah', pp. 459–75; G. N. Knoppers, *Two Nations under God: The Deuteronomistic History of Solomon and the Dual Monarchies* (HSM, 53; Atlanta: Scholars Press, 1994), pp. 121–28. The last work contains an extensive bibliography and survey of earlier views.
18 The reform program of 2 Kgs 23.4-24 seems to reflect the laws of Deut. 12 (centralization), 16.1-7 (passover), 18.1-8 (the Levites' privileges) and 18.9-14 (prohibited religious practices). The problem of the core law will be taken up again in Chapter 8.
19 Cf. Römer, 'Transformations'.
20 Baltzer, *Das Bundesformular*; McCarthy, *Old Testament Covenant*; Nicholson, *God and his People*.
21 Perlitt, *Bundestheologie im Alten Testament*.
22 Nicholson, *God and his People*.
23 See Mayes, *Deuteronomy*, pp. 30–34.
24 R. Frankena, 'The Vassal Treaties of Esarhaddon and the Dating of Deuteronomy', *OTS* 14 (1965), pp. 122–54.
25 See Weinfeld, *Deuteronomy 1-11*, pp. 9–13; Preuss, *Deuteronomium*, pp. 45–74; Mayes, *Deuteronomy*, pp. 30–34.
26 As we will see below, this personal style of demand and prohibition is not a feature of the Near Eastern law codes and its presence within the biblical codes, especially Deuteronomy must have another explanation, which the loyalty oath form provides.

27 A useful summary is W. G. Dever, 'Temples and Sanctuaries—Syria-Palestine', *ABD*, VI, pp. 378–80. For a fuller discussion see J. S. Holladay, Jr, 'Religion in Israel and Judah under the Monarchy: An Explicitly Archaeological Approach', in P. D. Miller, Jr *et al.* (eds.), *Ancient Israelite Religion* (Philadelphia: Fortress Press, 1987), pp. 249–99.

28 There is a second inscription at Kuntillet 'Ajrud with a similar blessing, 'By Yahweh of Teman and his Asherah', which suggests widely dispersed cult places where Yahweh and his consort were worshiped.

29 See J. M. Hadley, 'Yahweh and "His Asherah": Archaeological and Textual Evidence for the Cult of the Goddess', in W. Dietrich and M. Klopfenstein (eds.), *Ein Gott allein?* (Freiburg: University Press, 1994); S. M. Olyan, *Asherah and the Cult of Yahweh in Israel* (SBLMS, 34; Atlanta: Scholars Press, 1988); B. B. Schmidt, 'The Aniconic Tradition: On Reading Images and Viewing Texts', in D. V. Edelman (ed.), *The Triumph of Elohim: From Yahwisms to Judaisms* (Kampen: Kok, 1995), pp. 96–105.

30 This political ideal is so at variance with the political reality of the late Judahite monarchy that some have argued for an exilic date for this section of laws. We will return to this question below.

31 Braulik, 'Deuteronomy', pp. 99–130. While my presentation here is indebted to Braulik's study, I do not agree with his view of J texts, such as Exod. 34, as precursors of Deuteronomy.

32 Contra Braulik, none of these divine epithets constructed with the element *'ēl* is inherited from tradition but is the special development of the Deuteronomic theology.

33 Van Seters, 'The So-called Deuteronomistic Redaction'; *idem, Prologue to History*, pp. 227–45.

34 Römer, *Israels Väter*; Van Seters, 'Confessional Reformulation in the Exilic Period', pp. 448–59; *idem*, 'The So-called Deuteronomistic Redaction', pp. 58–77.

35 J. Van Seters, 'The Terms "Amorite" and "Hittite" in the Old Testament', *VT* 22 (1972), pp. 64–81.

36 In the other Pentateuchal sources the term 'Canaanite' acquires this same ideological sense.

37 The closest analogy to this understanding of identity is the claim by the Assyrian king that all of those under his domain who swear allegiance to him are Assyrians. See K. L. Sparks, *Ethnicity and Identity in Ancient Israel* (Winona Lake, IN: Eisenbrauns, 1998). The religious allegiance has now displaced the external political one. See also E. T. Mullen, Jr, *Ethnic Myths and Pentateuchal Foundations* (Atlanta: Scholars Press, 1997).

38 See A. de Pury, 'Erwägungen zu einen vorexilischen Stämmejahwismus: Hos 12 und die Auseinandersetzung um die Identität Israels und seines Gottes', in W. Dietrich and M. A. Klopfenstein (eds.), *Ein Gott allein?* (Freiburg: University Press, 1994), pp. 413–39. De Pury argues for the displacement of the forefather tradition by the exodus tradition as a basis of identity.

39 While the Horeb pericope in 5.1–6.3 is increasingly regarded as the work of Dtr, it only makes explicit what is implicit in Moses' role as revealer of the divine will in the rest of Deuteronomy.

40 What is important to realize and to face honestly is the fact that the religious intolerance reflected in Deuteronomy is the origin of the fundamentalisms in Judaism, Christianity and Islam. This militant religious intolerance of Deuteronomy becomes a basic attitude of Judaism in its conservative form, passes into Christianity and from both of these into Islam. When it combines with other ethnic overtones, it wreaks the havoc that we see so much of in the world today.

41 See A. Dearman (ed.), *Studies in the Mesha Inscription and Moab* (Archaeology and Biblical Studies, 2; Atlanta: Scholars Press, 1989). See esp. in this volume the remarks by G. L. Mattingly, 'Moabite Religion and the Mesha' Inscription', pp. 232–37.

42 See B. Albrektson, *History and the Gods: An Essay on the Idea of Historical Events as Divine Manifestations in the Ancient Near East and Israel* (Lund: C.W.K. Gleerup, 1967); M. Weippert, ' "Heiliger Krieg" in Israel und Assyrien', *ZAW* 84 (1972), pp. 460–93; M. Weinfeld, 'Divine Intervention in War in Ancient Israel and in the Ancient Near East', in H. Tadmor and M. Weinfeld (eds.), *History, Historiography and Interpretation* (Jerusalem: Magnes Press, 1983), pp. 121–47; S. M. Kang, *Divine War in the Old Testament and in the Ancient Near East* (BZAW, 177; Berlin: W. de Gruyter, 1989).

43 See my earlier treatment: 'Joshua's Campaign and Near Eastern Historiography', *SJOT2* (1990), pp. 1–12.

44 See also Weinfeld, *Deuteronomy 1–11*, pp. 62–65. He emphasizes the close association of Deuteronomy and the wisdom tradition in its humanitarian laws.

6

The Yahwist (J)

Bibliography

Aurelius, E., *Der Fürbitter Israels: Eine Studie zum Mosebild im Alten Testament* (ConBOT, 27; Stockholm: Almqvist & Wiksell, 1988).

Balentine, S. E., 'The Prophet as Intercessor: A Reassessment', *JBL* 103 (1984), pp. 161–73.

Blenkinsopp, J., *The Pentateuch* (1992).

Blum, E., *Die Komposition der Vätergeschichte* (1984).

—— *Studien zur Komposition des Pentateuch* (1990).

Boorer, S., *The Promise of the Land as Oath* (BZAW, 205; Berlin: W. de Gruyter, 1992).

Carr, D. M., *Reading the Fractures of Genesis* (1996).

Childs, B. S., *The Book of Exodus* (OTL; Philadelphia: Westminster Press, 1974).

—— 'Deuteronomic Formulae of the Exodus Tradition', in *Hebräische Wortforschung* (VTSup, 16; Leiden: E. J. Brill, 1967), pp. 30–39.

Clements, R. E., *Abraham and David* (SBT, 2.5; London: SCM Press, 1967).

Coats, G. W., *Moses: Heroic Man, Man of God* (1988).

Crüsemann, F., 'Die Eigenständigkeit der Urgeschichte: Ein Beitrag zur Diskussion um den "Jahwisten"', in J. Jeremias and L. Perlitt (eds.), *Die Botschaft und die Boten (Festschrift H. W. Wolff*; Neukirchen-Vluyn: Neukirchener Verlag, 1981), pp. 11–29.

Emerton, J. A., 'The Source Analysis of Genesis XI 27–32', *VT* 42 (1992), pp. 37–46.

Gressmann, H., *Mose und seine Zeit* (1913).

Holladay, J.S., Jr, *Cities of the Delta, Part III: Tell el-Maskhuta. Preliminary Report on the Wadi Tumilat Project 1978–79* (ARCE Reports, 6; Los Angeles: Undena Publications, 1982).

—— 'Maskhuta, Tell el-', *ABD*, IV, pp. 588–92.

Mann, T., 'The Pillar of Cloud in the Red Sea Narrative', *JBL* 90 (1971), pp. 15–39.

—— *Divine Presence and Guidance in Israelite Traditions: The Typology of Exaltation* (Baltimore: The Johns Hopkins University Press, 1977).

Nicholson, E.W., *God and his People* (1986).

Noth, M., *A History of Pentateuchal Traditions* (1972 [1948]).

Pury, A. de, *Promesse divine et légende culturelle dans le cycle de Jacob* (2 vols.; Paris: J. Gabalda, 1975).

Rad, G. von, *Genesis* (Philadelphia: Westminster Press, rev. edn, 1972).

—— *Old Testament Theology* (1962).

Redford, D. B., 'Exodus I 11', *VT* 13 (1963), pp. 401–18.

—— *A Study of the Biblical Story of Joseph (Genesis 37–50)* (VTSup, 20; Leiden: E.J. Brill, 1970).

—— 'Pithom', *LÄ* 4 (1982), pp. 1054–58.

—— *Egypt, Canaan, and Israel in Ancient Times* (Princeton, NJ: Princeton University Press, 1992).

Römer, T., *Israels Väter* (1990).

Schmid, H. H., *Der sogenannte Jahwist* (1976).

—— 'Vers une théologie du Pentateuque', in A. de Pury (ed.), *Le pentateuque en question* (Geneva: Labor et Fides, 1989), pp. 361–86.

Van Seters, J., 'The Terms "Amorite" and "Hittite" in the Old Testament' (1972).

—— 'Confessional Reformulation in the Exilic Period' (1972).

—— ' "Comparing Scripture with Scripture" ' (1988).

—— *Prologue to History* (1992).

—— *The Life of Moses* (1994).

—— 'The Theology of the Yahwist: A Preliminary Sketch', in I. Kottsieper *et al.* (eds.), *'Wer ist vie du, Herr, under den Göttern? Studien zer Theologie und Religionsgeschichte Israels* (Festschrift Otto Kaiser; Göttingen: Vandenhoek & Ruprecht, 1995), pp. 219–80.

—— 'In the Babylonian Exile with J: Between Judgment in Ezekiel and Salvation in Second Isaiah', in B. Becking and M. C. A. Korpel (eds.), *The Crisis of Israelite Religion: Transformations of Religious Tradition in Exilic and Post-Exilic Times* (OTS, 42; Leiden: E.J. Brill, 1999), pp. 71–89.

—— *The Yahwist* (2013).

—— 'Is There any Historiography in the Hebrew Bible? A Hebrew-Greek Comparison', in *idem, The Yahwist*, pp. 143–63.

—— 'The Joseph Story: some Basic Observations', in *idem, The Yahwist*, pp. 244–66.

—— Dating the Yahwist's History: Principles and Perspectives' *Biblica* (forthcoming).

Westermann, C., *Genesis 1–11* (trans. J. J. Scullion; Minneapolis: Augsburg, 1984).

—— *Genesis 12–36* (Minneapolis: Augsburg, 1985).

—— *Genesis 37–50* (Minneapolis: Augsburg, 1986).

1. National 'antiquities' as a literary form

According to the analytic model advocated in this book, the next phase in the Pentateuch's growth is to be found in the work of the non-P portion in the books of Genesis–Numbers, whose author I will refer to henceforth as the 'Yahwist' or J. In contrast to Deuteronomy, which is a retrospective farewell address by Moses to the Israelites at the end of the wilderness journey, Genesis–Numbers is in the form of a historical narrative that stretches from the beginning of human history to the end of that same wilderness journey. We shall begin by considering what particular kind of history it is that we have in the work of the Yahwist, and especially in Genesis.

The genre of the book of Genesis has long baffled scholars. The tendency since the form-critical work of Gunkel has been to treat it as a unique collection of folkloristic materials: individual stories, genealogies, lists of various kinds, cultic lore and anecdotes. Many of the individual units in the book have close parallels from the surrounding world of the Near East, but these parallels do not explain the form of Genesis as a whole. As we have argued above (Ch. 4), the model for this type of literature lies in the classical world of ancient Greece. It is a type of literature known in Greek as 'archaeology' and in Latin as 'antiquities'. Such antiquarian histories became very popular in the ancient world.[1]

There are a number of common features of antiquarian histories that may be compared with Genesis. They tell of the earliest appearance of human beings on earth who are the ancestors of the various peoples and nations of later times. The names of these ancestors are often in the form of *eponyms*, like Jacob/Israel, who give their names to all their descendants. These early histories are set forth in elaborate genealogies of eponymic ancestors and heroes that are traced from earliest origins down to historic times. (Because of their form these books are often called 'genealogies' in ancient book catalogues.) Within the framework of the genealogical structure are placed stories, anecdotes and other pieces of tradition about the various heroes and ancestors. The genealogy thus serves as a kind of chronology. The subject matter of the histories has to do with the invention of culture, founding of cities, origins of sacred places, and so forth. The relationships of ancestors to each other foreshadow relations of nations in later times. The wandering of heroes and ancestors is one way of explaining the origins of nations, for example Aeneas as the founder of Rome and Abraham as the father of the Hebrews. This involves the migration of an ancestor or his group from one place of high culture to a new land, often at the impulse of a deity. Such journeys ('itineraries') are an important means of providing additional structure, along with genealogies, to the literary work.[2]

It is my thesis that Genesis represents just such an 'antiquities' of the Hebrew people and their neighbors. The form of this history is derived from the learned traditions of the Eastern Mediterranean region (Phoenician/Canaanite). These were combined with Mesopotamian traditions of primeval times, such as the flood story. This diversity of forms and sources accounts for both the framework of genealogy and itinerary and the mixture of traditional stories within it. The book of Genesis was produced in two stages, an earlier version, the Yahwist (J), and a later, supplemented edition by the Priestly Writer (P). Thus, the second edition was not a separate literary work but existed only as a supplementation of the J edition, with new material added.

This proposed form of 'antiquarian' history explains the nature of Genesis better than any previous suggestion and it will guide our discussion of its literary character. Within the limitations of this literary genre we will try to understand what the Yahwist has to say about Israelite religious and social identity within the context of humanity as a whole and the world of its immediate neighbors.

2. Myth and history

Before we begin to deal with the Yahwist's treatment of the history of humanity in Genesis, we must face up to another issue: his use of *myth*.[3] Long before nations like Israel and Greece began to write history as a way of explaining the present by reference to causes in the past, they had their myths to account for origins.[4] In myth, present reality is based upon what happened to gods and heroes in the primeval time and this establishes an eternal precedent or paradigm. There is an explanation in myth and legend for every custom, institution and other important aspect of life. Myths are usually separate stories, units of tradition, handed down without any connection to each other. Consistency of chronology and the ordering of events between myths are not important. They are basically *symbolic* stories.

Modern readers have no difficulty with myth or legend as symbolic story if it is told 'once upon a time'. But when they are placed in a historical sequence of events, we find the mixture of genres inappropriate. However, that distinction is not yet part of the thinking of the earliest historians, including biblical authors. When they began to put together accounts of the nation's past, they had very few historical traditions and only those about the recent past. Thus, they had to use myths and legends for earlier periods. This often left them with the task of making sense out of the variety of different and often conflicting versions of stories. The tensions between such conflicting traditions can still be seen in the antiquarian's history. Furthermore, in order to relate the separate stories to each other, they fitted them into a genealogical chronology.

3. The primeval history

There has recently been a tendency in Pentateuchal studies to consider the literary development of the primeval history as separate from the rest of Genesis.[5] This is largely a consequence of the block model of compositional analysis in which the patriarchal stories developed within the Pentateuch as an independent block and only subsequent to its connection within the exodus-conquest traditions did the primeval history become attached to it. However, as I have argued above, this block model of literary development is debatable and, without a strong commitment to the block model of analysis, there is no reason to dispute the continuity between the primeval history and the patriarchal stories.[6]

Several arguments in support of the connection between the primeval history and the patriarchal stories may be mentioned. First, like the rest of Genesis and the Pentateuch, the primeval history also has two clearly distinguished non-P and P strata. While the continuities between the two parts of Genesis within the P strata are particularly strong, those continuities for non-P (J) are also significant. Furthermore, the relationship of P to non-P is the same throughout Genesis, as we shall see. Secondly, the genre of antiquarian historiography suggests that both parts belong together. The subject matter of such histories often includes the kind of material and themes that are present in both parts. Thirdly, the use of genealogy as a basic structuring device is characteristic of both parts of Genesis and is used by both sources. The P source has taken over part of the non-P material for its own genealogy at two important points and disturbed the earlier genealogical continuity of the narrative, but there seems little doubt that J provided a continuous genealogical sequence from creation to the patriarchs. Fourthly, there are strong features of narrative style that are characteristic of the J source in both parts of Genesis. Thus, one finds only in J the use of divine soliloquy in the flood story (Gen. 6.5-7; 8.21-22) and in the story of the destruction of Sodom and Gomorrah (Gen. 18.17-19). There are other interconnections between the primeval history and this story. Finally, there has been much discussion about the thematic continuity between the history of primeval curses and the contrast this provides for the promise of blessing to Abraham and through him to all the families of the earth (Gen. 12.1-3). These 'families' seem to be tied rather closely to the prior enumeration of the families of the earth in the table of nations (Gen. 10).

These arguments do not deny the fact that J has used very different traditions for his primeval history from those found in the patriarchal stories. It is within the primeval history that scholars have long noted the strong influence of Mesopotamian themes and stories. In particular the flood story (Gen. 6–8) has such a close parallel with the Babylonian flood story that there must be a direct literary relationship between the two. In addition, however, there are other parts of the primeval history that have their parallels with corresponding traditions of primeval times in early Greek and Phoenician lore. Of particular note are the anecdotes about the union of the gods with mortal women to produce heroes (Gen. 6.1-4), the table of nations (Gen. 10) and the 'history' of inventions (Gen. 4.19-22; 9.20). As I have argued elsewhere,[7] J seems to have drawn his traditional material for this part of his history from both Eastern Mediterranean and Mesopotamian sources.

I will not attempt a detailed commentary on the various episodes of J's primeval history but will limit myself to some general observations.[8] As indicated above, the basic structure of the primeval history is the genealogy. All these stories are made to stand within this framework and most of these stories have the character of etiology. Thus, the story of Adam and Eve tells of the origins of humans, the two sexes, and union in marriage. It accounts for the origins of vegetation and the animal world. In addition, it explains the origin of sin and guilt and the hardships of life, particularly the life of the peasant, as a consequence of the first disobedience to the divine commands. It accounts for the similarity between humans and the gods in their capacity to make moral decisions, but also in the sense of shame symbolized in the wearing of clothes. Yet unlike the gods, humans are mortal. In the sequel, the Cain and Abel story treats the origin of conflict among 'brothers', resulting in murder and the beginnings of violence as well as the distinction between settled society and the nomad. While these initial etiologies are developed in extended narratives, there are more anecdotal origins in the founders of culture within the genealogy of Cain (Gen. 4.17-19) and with Noah, the first viticulturalist in the line of Seth (5.29; 9.20), in the origins of heroes as the offspring of mortal women and gods (Gen. 6.1-4) and in the hero Nimrod as the founder of empires (Gen. 10.8-12). The Table of Nations (Gen. 10) sets out in genealogical form the origins of the peoples and nations as descendants from Noah's three sons. The basic components of this history J took over from the East Mediterranean antiquarian tradition.[9]

There are two major genealogical series that separate three important time periods in J's history. These are located between the time of Adam and Eve (and their children) and the time of the flood, and between the time of Noah and the time of Abraham. In both cases, P has followed this scheme, but in doing so, he has modified the J genealogies. Originally in J there were two parallel genealogies of Cain and Seth, probably of seven generations each. In the case of Seth, it is clearly fragmented with only the beginning left (Gen. 4.25-26), with the rest borrowed and modified by P in Genesis 5. It is clear that one of these fragments can be seen in Gen. 5.29, which goes together with the story in 9.20-27. Another piece is probably in the comment on Enoch in 5.24. Thus, J had a genealogy that connected Adam with Noah and the flood. The second genealogy of J is the Table of Nations. This is now a mixture of J and P in which P has again modified certain parts of it for his own purposes. Yet the basic form of a tripartite division into the eponyms of the nations clearly belongs to J. The last segment, which gives the genealogy of Shem, traces the line down to two brothers, Peleg and Joktan. It then deals with the line from Joktan, the forefather of the peoples of the Arabian Peninsula. But it says nothing of Peleg's line. Yet P gives a second Shem genealogy that follows the Peleg line and ends with Abraham (Gen. 11.10-27). This genealogy is followed by a J piece (11.28-30) that is typical of anecdotes about family relations of deaths and marriages within genealogies and almost certainly belongs to J's larger genealogical scheme.[10] If one supposes that in J Peleg was, in fact, the father of Terah, then we would have seven generations from Shem to Abraham, ending in a triad of brothers. This is also a common feature of the Greek genealogies and seems to me the likely original pattern here.

Into this largely western tradition of genealogies and origins J introduced three major modifications from themes of Mesopotamian origin. One was that of the divine garden of Eden ('pleasure') as a context for the special trees. This was not a separate 'paradise story' alongside a 'creation story', as some scholars have argued. Instead, it was a set of motifs that were skillfully combined with elements of the 'western' tradition to create the present narrative. A second modification was the story of the flood, and to this we will turn below. A third, the Tower of Babel, makes a break in the genealogical continuity between Noah and Abraham and is set in a very vague time frame. Yet, the Tower story relates to the very region from which Abraham's family is to migrate west and the theme of dispersal likewise fits with the theme of migration. In all three cases, the geography of the stories makes the eastern connection clear.

The Yahwist's treatment of the Mesopotamian flood tradition in Genesis 6–8 calls for special comment. The many similarities between the Genesis account and the version of the flood story in the Epic of Gilgamesh can be seen from the following table:

Gilgamesh tablet XI	*Genesis 6–8 (J)*
1. Divine warning and instructions to build a boat followed by detailed description: size of boat, seven levels, nine compartments in each level, pitch used to secure the boat.	1. Divine warning and command to build the ark with details given: size of the ark, with compartments, roof, door and three levels, covered with pitch.
2. Animals brought to the boat to preserve 'the seed of all living creatures'. Family and animals enter the boat. Utnapishtim shuts the door. In some versions there is a seven-day respite before the flood.	2. Animals and birds brought on board 'to keep alive seed upon the face of the earth'. Noah brings his family on board. Yahweh shuts the door. After seven days the flood comes.
3. Great storm of wind and rain for seven days. Flood destroys humankind.	3. Rain for forty days produces flood with destruction of all life.
4. Storm subsides. Utnapishtim opens the window. Boat lands on Mt Nisir. After seven days birds are sent out: dove, swallow, raven.	4. Flood subsides. Ark lands on Mt Ararat. Noah opens the window and releases birds: raven and dove with seven-day intervals.
5. Utnapishtim and all with him leave boat. He offers sacrifice to the gods who smell the sweet savor and decide never to bring another flood.	5. Noah and family leave ark and offer sacrifice. God smells pleasing odor and promises never to bring another flood.
6. Utnapishtim is granted eternal life.	6. Noah becomes new founder of human race.

The above table shows clearly that the biblical story of the flood must be directly dependent upon that of the Babylonian version. Some parts of what I have listed as belonging to the J version are sometimes attributed to P. This is particularly the case with the instructions to Noah to build the ark. Such a source division, however, is based entirely upon the use of Elohim for the deity in 6.13, which introduces the deity's speech to Noah. But this alone is a very weak basis on which to reject the attribution to J, as we have seen. Against assigning the description of the ark's construction to P is the fact that it is hardly likely that J would omit such an important detail from his source and leave an unexplained gap before the deity's command to enter the ark with the animals. Furthermore, P's version of the flood story does not otherwise follow the Babylonian version but merely builds on those details that are already present in the J version.

The J version modifies the Babylonian tradition in ways that make it conform to his own monotheistic tradition. For this reason there is no divine rivalry and the god who brings the flood is the same as the god who rescues humanity and the animals. The motivation for the divine judgment of the flood is the pervasive violence and lawlessness of humanity and not the noisy disturbance of the deity's sleep, as in the Babylonian tradition. The promise to avoid any future universal flood is not the result of the deity's remorse over the loss of humans to serve the deities but an expression of mercy and forbearance.

Thus, even in a case where J is heavily dependent upon a foreign tradition for all of his essential details, he is able to modify it in significant ways to make it fit his larger history. The extensive flood narrative is incorporated into the 'western' genealogical tradition by making Noah, a culture hero, also the hero of the flood story and by fitting it between the anecdote about the birth of the heroes and the Table of Nations. As the parallel Greek tradition shows, the Table of Nations was originally introduced by the birth of heroes as the ancestors of peoples and nations. In J's new arrangement, the mighty deeds of the heroes (Gen. 6.4) become part of the collective human violence that brings the judgment of the flood.

The Yahwist has shaped out of the traditional material a thematic unity, with only slight modification of the stories in some cases, in order to yield a series of five stories of crime and punishment.[11] These have to do with disobedience of a divine, 'apodictic', command in the Creation and Fall story (Gen. 2–3), the murder of a brother in the Cain and Abel story (ch. 4), the widespread violence and corruption in the flood story (chs. 6–8), violation of a sexual taboo in the story of Noah's drunkenness (9.20-27), and the sin of hubris in the Tower of Babel story (11.1-9). To these crimes there are various divine responses, often dictated by the story itself. In some cases it is expressed by a divine curse, but in one case the curse of Noah fulfills the function of divine judgment instead. There is no effort to make all of the crimes the same or to build them into a climax.

The idea of presenting a series of offences and their punishment as a way of ordering diverse traditions is not exceptional in the Old Testament. The most striking example outside the Pentateuch is the series of stories in the book of Judges. There DtrH has made use of the pattern with much greater uniformity, where disobedience to the divine laws and commandments (= Deuteronomy) is followed by defeat and servitude to a foreign power, followed in turn by salvation through a divinely appointed deliverer. A similar pattern occurs in J's treatment of the wilderness rebellions, so it is not remarkable that J should organize the primeval history in a similar fashion. In comparison with DtrH's series in Judges, however, J has allowed for greater diversity of crimes and a greater scope in shaping the stories to fit the crime-punishment theme and has given them a broad, universal application. The crime-punishment scheme applies not just to Yahweh as a national god and his people but to Yahweh as the deity of all humanity.

There is, likewise, a strong prophetic character to J's treatment of the primeval history. In the story of the Fall, failure to obey the word of the god brings the threat of death and exile from the god's land (the garden). This word stands in opposition to the advice of the wisest counselor (the snake). In the Cain and Abel story, the deity's advice to Cain is that 'doing good' is more acceptable to the deity than any form of sacrifice (see Amos). The flood story shows that human violence brings down divine judgment on all flesh (Gen. 6.13). But in judgment there is also mercy for the righteous remnant, a theme that also occurs in the story of Sodom and Gomorrah (cf. Gen. 18.17-33). The Tower of Babel story is about the hubris of nations that experience humiliation by the deity. All these themes are familiar from the prophets, usually directed at Israel or Judah, or at one of the imperial powers threatening them. By incorporating them into the primeval history, they have become universal principles applicable to all humanity. In this way, the national religion of the prophets is also given universal scope.

a. The social context of the Yahwist's primeval history

One of the indicators of J's social context is the antiquarian traditions that he uses for his primeval history. It is possible that the 'western' antiquarian tradition of genealogy and etiology that we have identified above was native to the general region of the Levant, including Palestine, although there is nothing distinctively Israelite in this material. The Babylonian tradition, however, reflects a quite different context and would fit best in the time of the Babylonian exile. In particular, the degree of correspondence between the flood story in J and the Babylonian versions suggests a close literary relationship. It has been argued in the past that such Babylonian traditions could have found their way into Palestine in the Middle or Late Bronze Age and been part of the inherited native tradition. This proposal of a literary inheritance seems very doubtful to me.[12] The placement of the Babylonian tradition within the 'western' tradition looks like the work of the J author himself and not the result of a long transmission process. This also applies to the Tower of Babel story, which contains an implied polemic against the world domination of Babylon and points to the Neo-Babylonian period. It was precisely at this time that the great Babylonian ziggurat, Etemenanki, was under construction by the Babylonian kings.[13]

The negative theme of crime and punishment in J also points to an exilic context. The emphasis throughout is on the curse on humanity, on exile and banishment from the land, on wandering and dispersement. The general human condition is one of exile from the 'garden' to endure the hardships of life and all peoples have been dispersed throughout the earth from the time of 'Babel' onwards. The notion of cataclysmic judgments and of the salvation of the righteous remnant are themes that come increasingly to the fore in the exilic period (Ezek. 14.12-20; Isa. 54.9). The theme of Yahweh as creator and god of the nations, which is reflected so strongly in Second Isaiah seems a most appropriate context for the universalistic emphasis in J. There is scarcely any hint of this in the theology of DtrH except in Deuteronomy 4, which gives some thought for the relationship of Yahweh to the nations. It also has a single reference to the primeval time when an unnamed god created man upon the earth (Deut. 4.32). It is the Yahwist who identifies this creator god as Yahweh-God and this theme of Yahweh as creator is also taken up by Second Isaiah in the same way. As we have seen above, there is an extension and transformation of Dtr and prophetic themes to give them a universality such that the national deity becomes a universal deity. Such a deity passes judgment upon all humanity. But this also means that, as in the case of Noah, righteousness and divine favor are possible without the Deuteronomic law.[14]

4. The patriarchs in J

a. The basic structure of the patriarchal history

The basic structure of J's composition of the patriarchal stories consists of three elements: (1) a genealogical framework, (2) itineraries, and (3) the theme of divine promises. The first two of these are easily recognized as the most important features of the western antiquarian histories. But even the third has its counterpart in the oracles that regularly accompany the quest for new homelands and the establishment of new settlements. We will look at each of these structural elements in turn.

The patriarchs are the forefathers of Israel, presented in Genesis 12–50 as four successive generations of ancestors: Abraham, Isaac, Jacob (Israel), the twelve sons of Jacob (= the twelve tribes of Israel). This simple scheme is part of a larger, more complex, genealogical structure.[15] At its beginning in Gen. 11.27b-31, it makes the connection with a wider scheme that ties it to the primeval history. At the same time, it gives a number of family connections and details, such as the barrenness of Sarah and Abraham's Mesopotamian relatives, which are important in the later narratives. In Gen. 22.20-24 a second genealogy is tied to the first by means of the reference to Abraham's brother, Nahor, and his offspring through Milcah. Within this genealogy a note is added to make a reference to Bethuel's daughter, Rebecca, in order to anticipate the story of her marriage to Isaac in ch. 24.

For the most part, the rest of the genealogy is based on the narratives of births and marriages. These can be set out in a segmented genealogy, as illustrated by the following chart.

Chart of patriarchs

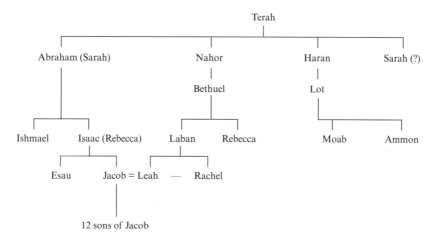

Within this genealogical framework one can place all the stories of the patriarchs. It provides a convenient generational chronology for the sequence of events. It also provides an etiological explanation for the origins of such neighboring peoples as the Ammonites and Moabites (sons of Lot), the Edomites (son of Esau), Arameans and Arabs.

The itinerary may be used as a simple literary device to connect together the stories of a particular patriarch that are associated with a number of different places. Furthermore, it gives the patriarchs an association with the whole land by their movement from place to place within it, even though their traditions were originally more regional in character. In addition, it links them with the neighboring regions, particularly Egypt. Most important for J, however, are the connections that he makes with distant Mesopotamia, both for Abraham and Jacob. For Abraham this connection is made within the initial genealogy in Gen. 11.27b-31, which tells of the family migration from Ur of the Chaldees to Harran and from there to Canaan. Likewise, Isaac's connection to Mesopotamia through Rebecca's migration to Canaan to be his bride, and Jacob's forced flight to Mesopotamia where he marries into the family of Laban make genealogy and itinerary inseparable. This larger world of travel is not the stuff of local traditions but the grand scheme of J, the composer of the larger patriarchal history. The final move in the itinerary of the patriarchs brings the whole family of Jacob and his sons to Egypt and makes the connection with the exodus tradition.

The third structuring device is the theme of the divine promises to the patriarchs. I will not repeat what was said above about the importance of this theme in the discussion of the composition-history of the Pentateuch. I will limit myself to a few observations on the use of the theme in J. By means of a series of divine speeches that offer promises and blessing (12.1-3, 7; 13.14-17; 15; 18.17-18; 22.15-18; 26.3-5, 24; 28.13-15; 32.13 [12]; 46.1-4) and numerous other allusions to them, repeated at important points in the patriarchal stories, J provides a 'red thread' that runs through his entire work. The promises include the gift of the land to their descendants, the promise of numerous offspring to become a great nation, and blessing of prosperity.

The promise theme is the most extensive within the Abraham story. It first occurs in the call of Abraham (12.1-3). The primary emphasis is on the divine promise of blessing that will make Abraham and his offspring into a great nation and will make them prosperous and at peace with other nations, to whom they will be a blessing. The 'families of the earth', mentioned in v. 3 as the recipients of blessing through Abraham, bring to mind the previous Table of Nations, and the blessings for such peoples contrast with the curses in J's primeval history. As with the prior genealogy and itinerary, the call narrative serves as a bridge between the primeval history and the stories of the patriarchs.

The land promise (12.7; 13.14-17) is given to Abraham when he arrives in the land of Canaan, and the extent is spelled out after he separates from Lot, who chooses the Jordan plain. The promise of land is already implicit in the call to 'go to a land that I will show you' (12.1), and the extent of the land is national and corresponds to the size of the descendant population that will inherit it. In fact, the two promise themes cannot be separated.

In the account of Yahweh's covenant with Abraham (ch. 15), the deity repeats to Abraham his promise of numerous offspring and makes a covenant with him to give him the land from the Nile to the Euphrates. Some want to relate this land promise to the empire of David,[16] but there is little reason to believe that David ever controlled more than a small part of this region. The promise of numerous offspring is related to the theme of Abraham's concern for a son, which is a subject that dominates a number of the story episodes and gives an added dimension to these narratives.[17] The rest of the promise texts (18.17-18; 21.13, 18; 22.15-18; 24.7, 60) are embedded in these stories. In the Isaac story, the promise theme is restricted to Gen. 26.3-5, 24 within a series of episodes that are modeled on the life of Abraham. The Isaac tradition has little independence from the story of Abraham. It emphasizes the transmission of the promise from Abraham to Isaac of the next generation.

The promise theme in the Jacob story is initially given in the context of a theophany at Bethel (Gen. 28.10-22). In it the deity, Yahweh, now appears as the god of Abraham and Isaac, so that again the promises are passed on to the next generation. They include the promise of land, which is tied to the promise of numerous offspring that will take possession of the land in all directions. A third promise of divine protection relates directly to the larger story of Jacob's flight and journey to Mesopotamia. This theophany is then recalled at various points in the following episodes of his sojourn with Laban, his anticipated encounter with Esau and his final return to the homeland (31.3, 5, 13, 29, 42; 32.10-13 [9-12]; 35.1-7).[18]

The final revelation and promise to Jacob occurs within the Joseph story at the point when Jacob is moving his family to Egypt (46.1-4). It prepares for the larger narrative of the Egyptian sojourn. A final allusion to the promises sworn to Abraham, Isaac and Jacob occurs in the deathbed scene of Joseph (Gen. 50.24-26) and leads directly into the exodus tradition.

The three structuring elements of genealogy, itinerary and promises are so interconnected that they must be the deliberate and careful construction of J's composition. The promises often come at critical points in the travels of the patriarchs and occur in theophanies at various points in the itineraries from north (Shechem) to south (Beersheba). They emphasize the generational transmission of the promises from one patriarch to another and are linked to the typical subjects of genealogies, birth, marriages and death.

b. The compositional history of J's patriarchal stories

A careful reading of J shows that the narrative is not a unified story but combines many stories and traditions. The patriarchal stories have developed into their present corpus through various stages of growth that are sketched here.[19]

1. *Pre-J traditions in the Abraham and Isaac stories (Genesis 12–26).* The pre-J traditions in this section correspond to Gunkel's smaller units, the 'fragments', and develop in two phases. The first phase consists of an early collection of folktales about Abraham represented by three stories. The first, Gen. 12.10-20, is a little folktale about Abraham's journey to Egypt in a time of famine in Canaan. To protect himself against being murdered by the Egyptians because of his beautiful wife Sarah, he pretends that she is his sister and he is her guardian. As a consequence, Sarah is taken by Pharaoh into his harem, for which Abraham is paid a handsome bride price. When a divine plague strikes Pharaoh's household because he has committed adultery (inadvertently), he is forced to return Sarah to Abraham and send them out of the country. Abraham gets his wife back and he keeps his wealth. The story was originally independent of its present context. In the second story (16.1-12), Sarah, who is childless, provides Abraham with her Egyptian maid Hagar in order to have children through her. When Hagar becomes pregnant, however, ill-feeling develops between the women and Sarah forces Hagar to flee. Hagar's child, Ishmael, is promised a great destiny by a divine being. He will be the father of the Arabs. The third story, 18.1a, 10-14; 21.2, 6-7, tells of a divine promise to Abraham and Sarah of a child in their old age. In spite of Sarah's doubts, attested by her laughter, she gives birth to a son, calling him Isaac (= 'laughter'). These three stories together represent an early pre-exilic collection of folktales about an ancestor, Abraham.

2. *The J additions.* To this small written collection of Abraham stories J has added a number of major episodes of his own and fitted them all into the framework of

genealogy-itinerary-promises that I mentioned earlier. The additional J stories are of two kinds. Some are doublets that are modeled on parallel episodes in the received patriarchal tradition; others are developed on folkloristic motifs that are common to the eastern Mediterranean world or they make use of well-established traditions of the region. Furthermore, unlike the earlier stories, these use elements of J's framing devices and make them integral to the narratives themselves. Let us review J's expansion of the Abraham story to see how these principles apply.

The story of the destruction of Sodom and Gomorrah (Gen. 19) uses the familiar myth about how gods in disguise come to earth on an inspection tour and are rudely received. The myth tells how a righteous couple show the gods hospitality and are rewarded or spared, while the rest of the region is violently destroyed. The doubling of the visitation (Gen. 18) allows Abraham to become part of the deliberation in the divine council before the sentence is passed. The prophets also attest to the fact that J used a well-known tradition about the destruction of Sodom and Gomorrah (see Isa. 1.9-10). The concluding episode about the incest between Lot and his daughters (19.30-38) is a mocking ethnographic etiology for the origin of the Moabites and the Ammonites. It is likely that in the original Moabite/ Ammonite version, the daughters were 'visited' by a deity (as in the Greek myths) and gave birth to heroic ancestors (cf. Gen. 6.1-4). If so, this rationalized version substitutes a drunken father for the foreign deity.

The story of Sodom and Gomorrah is tied into the larger J story of Abraham in two ways. First, Lot's separation from Abraham (Gen. 13), in which Lot chooses to live near Sodom in the Jordan valley, anticipates the account of Sodom's destruction. But Lot's travels with Abraham up to this point depend upon the introductory genealogy and itinerary in Gen. 11.28-31 and 12.4b-5, and Lot's separation from Abraham leads directly to the affirmation of the promises in 13.14-17. Secondly, in order to incorporate the Sodom and Gomorrah story into the earlier material, J divided the account of Isaac's birth into two parts, placing the Sodom and Gomorrah story between the promise of the child (18.1a, 10-14) and its fulfillment (21.2, 6-7). Thirdly, the double visitation of the divine strangers allows for the dialogue between Abraham and Yahweh (18.16-33) that includes a reference to the promise theme (vv. 17-19). At this point, ch. 20, the story of Abraham and Sarah in Gerar, was included, though it hardly fits between chs. 18 and 21, which indicate that Sarah is both very old and very pregnant. The king of Gerar would hardly be inclined to take her into his harem. She gives birth to Isaac in 21.1-7.[20]

The story of Hagar's expulsion (21.8-21) is added as a sequel to the birth story of Isaac and is composed as a parallel to ch. 16. In the earlier story Hagar was told by a divine being to return and submit to her mistress. This second episode is not just a variant of the other but builds on the prior knowledge of that event and the principals involved. The issue in this story is not just which child will be the heir to Abraham's goods, but which will be the recipient of the divine promises. By divine decree this must be Isaac. Nevertheless, because Ishmael is also a son of Abraham, he, too, receives a divine promise that he will become a great people (= Arabs). The promise theme is basic to the composition of the story.

The sacrifice of Isaac (Gen. 22.1-19) makes use of the very popular 'Iphigenia' motif in which the god demands the sacrifice of a beloved child and then at the last moment an animal is miraculously substituted for the human. The story is introduced as a test of Abraham's faith (v. 1), and, as a reward for his obedience, the divine promises are renewed and guaranteed to all his descendants. The passing on of the promises to Isaac is directly based upon Abraham's obedience in this event (Gen. 26.5, 24).

The story of the quest for a bride for Isaac (Gen. 24) among Abraham's kinfolk in Mesopotamia illustrates the theme of divine guidance in answer to prayer. The story, with its primary point of concentration in the scene at the well, is a doublet to a similar scene in the Jacob story in Gen. 29.1-14.[21] In both cases the encounter with the woman at the well leads to a marriage in the same family of relatives one generation apart. The Aramean marriages of Jacob belong to the pre-J material of the Jacob story (see below), so that J is modeling his Isaac story on the older account. The story makes use of J's larger genealogical scheme of Aramean relatives and the setting in Harran provides important material for his itinerary in the Jacob story. Some scholars want to treat the chapter as a late addition to the patriarchal tradition, but it cannot be easily separated from J's larger work. It also depends heavily upon the theme of patriarchal promises.

The story of Isaac in Gerar (Gen. 26) contains the *second* version of the wife–sister motif (vv. 1-11). This account imitates the first story but this raises a serious problem. Isaac and Rebecca are supposed to have two full-grown sons (ch. 25) but nothing is said about them. The rest of the chapter recounts dealings with Abimelech. In this episode J makes explicit reference to the prior visit of Abraham to Egypt and is meant to construct a life of Isaac parallel to that of Abraham and make the connection between Abraham and Jacob. Apparently, there were no independent traditions about Isaac for J to use. Again, the divine promises and the deity's blessing of the patriarch are basic to the whole narrative.

3. *The Pre-J traditions in the Jacob stories (Genesis 25, 27–35).* The same literary process is at work in the Jacob stories that we saw in the Abraham stories. Thus, the Jacob story also has pre-J traditions derived from an older body of local folklore. The story of the birth of Jacob and Esau (Gen. 25.11, 21-35) is completely transparent in representing the rivalry of the brothers as the rivalry between the two nations of Israel and Edom. Jacob (= Israel) bargains with Esau (= Edom) for the birthright and, therefore, the best land. Edom is a much less fertile region than Israel. It is a typical piece of antiquarian lore. The link through Isaac back to Abraham is the work of J.

The story of Jacob's vision at Bethel (Gen. 28.10-20) is viewed by many scholars to consist of more than one source or literary stratum.[22] In the oldest version of this story (vv. 11-12, 16aα, 17-19), Jacob gives the name Bethel (house of god) to the place where he has a nocturnal vision of a great staircase with heavenly beings going up and down on it. He anoints a stone pillar to mark its holiness. Similar traditions of divine encounter are associated with Mahanaim (32.2-3 [1-2]) and Penuel (32.25-33 [24-32]).

The story of Jacob and Laban (Gen. 29–31*) was originally about Jacob's sojourn with his uncle Laban in the region of southeastern Syria, where he met and married his wives Leah and Rachel. It explains the historical border between the Israelites and the Arameans near the town of Rammoth Gilead (close to the present border between Jordan and Syria). Within this story is an account of the birth of the twelve sons (and one daughter) of Jacob (29.31–30.34). This is an old tribal genealogy with etiologies for all the names of the tribes.[23] Finally, a story about the slaughter of the inhabitants of Shechem by the sons of Jacob as revenge for the rape of their sister Dinah (Gen. 34) is a typical tale of early times. However, in its present form, it is the work of J. It actually belongs to the generation of the sons of Jacob but is located by J within the Jacob story.

This group of stories does not form any continuous series of episodes with a common theme. They are individual pieces of folklore. The Yahwist has fitted them into his larger framework by making the locations of various episodes, such as the theophanies at Bethel, Mahanaim and Penuel, places on the itinerary to and from Mesopotamia. The conflict with Shechem is placed at the time of Jacob's return to the land of Canaan, even though the fact that all the sons and daughter are adults conflicts with what precedes and follows.[24] The homeland of Laban is placed in Harran, in agreement with the Abraham story. The story of the birth of Jacob and Esau and the sale of Esau's birthright to Jacob in Gen. 25.20*-34, however, is made part of the story of Isaac by the separation from the rest with the intervention of ch. 26, which deals entirely with the life of Isaac.

4. *J's additions to the Jacob story.* As in the case of the Abraham story, J's additions are all made an integral part of his framework of genealogy, itinerary and promise theme. The stories are modeled on parallels in the older tradition or extensions of the earlier stories, and J likewise makes use of common folklore motifs to create his own stories.

J begins by developing the theme of rivalry between the brothers, already suggested in Genesis 25. He does this by constructing a parallel story in ch. 27.[25] The story of Isaac in Gerar in ch. 26 belongs to the Abraham stories and has little to do with Jacob. In ch. 27 Jacob steals the blessing from Esau by deceiving his blind father Isaac. The parallel with the earlier story is actually made quite explicit in the words of Esau: 'Twice he has supplanted me. He took my birthright, and now he has taken my blessing' (Gen. 27.36). As a result, Esau threatens Jacob so that Jacob is sent by his mother Rebecca to her brother Laban's family in Harran. This establishes the link between the Jacob and Esau story and the Jacob and Laban story. It also creates the connection between the Abraham story, recalling Rebecca's origins in Harran (Gen. 24).

In the course of his flight to Harran, Jacob spends the night at Bethel.[26] J now expands the older story of the vision to include Yahweh's appearance to him as god of the fathers, Abraham and Isaac, and his promises to Jacob of land and great progeny and of a safe return (28.13-15). J further adds a vow by Jacob in the form of a covenantal commitment to make Yahweh his god also. Note that the unit, by stating in v. 10 that Jacob came from Beersheba and was on his way to Harran, is now integrated into J's larger itinerary framework. Beersheba is given as Isaac's home in 26.35 (within the Abraham-Isaac story) and Harran is J's link between the Abraham and Jacob stories. Furthermore, the old vision story is made the basis of the declaration at the primary promises in the Jacob story, to which frequent reference will be made in the following narrative. And it confirms the sequence of promise transmission from Abraham to Isaac to Jacob.

In J's story, Jacob now proceeds to his uncle Laban, who is placed by J in the more distant region of Harran in Mesopotamia. Jacob's experiences in Harran— his marriages, the birth of the children, the seven additional years that he worked for Laban and by trickery became rich at his uncle's expense, and his sudden flight—are all part of the older story. Yet Jacob's return to Canaan is given a new motivation by making it the response to the command of the deity who appeared to him in Bethel (31.3, 5b, 13). After departing from Laban, Jacob proceeds south in Transjordan and has an encounter with a divine being at Penuel (another old tale) in which his name is changed to Israel (32.24-33 [23-32]). To all of this J adds his own story of Jacob's encounter with his brother Esau and their reconciliation (Gen. 32–33). Before Jacob's meeting with his brother, of which he is very fearful, Jacob offers a prayer for divine protection (32.10-13 [9-12]), which again takes up the promises theme. When Jacob finally meets a friendly and forgiving Esau, Jacob describes the encounter as seeing the 'face of a god', which is clearly a play on the old story of his struggle with the divine being at Penuel (the name means 'face of god'). Jacob crosses the Jordan and arrives back in Canaan.

J has skillfully shaped both old and new elements into one continuous *adventure story*, a genre common to other peoples as well.[27] Among its typical features are the rivalry of brothers (often over who will be heir of a kingdom) forcing one brother to flee while the other takes control. The brother who flees goes to a foreign land, marries the daughter of the ruler, makes his fortune and returns to claim his inheritance. The story often ends in a reconciliation of their rival claims and the establishment of their separate kingdoms. The application of this genre with modification for the older elements of the tradition seems obvious.

J's itinerary of Jacob's return to Canaan places him at Shechem, where he camps and builds an altar (33.18-20), parallel to the itinerary of Abraham (12.6-7). Here he places the story of the rape of Dinah (ch. 34), which is then used as the motivation for moving from Shechem to Bethel, where the promise is renewed

(35.1-8). Finally, the family moves to the southern region of the land (that will become Judah), thereby giving to the Jacob stories a southern connection and anticipating the Joseph story. J's elaborate itinerary-based framework of the Jacob story is now complete.

5. *The stories of Joseph (Genesis 37, 39–50) and Judah (Genesis 38)*. The Joseph story is a pre-J composition more elaborate and developed than the previous units of folklore in the patriarchal stories and for this reason was designated by Gunkel as a *novella*.[28] Not so long ago, as reflected in von Rad's commentary on Genesis, this literary masterpiece was thought to reflect the time of the 'Solomonic enlightenment' and to contain elements of Egyptian custom and coloration from an even more ancient period. However, the study of the Joseph story by the Egyptologist D. B. Redford[29] has shown that the Egyptian elements in the story are all of late date, corresponding in time to the period contemporary with the late Israelite and Judahite monarchies. The fact that Joseph is the hero would suggest a northern rather than a southern provenance for the original story.

In the past, documentarians had attempted to divide it into separate J and E sources, but that approach has now been largely discredited, and it is seen as a unified story with a number of secondary additions and expansions, which I attribute to J and P. For instance, Judah tends to replace Reuben as the older brother in charge of the rest, an alteration made by the Judean Yahwist. J also added the theme of the divine promises in 46.1-4 and used the Joseph story as a bridge between the patriarchal stories and the exodus tradition to account for how the Israelites ended up in Egypt and became a nation there. The final scene between Joseph and his brothers (50.15-26), modeled on the earlier version of reconciliation in 45.1-15, is used again to tie the divine promises to the exodus theme.

Into the Joseph story J has fitted the independent, pre-J story about Judah in ch. 38. It is an etiology for the origin of the clans of Judah and is clearly intrusive in its present context.[30] The story knows nothing of the Egyptian sojourn and the exodus. It contrasts rather sharply with the prominence given to Judah in the Joseph story and suggests that the reason for highlighting Judah's role is to compensate for the impression of the Judah story that Judah was not part of the Israelites in Egypt.

6. *Basic principles of compositional history*. What I have tried to show by the above analysis is that the patriarchal stories of the J (non-P) stratum grew by a system of literary supplementation. I have identified a number of largely independent pre-J 'fragments', single units of tradition within the Abraham and Jacob stories (none in the Isaac story), the Judah story and the larger Joseph story. Only in the Abraham story was there a second pre-J stage that collected and supplemented the earlier tradition. It was J who constructed the continuous patriarchal history from Abraham to Joseph with his framework of genealogy, itineraries and divine

promises. He greatly expanded the stories by creating new episodes as parallels to older ones or as segments based on popular folklore motifs.

c. The social context of J's patriarchal history

Both the genealogy of nations and the itineraries in the patriarchal stories of J reflect the geography and social world of the mid-first millennium BCE. Even the older pre-J stories recognized the reality of Israel and Judah with its immediate neighbors, the Transjordanian peoples, the nomadic Arabs, the Egyptians and the Arameans in the northeast. The oft-contested border between Aram and Israel in Gilead in the late ninth and early eighth centuries BCE is specifically mentioned in the Jacob-Laban story.[31]

This rather limited world of the middle monarchy period is greatly expanded by J when the primary focus of the Aramean region shifts to the much more distant locality of Harran and Upper Mesopotamia. This is the region to which exiles from the Northern Kingdom of Israel were taken by the Assyrians after the fall of Samaria (2 Kgs 17.6). Harran in the late Neo-Assyrian period became a major city of the empire. It continued to have importance under the Chaldean rulers of the Neo-Babylonian period and with the last Babylonian ruler, Nabonidus, both the city of Ur in Lower Mesopotamia and Harran were given special honor as major cult centers of the god Sin. The fact that Abraham's family is said by J to have migrated from Ur to Harran and from there to Canaan seems to reflect this political and geographic reality of the late exilic period.

The social world of J is also seen in the ideological transformations within the theme of the divine promises. In our review of Deuteronomy above, we saw that one of the principal themes of this work was that of the 'promised land' that was given to the Israelites through the conquest and was to be theirs on condition of obedience to the Mosaic covenant. The land had been promised to the fathers, the generation that came out of Egypt, but through disobedience in the wilderness it was only their sons who would be heirs of this promise. It is J who has reinterpreted the term 'fathers' to mean the patriarchs Abraham, Isaac and Jacob and who has introduced into his patriarchal history the theme of land promise.[32] In doing so he has intended to transform the old land promise scheme in two important respects. This can be seen especially in Gen. 15.7-21. First, the deity declares to Abraham, 'I am Yahweh who brought you out from Ur of the Chaldeans to give you this land as your possession' (v. 7). What is remarkable about this declaration is that it uses the same language as the common D formula, 'I am Yahweh who brought you out of the land of Egypt to give you this land as your possession.' In this way the patriarchal tradition has replaced the exodus tradition as the basis of the deity's gift of the land. Secondly, directly connected with this promise of the land is Yahweh's unconditional covenant to Abraham that the land will belong to his offspring. This would seem to override the conditionality of the land promise in

Deuteronomy. The dimensions of the promised land (vv. 18-21) from the borders of Egypt to the Euphrates River, including the list of aboriginal nations, are the same as those found in D and DtrH.

Some have attempted to use the claim to such a large promised land (covering the whole of Syria–Palestine) as a reflection of the Davidic empire and to date the patriarchal land promise to that political and social milieu as a legitimation of David's reign. Such a Davidic empire is now regarded by biblical historians as very doubtful, and the language that attributes such a large territory to David and Solomon in the biblical text belongs to the DtrH and is reflective of his ideology. The whole notion of such an extensive 'land of the Amorites' is actually derived from the Neo-Assyrian royal inscriptions.[33]

There was an attempt in the early exilic period to use the Abraham tradition as the basis for a claim to the land by some of the Jews in Judah who were not part of the Babylonian exile (Ezek. 33.24).[34] This claim is rejected by Ezekiel as contrary to the conditional tenure of the land, as in Deuteronomy. By the time of Second Isaiah, however, both Jacob and Abraham could be cited as having been called by Yahweh from their places in Mesopotamia and their election and covenant had not been revoked (Isa. 41.8-9).

In Deuteronomy the promise of future blessedness, including numerous offspring, prosperity and agricultural fruitfulness, is not based on the promises to the patriarchs but on the gift of the land and is conditioned upon obedience to the law (7.12-16; 28.1-14). These too have been transferred to the patriarchs by J, who includes within the promise numerous progeny, general blessedness, and especially the promise of nationhood. The latter is closely tied to the promise of land, for a nation cannot exist without a land. The patriarchs themselves are promised a great name that can even be invoked in blessing by other peoples. These features are particularly characteristic of royal ideology (see Ps. 72.17) so that J has also transferred royal prerogatives to the first ancestors and in this way to the people as a whole. In all of these respects, J stands close to Second Isaiah, who emphasizes the blessedness of Abraham and Sarah as the hope of future nationhood (Isa. 51.1-2). In an image of Israel as the barren one who will have many children (Isa. 54.1-3), one is reminded of the barren Sarah. The language used to describe the repopulation of the land (v. 3) is very similar to that used in the deity's promise to Jacob that his descendants would 'spread abroad to the east and west and the north and the south' (Gen. 28.14). It is also in Second Isaiah that we find that the Davidic royal ideology has been democratized and applied to the people as a whole (Isa. 55.3-5). All of this suggests that J and Second Isaiah are contemporaries.[35]

As with Deuteronomy, the gift of the land is closely linked with the covenant between god and people. But the covenant that Yahweh makes with Abraham and his offspring is an *unconditional* commitment to fulfill the promises of land and nationhood (Gen. 15.7-21). In Jacob's response to the theophany at Bethel in which Yahweh promises both land and nationhood with great progeny, Jacob makes a vow that Yahweh will be his god. The language is reminiscent of covenantal language in Deuteronomy (Deut. 26.16-19), but in D it is conditional upon the people's obedience to the laws. In J, the conditions are all placed on Yahweh and the fulfillment of his promises to Jacob.

The promises are repeated to each subsequent patriarch so that Yahweh becomes the 'God of Abraham, Isaac and Jacob'. In this way the Yahwist fashions a new identity for Israel, which is chosen not primarily through the exodus, as in D, but through the call of Abraham and the covenant with the forefathers. This is an *ethnic*, not a national, identity. The nation was destroyed by the Babylonians, the people are now scattered and in exile. But as sons of Abraham and Jacob they are still a people, and in this way the Yahwist gives them a sense of identity that will overcome this crisis and be a hope for the future.

In each of the various narrative episodes that J has created, as compared with those that he merely took up and modified, J has used the occasion to present a theological problem, often one that was of particular concern to those in the exilic community. Thus, the destruction of Sodom and Gomorrah poses the question about whether the righteous will perish with the wicked or whether the goodness of the few can prevent divine judgment on the many (Gen. 18.22-33). The verdict of Ezekiel is that only the righteous themselves would be delivered (Ezek. 14.12-23), whereas Second Isaiah speaks of a righteous servant whose intercession and suffering can make many righteous (Isa. 53). The fact that the legendary destruction of Sodom and Gomorrah is often used in prophecy to symbolize Jerusalem's destruction makes the theological dialogue between Abraham and Yahweh all the more poignant.[36]

The test of Abraham's faith in Yahweh and obedience to the divine command (Gen. 22) must be set over against D's notion of the wilderness experience as a test of Israel's obedience to the laws of Yahweh (Deut. 8). The verdict of Dtr (Deut. 9.7-29) and of Ezekiel (Ezek. 20) is that Israel repeatedly failed the divine tests and thus put the promises of land and nationhood in jeopardy, as it was with the exile. J suggests that, because of Abraham's obedience to this one command (which was the equivalent of all the divine commandments, statutes and laws), the benefits would come to his offspring (Gen. 22.15-18; 26.5, 24).

The story of how Abraham's servant procured a bride for Isaac (Gen. 24) deals with the theme of divine guidance in the absence of cult, prophecy and oracle. In their place is the personal piety of prayer, whose answer in the coincidence of events is interpreted as the unseen 'angel of Yahweh'. The story also highlights the theme of prohibition against mixed marriages, a major concern of the exilic period as the greatest threat to ethnic identity.

The story of Jacob and Laban is a paradigm for Israel's exile in Mesopotamia in which J emphasizes the theme that Yahweh will be with Jacob, protect and prosper him and bring him back to the land of his fathers, and in return Jacob will worship Yahweh as his god. All the gods acquired in the foreign land will be buried (35.2-4) in the true worship of the one deity, Yahweh. The theme here is similar to that of periodic religious revival that one finds in DtrH (1 Sam 7.3-4; cf. Josh. 24). The story of Jacob and Esau (Gen. 27, 32–33) highlights the theme of forgiveness and reconciliation, a major concern of the exilic period. To experience such forgiveness is like seeing the 'face of a god'.

While J only makes a few additions to the Joseph story, mostly having to do with the divine promises, he does highlight the theme of providence. It is likely that Joseph's interpretation of the events of his life as providential (a wisdom theme) belongs to the original pre-J story (Gen. 45.5), but it is J who extends this theme to make it particularly appropriate for a people in exile. It is the exilic community who are the remnant and the many survivors (45.7) who will be kept alive to become a numerous people by this strange act of divine providence (Gen. 50.19-21). The Egyptian sojourn becomes a paradigm for their own experiences.

5. The story of Moses in Exodus–Numbers according to J

a. The basic structure of the life of Moses

The Yahwist has structured the history of the exodus and wilderness period as a biography of Moses.[37] The story opens with a brief exposition of the circumstances in Egypt preceding his birth, followed by the birth itself (Exod. 1–2), and it ends with Moses' death at the end of the wilderness journey (Deut. 34.1-12*). With only a few exceptions, Moses dominates all of the scenes of the narrative. Superficially, one could divide up this story into various blocks, as was done by Noth in his traditio-historical approach to this material. Thus, the account of the rescue of the people through Moses and their departure (Exod. 1–14) is the first obvious block. A second is the wilderness journey, which has two principal phases, one before Sinai (Exod. 15–17 [18]) and one after Sinai (Num. 10.29–14.45*; 16.1-34*; 21.4-9; 25.1-5). Within the wilderness journey has been set the Sinai theophany and the giving of the law (Exod. 19–24*) along with the breach of the covenant and its renewal (Exod. 32–34). Finally, there is the march around Edom and Moab and the conquest of the eastern kingdoms (Num. 20.14-20; 21.10-35; [22–24]; 32*).

The story of the rescue from Egypt (Exod. 1–14*) is made up of a series of episodes that build in stages from a general situation of need to the birth and call of a leader, the contest between Yahweh and Pharaoh in the plagues, and finally to the resolution in the event at the sea. The wilderness journey takes a quite different form of a series of episodes loosely tied together by means of an itinerary. Many of the events are characterized by a common form of murmuring story in which either the people are in need and cry to Moses and Aaron for help and Moses intercedes with Yahweh for relief, or the people act in such a way as to displease the deity and are threatened by divine punishment. In this case, Moses intercedes to obtain their forgiveness or mitigation of the punishment. All the instances of the first form occur before Sinai and all the examples of the second after Sinai.[38]

The Sinai event centers on the occasion of the theophany at the divine mountain and the giving of the law and covenant-making (Exod. 19–24*) followed by an act of apostasy and covenant-breaking (ch. 32) and then covenant renewal (chs. 33–34). All of it belongs together, and scholarly attempts to see parts of it as derived from different sources or traditions have not been successful. The laws have often been treated as an independent corpus and secondary, but I cannot agree with this assessment. To this issue we will return below. The theme of the conquest of territory in Num. 20.14-21; 21.21-35; 32* seems incomplete without a corresponding conquest of the western territory, which it clearly anticipates. It is also interrupted at various points, but particularly with the Balaam story (Num. 22–24), one of the few places where Moses is completely missing. The literary structure of this part of the Moses story seems particularly awkward. It can only be accounted for by its composition history, to which we will return below.

The division into these major tradition blocks by some tradition-historians does not conform to J's use of literary devices to structure his narrative. These overlap all of the blocks into which the material is usually divided. For instance, the use of itinerary to link all of the events of the wilderness together begins with the Israelites' movement out of Egypt before they get to the sea (12.37; 13.20); it links the Sinai unit with the rest of the wilderness route (Exod. 19.2; Num. 10.33), and it continues throughout the account of the conquest (Num. 20.14–21.35*). Likewise, most characteristic of the wilderness tradition is the murmuring motif, in which the people complain to Moses and Aaron about their difficulties or dissatisfactions. In these events Moses acts as intercessor to call upon Yahweh for divine aid or to ask for divine forgiveness when there is a threat of the deity's wrath and punishment. Again, the murmuring motif and Moses' role as intercessor occurs already in the story of the deliverance, when God threatens his plagues (Exod. 5.20–6.1) and at the sea (Exod. 14.10-14). The same applies to the story of the golden calf, where much is made of Moses' intercession to spare the peoples' from complete destruction. The final instance of their murmuring in Num. 21.4-9 is occasioned by their need to take a detour around Edom, which is part of the conquest theme.

b. The composition history of the story of Moses

There is a fundamental difference between the composition history of the patriarchal stories and that of the story of Moses. In the former it was possible to isolate a body of pre-J tradition in the form of short independent units, in the case of Abraham, Jacob and Judah as well as the larger Joseph story. In the Moses story a pre-J tradition of smaller units cannot be recovered, and efforts to do so are

doomed to failure. It is the traditio-historical approach by Gressmann, supported
and modified by Noth, that has led so many astray. More recently, Blum[39] has
abandoned any attempt to isolate such early traditional material, as he did for the
patriarchs, but he still expresses the belief that such a body of tradition exists
within the present corpus. Yet a close scrutiny of any part of J's Moses story reveals
that an earlier level cannot be found.

However, what is very similar in the Moses story to J's method of inventing new
episodes in the patriarchal stories is his use of parallel accounts from other sources,
in this case primarily the DtrH, and the use of popular folkloristic motifs. Together
they account for most of the material in J. An exhaustive analysis cannot be
undertaken here, but a number of examples should be enough to demonstrate J's
method of composition.

The opening remarks of J in the story of the exodus (Exod. 1.6, 7*, 8) provide a
transition from the time of the patriarchs (Joseph and his brothers) to that of the
oppression and the exodus. As scholars have observed, this unit has its closest
parallel in DtrH in the transition from the time of Joshua to the Judges (Josh.
24.29-31//Judg 2.6-10). Yet it is clear from this parallel that the full scheme also
includes a speech by Joshua, followed by his death at 110 years of age and his
burial, so that one must likewise view Gen. 50.24-26 (which has Joseph's speech to
the Israelites, his death at 110 years of age and his embalming) as part of this
transition. J has modeled his transition from the patriarchal age to the time of
Moses on the transition form in DtrH.

Furthermore, it is clear that one cannot regard this transition formula as
secondary to the narrative about the Israelite oppression. The 'Pharaoh who did
not know about Joseph' (v. 8) is the one who is responsible for the oppression and
who orders all of the measures taken in the rest of the narrative in ch. 1. Likewise,
the theme of the great increase of the people introduced in v. 7, which links the
unit to the patriarchal promises, is continued as the primary motivation for
Pharaoh's actions in what follows. The threat is that they will become more
numerous and stronger than the Egyptians. The oppression theme is common to
Deuteronomy (Deut. 26.6) and belongs to the older tradition of the exodus. The
form the oppression takes is hard labor building Pharaoh's 'store-cities'. This
parallels DtrH's description of Solomon's construction of store-cities, using the
foreign labor in Israel (1 Kgs 9.19-23).

A new element in the oppression theme, however, is the genocide motif. This is
combined with the hard labor motif as a way of controlling the population, which
is hardly appropriate. A second method of population control is that of instructing
the two midwives attending on the Hebrew women to kill the male babies. This
also seems quite inappropriate for a large population and is unsuccessful. The last
resort is a general command to the Egyptians to drown all Hebrew male infants in
the Nile. It has long been recognized that the genocide theme is introduced entirely
for the purpose of providing a suitable background for the birth and rescue of the

infant Moses. Once this episode is told, the genocide theme disappears from the oppression and hard labor alone remains (cf. Exod. 5).

It is widely recognized that the story of Moses' birth and rescue belongs to a common folkloristic theme of the foundling who is rescued and grows to become the ruler of his people. The cause of his exposure is often the cruel policy of a prior ruler who fears some future usurper and who plots to kill the child who poses such a threat. The genocide motif of killing all male children is a modification of this more limited element of the theme. Yet the use of two midwives for this purpose seems to derive from the original folktale. The fact that Moses is rescued by Pharaoh's daughter and reared within the royal household and becomes the Pharaoh's undoing seems to owe its poignancy and irony to the foundling theme. I am not suggesting that there was an older story of Moses' birth that has been modified by J. The story does not follow the usual form of birth stories in which the parents are known and the child is named at birth by one of the parents. The unusual form of this story is explained by its creation by J for just this particular context.

One would expect that the sequel to the birth story would be an account of the hero's exploits in defeating the tyrant and rescuing his people. Instead, Moses' failed heroics lead to his flight from Egypt to Midian. At a well in the desert he encounters seven daughters of the priest of Midian, defends them against some unruly shepherds, helps them water their sheep and is subsequently introduced into the Midianite household. This scene is built upon the model of Jacob's encounter at the well (Gen. 29.1-14), which is the more original. All of this is merely by way of exposition for the experience of the theophany at the divine mountain in the land of Midian (Exod. 3.1).

Advocates of the Documentary Hypothesis find two sources, J and E, in the call of Moses (Exod. 3.1–4.17) and use this distinction here, based upon the revelation of the name of Yahweh as the basis for source separation elsewhere. In my view, however, it is the one author J who has combined a number of different motifs and models to produce his rather complex narrative. The call of Moses consists of two basic components: a theophany at the mountain in vivid narrative style (3.1-6) and a long dialogue between Moses and Yahweh (3.7–4.17). Once again, both parts are modeled upon narrative episodes that are found elsewhere. Within the theophany (3.1-6) J has combined two motifs. The one has to do with the way in which Moses is addressed by name, 'Moses, Moses', followed by Moses' response, 'Here I am', together with the identification formula, 'I am the god of your father, the god of Abraham, Isaac and Jacob.' This same pattern occurs in Gen. 46.2-3 in a vision to Jacob and in similar divine appearances to the other patriarchs. A second motif consists of the dramatic theophany in which the angel of Yahweh commands Moses, 'Remove your sandals for the place where you are standing is holy ground' (v. 5). In a similar episode in which Joshua is confronted by a divine being, he also is given the same command (Josh. 5.13-15). The latter is the original upon which

J has modeled his scene and combined it with the revelation of Yahweh as god of the fathers.[40]

The commissioning of Moses as leader in the dialogue that follows also uses elements from two different types of call narratives. The one is the commissioning of a military deliverer, such as Gideon (Judg. 6.11-24; cf. 1 Sam. 9.15-21; 10.1-8). In the Gideon story, an angel of Yahweh appears to Gideon and commissions him to deliver the Israelites from the Midianites. Gideon objects on the basis of his lowly status and is given divine assurance of protection and a sign, which is the disclosure that it is a divine being who has addressed him. Moses, too, is commissioned to lead his people, is assured of the god's protection and is given a sign (Exod. 3.9-12) to overcome his initial objection to the task. Yet Moses is not called upon to lead his people in military combat but to speak as a prophet of judgment to Pharaoh.

This leads to the second motif, that of the prophetic call. Of all the examples of such prophetic call narratives, the one that stands closest to the call of Moses is that of Jeremiah. Here much is made of the prophet's objections to his calling, particularly his difficulty in speaking, and the way that Yahweh overcomes this difficulty. J has used the Jeremiah model with the motif of a speech impediment, but he has also added several other objections. Furthermore, Moses embodies two different kinds of prophets in a single person, a prophet of judgment (like Jeremiah) to Pharaoh and the prophet of salvation (like Second Isaiah) to the people.

In J's account of the plagues there are seven in number: the Nile turned to blood (7.14-24*), the frogs (7.25–8.11* [= ET 7.25–8.15*]), the flies (8.16-28 [= ET 8.20-32), the pestilence (9.1-7), the hail (9.13-34*), the locusts (10.1-19*, 24-27), and the death of the first-born (11.1-8a; 10.28-29; 11.8b; 12.29-32). These plagues all follow a quite consistent pattern that allows them to be distinguished from P's plagues and from P's additions to J's plagues.[41] Scholars have often argued for a long tradition behind these plagues, but against this is the fact that Deuteronomy seems to know nothing of any plagues tradition. It mentions Yahweh's 'signs and wonders' in Egypt but it never specifies that these were plagues.[42] In fact, the mentions of the 'diseases of Egypt' in Deut. 7.15 and 28.60 refer to something that afflicted the Israelites. J, however, uses this same terminology in Exod. 15.26 to refer to the plagues suffered by the Egyptians. In this way J has transformed the D tradition about 'signs and wonders' and the 'diseases of Egypt' into a series of plagues by which Yahweh freed the people from servitude.

The plagues are divine judgments and in this they resemble a series of curses, such as one finds in Deut. 28.15-68, with many of the same afflictions mentioned. However, in the case of such curses there is no room for a change of heart, as there is in the plague story. The curses in the Holiness Code (Lev. 26), however, do allow for the possibility of repentance, but a lack of compliance will lead to a *sevenfold* punishment. There is also a theme in the prophetic tradition that suggests that divine punishment should lead to repentance (Amos 4.6-12; Ezek. 20). The form of prophetic speech, 'thus says Yahweh' and the prophet as messenger of the divine oracle are all features that are most at home in the prophets, Jeremiah and Ezekiel, and in the DtrH. Furthermore, the theme of obstinacy, in which it is said that Pharaoh repeatedly hardened his heart, is again derived from the prophetic tradition (Isa. 6.9-13; Jer. 5.3; Ezek. 3.7-9). All of these motifs suggest that the plagues narrative in J is a late composition, heavily dependent upon both DtrH and the prophetic tradition.

The motif of the crossing of the sea has often been regarded as one of the earliest and most important elements of the exodus tradition. This is not borne out by an examination of the earlier references to the exodus, which are silent about it. Deuteronomy makes no mention of it except in a single text, Deut. 11.4, which is suspected of being a late addition.[43] The earliest reference to it in the prophetic tradition is in Second Isaiah. There is, in fact, good reason to believe that the crossing of the sea at the point of departure from Egypt was developed as a counterpart to the crossing of the Jordan into the promised land. The crossing of the Jordan at the beginning of a military campaign is a motif within the larger story of DtrH's presentation of Joshua's conquest of the land. It was developed on the model of Assyrian royal inscriptions which describe imperial campaigns in much the same way.[44] The motif of the crossing of the Jordan is the invention of DtrH and J used it as a model for the exodus from Egypt.[45]

The sea event is not just the crossing of a boundary, but also serves as a military encounter between Israel and Egypt, with its infantry, cavalry and charioteers. Under the circumstances, defenseless Israel cries out to the deity and Moses for help and Yahweh intervenes. This makes it a 'holy war' in which the god fights for the people by protecting them with the pillar of cloud and fire and by terrorizing the enemy so that they flee to their deaths. All of these elements of holy war fit a style that is common to DtrH (see 1 Sam. 7; also 12.16-25).

In DtrH's account of the crossing of the Jordan, the author uses the ark of the covenant as a vanguard for the people to follow and as a symbol of the divine presence. J substitutes for the ark the pillar of cloud and fire, which is said to lead them out of Egypt (Exod. 13.21-22), protect them at the sea (14.19-20) and accompany them throughout their journey. When the ark of the covenant is mentioned later as a vanguard (Num. 10.33-36), it is closely associated with the pillar of cloud. This vanguard motif is probably to be derived from the Assyrian tradition of using the standards of deities on military campaigns, which were emblematic of the divine vanguards who led their armies to victory.[46]

In our review of all of the major components of the exodus tradition in Exodus 1–14, we saw that in every case the author J has made liberal use of models and parallels from DtrH and from the prophetic tradition as it existed down to the exilic period. In a few cases, he drew upon popular folktale motifs, as in the birth story of Moses and in some parallels from the Genesis stories. There is no basis for trying to uncover earlier levels in this block of material. All of the non-P text is primarily the work of one author, J.

Concerning J's treatment of the Sinai pericope (Exod. 19.2-11, 13b-19; 20.18–23.33; 24.3-8, 12-15, 18b; 32-34*), the unit divides between the events of Exodus 19–24 and 32–34 with a 40-day interval between. The usual treatment of the tradition history of the first unit is to consider the theophany as the older part and the law and covenant ratification as a secondary addition. This reconstruction, however, is unsupported by any evidence. The direct parallel to Exodus 19–24 is the account of the theophany and giving of the Ten Commandments in Deuteronomy 5, with a later version in Deut. 4.1-40. The accounts in D and J agree on certain basic points: (a) there was a great theophany at the sacred mountain accompanied by fire, smoke, cloud and lightning; (b) there was a pronouncement of divine law; and (c) at the conclusion of the theophany the people ask Moses to act as intermediary for them to receive the laws on their behalf to avoid a repetition of the experience, and this Moses does. On many other details, however, the accounts disagree.

Elsewhere I have argued that J has made use of both Deuteronomy 4 and 5 and has changed and expanded the account.[47] Assuming this view, let us look at the development of the Sinai pericope in Exodus. Deuteronomy says briefly that the people were gathered in assembly *on the mountain* at Horeb (Deut. 5.4, 22 [cf. v. 5]), or *at the foot of the mountain* (4.10-14, 33, 36), and that the deity spoke to them face to face from the midst of the fire. What the people heard was the Ten Commandments ('ten words') and these were then written by the god on two stone tablets and given to Moses. In Exodus, J elaborates this scene (Exod. 19.2-11, 13b-19; 20.18) by having the deity give Moses various instructions in preparation for the people to assemble *on the mountain* of Sinai after being specially consecrated to approach the deity. The people approach the terrifying theophany at the sound of the shofar (about which nothing is said in D), but they are too afraid to ascend the mountain and so remain *at the foot of the mountain* while Moses alone ascends the mountain to speak with the deity face to face. The people hear not words but only the divine voice as the sound of the shofar. There are no Ten Commandments in J.

Following the theophany in D (Deut. 5.23-31), the people's representatives approach Moses and ask him to act in the future as intermediary to receive the words from Yahweh so that they do not have to endure this experience again. Yahweh agrees with this arrangement and in this way Moses is to receive all the rest of the laws that are contained in Deuteronomy. This explanation legitimates the whole of Deuteronomy and Moses' role as prophet and revealer of the divine will. This same motif of making Moses an intermediary is taken up by J (Exod. 20.19-21), but here it is used merely to introduce the law code that follows (20.22–23.33) as the direct speech of Yahweh to Moses, which he in turn is to give to the people. It does not explain Moses' primary role since Moses has already served as intermediary from his call onwards and earlier in the pericope itself.[48]

Another motif that is emphasized throughout Deut. 4.10-20, 32-38 is that, since the people saw no shape or figure but only heard words, they are not to represent the deity in any earthly form: 'Out of heaven he let you hear his voice for your disciplining. ... from the heart of the fire you heard his words' (4.36). J picks up this same motif and combines it with the other. First, Moses tells the people that the experience of the theophany was a testing and a means to put the 'fear of god' into them (Exod. 20.20). Secondly, the deity tells Moses to say to the people, 'You have seen how I spoke with you from heaven; you are not to make along side of me or make for yourselves gods of silver or gold' (20.22-23). The connection between the speaking from heaven and the prohibition against idolatry is based entirely on the explanation in Deuteronomy 4. The dependence is obvious.[49]

J culminates his treatment of the law-giving at Sinai with a covenant ceremony in 24.3-8.[50] There is no counterpart to this in D, even though it regards the Ten Commandments as a covenant (Deut. 5.2). The covenant ceremony in J has been anticipated by the special consecration of the people in the previous unit (19.10-11, 14-15) and is needed for their formal acceptance of the law code, called the 'book of the covenant', which Moses has written for them. In D, there is provision made for frequent reading of the book of covenant law (= D) that Moses gives to them in Moab (Deut. 31.9-13). Only in some late additions to D in Deuteronomy 27 and to Joshua in Josh. 8.30-35 is there anything like the ceremony in Exod. 24.3-8. J has developed his own version of such a ceremony and used it to ratify the code of laws given to Moses at Sinai. (On the laws themselves see below.)

The law code is in two physical forms; the one is the 'book' written by Moses and the other is the version inscribed on stone tablets by the deity. In D these are two different law codes, given at different times. In J it is the same code, because the law code in Exod. 20.22–23.33 and not the Ten Commandments are the laws written on the two tablets (Exod. 24.12).

The episode of the golden calf in Exodus 32 and the covenant renewal in ch. 34 is based upon two sources, the one in Deut. 9.8–10.11* and the other in 1 Kgs 12.26-32. For lack of space, I will not attempt here a detailed argument of how J's account of the events is a combination of these two versions.[51] The most obvious indication of dependence is in the statement of the Israelites in the wilderness when they receive the one golden calf from Aaron: 'These are your gods, O Israel, that brought you up from the land of Egypt' (Exod. 32.4). The plural 'gods' makes no sense in this context. But in 1 Kgs 12.28 Jeroboam uses almost identical language where 'gods' here refers to the two golden calves made for Bethel and Dan. The direction of borrowing is clear. J has not only combined elements from the two accounts but has expanded it with a number of additional details.

For covenant renewal in D (Deut. 10.1-5), it is enough simply to have the Ten Commandments rewritten upon stone tablets and placed in the ark made for their conveyance. In J, an abbreviated version of the code is given as the content of the new version on the tablets (Exod. 34.1-28) and nothing is said about the ark, although it is later assumed to have been made (Num. 10.33-36). One might have expected the need for some sort of covenant renewal ceremony in J like the first one, but instead it is the word of divine forgiveness that reconstitutes the new basis for the covenant (34.5-10). This is a radically new emphasis in J to be discussed below.

The compositional history of the wilderness wanderings tradition has been badly misunderstood because, following Gressmann, scholars began by looking for small units as the earliest fragments and these seemed to be present in the etiologies and short independent episodes of the murmuring stories. In actual fact, there is good reason to believe that these stories do not belong to any early level, as we shall see, and it seems to be increasingly the case that many are suspected of being late creations. The matter can be greatly clarified if we resort to the procedure used above of comparing J with Deuteronomy. The historical prologue of Deuteronomy 1–3 presents us with a recapitulation of the events of the wilderness journey from Horeb (Sinai) to the conclusion of the conquest of the eastern Transjordan region and the preparation for the crossing of the Jordan. In this it parallels a series of episodes in J, some very closely, and these may be set down in table form.

Deuteronomy 1–3	*Numbers 10–32 (J only)*
1.6-8 Command to leave Horeb for promised land	Exod. 33.1-6, 12-17; Num. 10.29-36 Departure from Sinai *Num. 11.1-3 Trial at Taberah*
1.9-18 Choosing administrators	11.4-34 Choosing administrators + *story of quails* *Ch. 12 Dispute with Aaron and Miriam*
1.19-45 Failed southern campaign	Chs. 13–14 Failed southern campaign
2.1 40 years of wandering	*Ch. 16 Rebellion of Dathan and Abiram*
2.2-15 Passage through Edom	20.10-21 Refused passage through Edom *21.4-9 Trial of Serpents*
2.16-23 Passage through Moab	21.10-20 Route around Moab
2.24–3.11 Conquest of Sihon and Og	21.21-35 Conquest of Sihon and Og *Chs. 22–24 Story of Balaam*
3.12-20 Distribution of the land east of Jordan and charge to the eastern tribes	ch. 32 Distribution of land to eastern tribes and charge to them
3.21-29; 31.7-8 Joshua as Moses' successor	Deut. 31.14-15 Joshua as Moses' successor
ch. 34 Moses' death.	ch. 34 Moses' death.

From these parallel columns it is clear that everything in the historical résumé of Deuteronomy has its equivalent narrative account in J, but J also contains many more episodes about which D says nothing. These have been indicated in the table by the items under J in italics. Furthermore, D has a very simple, staightforward theme, that of the conquest of the land after the departure from Horeb. J has taken the conquest theme and interspersed it with a series of narratives, mostly about the trials or murmurings in the wilderness, which now completely obscures this theme. It would be remarkable indeed if Dtr had before him the J text and could just eliminate all the parts that did not suit his interest in the conquest and thus end up with the scheme we have in Deuteronomy 1–3. Moreover, the end of the J source is not in Numbers but is embedded as some additions within Deuteronomy itself. When one compares each of these parallel pieces[52] each one betrays clear evidence that the J version is dependent upon Deuteronomy.

A superficial solution would be to suggest that a redactor has taken an older murmuring tradition and has interspersed it into the later Dtr conquest tradition to create the present text. This, however, will not work for three reasons. First, the elements from the conquest tradition in D have been significantly changed at many points so that it is not just a question of a redactional combination but a conscious artistic recreation of the tradition. Secondly, at a number of points the elements of the conquest tradition have been used as the context for murmuring stories, whereas these are completely lacking in D. Thus, the spy story in J becomes the occasion of murmuring against Moses and Aaron (Num. 14.1-4), using language typical of such stories in place of the motif of rebellion with language very typical of D (Deut. 1.26-28). The selection of leaders in Num. 11.4-34 (J) is combined with the quail story, a murmuring episode, as its motivation, whereas in the parallel in Deut. 1.9-18 there is no mention of this. Thirdly, the murmuring stories are built into the itinerary of the journey from Horeb (Sinai), much of which is derived from the conquest theme of a march to the promised land. The forty years of 'wandering' contains only one such story, the rebellion of Dathan and Abiram (Num. 16) and the point at issue in this rebellion is that Moses has not brought the people to the promised land (vv. 12-14), the object of the conquest.

As noted earlier, there are two different types of murmuring traditions, the one in which the people are in real need and receive help from Yahweh and the other in which the people are in the wrong and are punished. These two motifs have their parallels in D but not in the historical prologue. The one motif of Yahweh's repeated intervention on Israel's behalf to deal with their hardships by giving them water from the rock and manna as bread and saving them from snakes is presented in Deut. 8.2-6, 14-16. Here the positive providence throughout the wilderness journey is stressed, and the hardships were a test of their trust in Yahweh. A different picture is given in Deut. 9.7–10.10, which suggests that the people were continuously rebellious from the time they left Egypt until the end of the journey, and it gives as an example the making of the molten calf at Horeb.

J has taken these two somewhat contradictory treatments of the wilderness period and suggested that in the time before Sinai the deity responded to the needs of manna from heaven and water from the rock. But with the golden calf episode, and from that point onwards, all of the murmurings were acts of rebellion and were punished. Even the snakes of Deut. 8.15 become a means of punishment in J (Num. 21.4-9).

An essential element of both types of murmuring stories is Moses' role as intercessor, one who prays to Yahweh on behalf of the people.[53] It also belongs to the earlier exodus tradition at the end of Moses' first encounter with Pharaoh (Exod. 5.22-23) and throughout the story of the plagues, when Moses petitions the deity on behalf of Pharaoh to end the plagues. The role of intercessor is applied to Moses once in Deuteronomy in the molten calf story (Deut. 9.18-20, 25-29), an addition by DtrH, and also elsewhere in DtrH, especially with Samuel in 1 Samuel 7 and 12. In the prophets it is rare until the book of Jeremiah, where it comes to particular prominence and even mentions the examples of Moses and Samuel as intercessors (Jer. 15.1). Everything points to the development of the murmuring motif in J as his own creation in the exilic period.

Finally, if one consults the table again, one can see that the end of the story for J is not in Numbers but in Deuteronomy. There is rather widespread agreement on the presence of J texts at the conclusion of D in conjunction with the appointment of Joshua (Deut. 31.14-15, 23) and the death of Moses in Deuteronomy 34. In the case of Joshua's installation, the tent of meeting is mentioned, which does not occur elsewhere in D but is characteristic of J. The reason for J's placement of these events within D is clear. The rest of D's historical account is a recapitulation of earlier events, but at the end of Deuteronomy the style shifts to report events as they happen so J could not place these earlier. In this way he ties his own historical narrative to the DtrH and with Joshua's installation anticipates the events of the conquest in Joshua. The whole of J is a supplement to DtrH.

c. The social context of J's life of Moses

Much ink has been spilled in the attempt to find within the exodus story some clues to the historical circumstances of Israel's origins as a group of escaped slaves from Egypt. The time period most favored for a proposed correlation between the biblical story and Egyptian history as known from the monuments is the time of Ramesses II. This is based largely upon the reference to the city of Rameses (Exod. 1.11), but in the Moses story no Pharaohs' names are given and there are no other elements of the biblical account that can be used to define the historical period more closely. The biblical chronology is of little help. The general situation of the use of foreign slaves in Egypt, usually the result of military activity on foreign soil, is so common over such a long period of time that it is useless as a historical datum. It is true that Ramesses II was a great builder, as were many other Pharaohs, and that he used slaves alongside the Egyptians themselves, but there is no evidence that one particular foreign group was singled out and treated differently from others or used exclusively for building cities. All such attempts to get history out of Exodus are a waste of time and are now widely acknowledged as such.[54]

It is also common to link the description of the oppression with a writer of the time of Solomon and to see in the Pharaoh a critique of Solomon's building activity.

In particular, a close connection can be made between the Israelites building store-cities for Pharaoh (Exod. 1.11) and the store-cities built by Solomon (1 Kgs 9.19-23). The parallel is significant, but not in the way that it is usually understood. The account in Kings states that Solomon did *not* use Israelites for this building activity but foreigners, the survivors of the aboriginal populations, and that the Israelites were the taskmasters over the work. That is parallel to the native Egyptians being the taskmasters over the foreign Israelites. The Kings account, however, describes the foreign workers in language that refers directly back to DtrH's presentation of the conquest. They are the survivors of Israel's genocide of these peoples. J, using the DtrH's account of Solomon's reign as a model, must have been written later than DtrH.

This observation is confirmed by J's mention of the two store-cities, Pithom and Rameses. Pithom is to be identified with the archaeological site Tell el-Maskhuta,[55] and recent excavations at this site have revealed that it did not exist before c. 600 BCE, at which time it was constructed as a large fortress and 'store-city'.[56] The reference in the same text to the store-city Rameses is more problematic because at that late date it might have been identified with any number of places in the eastern delta of Egypt that contained monuments of Ramesses II, including the ancient ruins of the old capital itself. To describe it as a store-city, however, would have been no more appropriate in the time of Ramesses II than to call Jerusalem a store-city in the time of Solomon. The incidental reference to Pithom, therefore, dates the story as a whole to several years after 600 BCE.

If the exile is the historical and social background for the exodus story, then the Babylonian rulers may have been the more appropriate models for the Pharaoh of Exodus 1. These Chaldean rulers from Nebuchadnezer to Nabonidus were active builders (almost exclusively in brick) and they used foreign levies. These foreigners, including the Israelites, often lived in their own communities and supplied corvée labor for such projects. Furthermore, the remark by Pharaoh that he feared an attack by their enemies in which such foreigners in Egypt would side with their enemies hardly fits the time of Ramesses II, who controlled much of the Levant. However, for the last Babylonian ruler, Nabonidus, this was a serious problem for Babylon, because the Persians under Cyrus were a constant threat, and it is clear from Second Isaiah that the Jews along with some of the Babylonians themselves were like a fifth column in support of Cyrus.

I have suggested repeatedly in my analysis that J is a contemporary of Second Isaiah. Consequently, it is noteworthy that Second Isaiah compares the future return from exile as a second exodus, using some of the details that occur in J's account. For Second Isaiah the return from exile is going to be an event greater than the first exodus. Unlike the first time, they will not go out of Babylon with haste and in flight (Isa. 52.12; cf. Exod. 12.31-34). Yahweh will also act as their vanguard and rearguard (Isa. 52.12b) and turn the night into day for them on the journey (42.16), just as the pillar of cloud and fire did when they came out of Egypt

(Exod. 13.21-22; 14.19-20). Second Isaiah is also the first prophet to mention the crossing of the sea and the defeat of Pharaoh's forces there (43.16-17), similar to J. Second Isaiah presents the return through the Syrian desert between Mesopotamia and Palestine as a grand procession on a highway constructed by the deity in which all their needs of food and water are met.[57] This is intended as a far more glorious desert journey than the earlier one. So important has the exodus model of J become for Second Isaiah that he regularly uses the epithet 'redeemer' (*go'el*) for the deity,[58] a reference to Yahweh redeeming the people from servitude, both in the past and in the immediate future.

There are a number of thematic continuities between the J material of Genesis and his life of Moses. As indicated above, J has integrated the patriarchal tradition with the exodus and built a bridge between the Joseph story and the oppression theme of Exodus 1. In the call narrative, Moses asks the deity to identify himself so that he can tell the people who it is who has appeared to him (Exod. 3.13). The deity responds with a double answer. The first (v. 14), 'I am that I am,' is clearly intended as an explanation of the name Yahweh as derived from the verb 'to be' and probably as an affirmation of monotheism.[59] The second (v. 15) identifies Yahweh as the god of the fathers, the god of Abraham, Isaac and Jacob. This is not intended to mean that the name Yahweh was revealed to Moses for the first time but that Yahweh, the god of the exodus tradition, was the same as the god of the patriarchs. The concluding remark, 'This is my name forever and this is my title in every generation', suggests a major theological shift from Yahweh as the god of the exodus tradition to Yahweh as the god of the patriarchs and of all of the promises that that title invokes. It is this name and title that Moses is to use when addressing the elders of Israel (v. 16) in order to persuade them to hope in their deliverance. This is very similar to Second Isaiah's invoking Yahweh's election of the patriarchs as their hope of deliverance from exile in Babylon (Isa. 41.8-10; 51.1-2).

It is true, as some have pointed out, that in the subsequent narrative, reference to the patriarchs occurs rather sparingly. In Moses' prayer of intercession at the time of the golden calf apostasy, Moses recalls the promises to the patriarchs as a means of persuading Yahweh to forgive his people (Exod. 32.13) and succeeds in doing so. In the deity's command for the people to set out for the promised land, it is identified as the land promised to the patriarchs (Exod. 33.1). And at the very end of the journey, when Moses views the land from Mount Nebo, it is again the land promised to the patriarchs. There is a tendency to dismiss these few references as the work of Deuteronomistic redactors.[60] However, nothing about the patriarchal promises is Deuteronomistic. These texts that refer to the patriarchs are not incidental. Furthermore, J has added an extensive narrative to the wilderness journey in the form of the Balaam story (Num. 22–24), the primary theme of which is that Yahweh has blessed Israel and there is nothing that can frustrate that blessing. The whole premise of that blessing is the promises of blessing to the patriarchs.

The exilic social context opened up the horizon of Israelite theology and ideology to a more universal perspective; and this is clearly evident in the prophecy of Second Isaiah. His emphasis on Yahweh as creator and as the only deity, and on the divine governance of the world fits very well with J's primeval history, as we have seen. This same perspective, however, is not lacking in this later part of J's work. His universalism is particularly evident in Moses' dealings with Pharaoh in the story of the plagues. Pharaoh and the Egyptians do not know Yahweh, the god of the Hebrews, at the beginning of the story, but through the events of Yahweh's signs and wonders they come to know him. The statement of divine self-disclosure, 'That you may know that I am Yahweh', is used in Ezekiel as a way of introducing a threat of punishment on Israel. With J, the formula is extended to apply to non-Israelites as well. J varies the formula: 'so that you may know that there is none like our god, Yahweh' (Exod. 8.6 [10]), 'so that you may know that there is none like me in all the world' (9.14), 'so that you may know that the earth belongs to Yahweh' (9.29), to emphasize the universal character of Yahweh's domain. This raises the theme of divine incomparability to the level of monotheistic assertion and the foreigners give grudging recognition of Yahweh as such a god through his judgments. Such language and perspective is similar to that found in the story of Sodom and Gomorrah, in which Abraham says to the deity, 'Shall not the judge of all the earth do what is right?' By contrast, another foreigner, the Midianite Jethro who was Moses' father-in-law, acknowledges Yahweh's greatness ('the greatest of all the gods') when he hears about all the events of Egypt (Exod. 18.11). There is an openness to foreigners in J that is missing from Deuteronomy.

There are a few themes present in this part of J's work that are particularly appropriate for the exilic period. The first of these is the theme of divine forgiveness. Once there was general acknowledgement within the religious community of Yahweh worshipers that the destruction of Jerusalem and the temple and the devastation of the land were the result of divine punishment, then the possibility of restoration and with it divine forgiveness became a major concern. This is already evident in the latest additions to Deuteronomy in Deut. 4.25-31, which 'predicts' the devastation and exile and suggests the possibility that a repentance can lead to forgiveness by a 'merciful god' and restoration. This theme is greatly expanded by J so that in a scene on the mountain (Exod. 34.6-9), Yahweh again proclaims to Moses his name and titles: 'Yahweh, Yahweh, a compassionate and gracious god, long-suffering, ever faithful and true, remaining faithful to thousands, forgiving iniquity, rebellion and sin.' This self-proclaimed title then becomes the basis upon which Moses now pleads for the people's forgiveness and receives from Yahweh the renewed covenant.

If Second Isaiah is a good reflection of the concerns of the exilic period, then the message to the exiles of divine forgiveness and pardon seems to have been a major preoccupation of this prophet. The prophecy opens on this note (Isa. 40.1-2) and it occurs repeatedly throughout. It represents the primary shift from the prophecy of judgment found in Jeremiah and Ezekiel to Second Isaiah's prophecy of forgiveness and hope.[61] This can also be seen as the primary difference between J and D/DtrH.[62] In telling the story of the failed invasion from the south (Deut. 1.19-46), Dtr reports the rebellion, Moses' vain attempt to change the people's mind and the divine judgment of forty years' wandering in the wilderness. In J's version, however, he adds a prayer by Moses in which Moses uses the deity's own self-proclamation as a forgiving god to extract forgiveness and a reprieve on the people's behalf (Num. 14.17-20). The forty years in the wilderness is now actually understood as a mitigation of the more severe sentence that would have resulted in complete oblivion. Since the 'wilderness' is also used as symbolic of the exile, one can understand the author as suggesting that the exilic experience was itself a reprieve and the promises of land and nationhood could still be realized by the next generation.

A second major issue of the exile was the problem of the divine presence with the destruction of the temple. How could the deity have an abode in the foreign land without a temple? The Yahwist reflects on this concern in Exodus 33 by speaking about the deity accompanying the people after they leave the sacred mountain. In J there is a rather temporary 'tent of meeting', which is one solution. No elaborate cultus is associated with it. Most of the discussion in the chapter, however, centers on the assurance that Yahweh will continue to be with his people. In addition to this, J suggests the symbolic representation of the divine presence in two ways. On Sinai, Moses experiences the presence of the deity as a burning bush that is not burnt up (Exod. 3.1-6). This seems to me to symbolize the menorah, a many-branched lampstand. Again, on Sinai, the people hear the speech of Yahweh as the sound of a shofar. These two sacred objects could be symbolic of the divine presence in an aniconic cult and could be used, as they were later in the synagogue, to symbolize the presence of the deity among the worshiping community.[63]

The social context of J also comes through his work in his presentation of the role of Moses. Some who have urged an early date for J have tried to cast Moses in the form of a monarch.[64] This, however, is a mistake, for even though Moses is the leader of his people and they are sometimes referred to as 'his people', there is scarcely a single royal attribute associated with him. He has no court, no crown prince or dynasty, and Joshua is not related to him in any way. He does not even lead his forces in battle. Even the law code associated with J in Exodus 21–23 makes no allowance whatever for a monarchy, as does D. The form of administration of 70 elders who share the rule with Moses (Num. 11.16-17, 24-25) has more in common with those republican constitutions in the Mediterranean world that have 'senates', such as Carthage and Rome.

The Yahwist follows D in understanding Moses' role as primarily that of a prophet, and it is in this capacity, and not as king, that he mediates the laws to the people. The manner of that mediation is treated in the Sinai/Horeb scene in the same way in J and D. Furthermore, Moses' role in the encounter with Pharaoh and the story of the plagues uses the very familiar language of the prophet as messenger and living oracle of the deity. The call narrative has its greatest similarity with that of the prophet Jeremiah. While Moses is associated with certain wonders in the Plagues story and in the wilderness tradition, they do not really belong to the *legenda* or tales of holy men such as one finds in the stories of Elisha.[65] The wonders are always subordinated to the model of the prophet as messenger.

There is, however, a major difference in emphasis in J's prophetic model from that of D. In Deuteronomy Moses as prophet is both the mediator of the law from the deity and also the one who admonishes and exhorts the people to keep this law with great diligence. The whole understanding of the prophet's role is bound up with this proclamation and admonition to keep the Deuteronomic law, particularly its injunctions against the worship of other gods and engaging in 'foreign' religious practices. By contrast, in J there are very few examples in which Moses is actually presented as announcing the law to the people or as exhorting them to obedience to the law. They are given the law in a 'book of the covenant' (Exod. 24.3-8) and are committed to keeping it, and when they violate its terms they are punished. But reminders, admonitions and warnings, which are the stock-in-trade of Deuteronomy, are lacking in J.

The most important aspect of prophecy stressed by J vis-à-vis the people itself is that of intercessor.[66] This intercessory role of the prophet shows up in DtrH's addition to D in the molten calf story of Deut. 9.8-29 and in the DtrH story of Samuel (1 Sam. 7 and 12). It is also common to the Dtr edition of Jeremiah.[67] Yet even here it is usually combined with the D theme of obedience to the law and to the people's repentance for having broken it. J, however, has greatly expanded the role of Moses as intercessor in which he prays to Yahweh for Pharaoh to mitigate the judgment of a plague, not because he has broken Yahweh's laws but because he has not heeded a specific command to let the people go. Moses prays for the Israelites in situations of physical hardship or when they are punished for specific wrongs or acts of rebellion that are not related to any set of laws. Only when J uses the molten calf story does the intercession have to do with the violation of the law in the covenant to which they have just committed themselves.

If Moses in D and the prophets in DtrH seem to stand over against the king and people as divine representatives to admonish and correct them, in J Moses is much more closely identified with the people and with all of their concerns and failings. This reflects a major shift in prophecy in the exilic period. It can be seen initially in Ezekiel's role as a 'pastor' within the exilic community, however harsh he may sometimes appear.[68] It is also reflected in Second Isaiah, in the Servant Songs and especially in the suffering servant of Isa. 52.13–53.12. Von Rad saw in this figure a kind of second Moses,[69] and this is particularly true of the portrayal of Moses in J. The prophet has become a leader of the social and religious community in the 'wilderness' (= exile).

The primary problem for such a leader in the exile is not the need to exhort the people to obedience to the law. It is rather the need to maintain the faith in the midst of a hostile world. This can be seen in the way in which Ezekiel attempts to deal with theological problems, justifying the ways of the god Yahweh to the exiles of Babylon. Second Isaiah's prophecy is dominated by disputation and theological argument to prove the worthiness of faith in Yahweh. The exiles' very survival as a people depends on maintaining the faith and their belief in Yahweh. In J, the call of Moses confronts this problem of belief by the people as the major obstacle to Moses' mission. How can he persuade the Israelites that the deity has appeared to him and is about to deliver them (Exod. 4.1-9)? There is a crisis of the people's faith in Moses after the first encounter with Pharaoh (Exod. 5) and again at the sea (14.10-14, 30-31). The murmuring tradition is presented primarily as a series of crises of faith that Moses as their leader must struggle to overcome. If it is possible to get some sense of the environment of the exilic community in Babylon, I think it comes to us most poignantly through the works of J and Second Isaiah.

Notes

1 See Van Seters, *Prologue to History*, pp. 86–103; Van Seters, *The Yahwist*, pp. 18–34.
2 For the works of the early Greek 'antiquarian' historians see the works of Lionel Pearson, *The Early Ionian Historians* (Oxford: Oxford University Press, 1939); *idem, The Local Historians of Attica* (APAPM, 11; Philadelphia: American Philological Association, 1942); and *idem, The Greek Historians of the West* (Atlanta: Scholars Press, 1987). The best-preserved example of such a history in that of Dionysius of Halicarnassus of the first century BCE, whose work rests on many older Greek histories. For a translation of his work see Loeb Classical Library; see also, 'Is There any Historiography in the Hebrew Bible? A Hebrew-Greek Comparison', in Van Seters, *The Yahwist*, pp. 143–63.
3 See Van Seters, *Prologue to History*, pp. 24–44.
4 For ancient Greece, see the works of M. I. Finley, 'Myth, Memory and History', in *idem, The Use and Abuse of History* (New York: Viking Press, 1975), pp. 11–33; P. Veyne, *Did the Greeks Believe their Myths?* (Chicago: University of Chicago Press, 1988).
5 Crüsemann, 'Die Eigenständigkeit der Urgeschichte', pp. 11–29; followed by Blenkinsopp, *The Pentateuch*; Blum, *Die Komposition der Vätergeschichte*, and Carr, *Reading the Fractures of Genesis*.
6 For my critique of Crüsemann, see *Prologue to History*, pp. 191–93.
7 *Prologue to History*.
8 For a different treatment of the primeval history with extensive survey of past discussion and bibliography one should consult Westermann, *Genesis 1–11*.
9 One of the most striking parallels to this material in early Greek literature is the Hesiodic *Catalogue of Women*. For a recent edition and discussion of this, see M. L. West, *The Hesiodic Catalogue of Women: Its Nature, Structure and Origins* (Oxford: Oxford University Press, 1985).
10 Emerton, 'Genesis XI 27–32', pp. 37–46.
11 See Westermann, *Genesis 1–11*, pp. 47–56.
12 Nowhere in the Levant do we find any continuity in the cuneiform scribal tradition or any overlap in the use of cuneiform with the development of the later alphabetic system. There is a significant gap between the widespread use of cuneiform of the

second millennium, in which the Mesopotamian traditions would have been preserved, and the alphabetic scribal tradition of the first millennium.

13 C. Ühlinger, *Weltreich und "eine Rede": Eine neue Deutung der sogenannten Turmbauerzählung (Gen 11,1–9)* (OBO, 101; Freiburg: University Press; Göttingen: Vandenhoeck & Ruprecht, 1990); Van Seters, *Prologue to History*, pp. 180–85.

14 Van Seters, 'The Theology of the Yahwist'.

15 For the latest discussion of the tribal genealogies, see U. Schorn, *Ruben und das System der zwölf Stämme Israels* (BZAW, 248; Berlin: W. de Gruyter, 1997).

16 Clements, *Abraham and David*.

17 There has been a tendency in recent years to regard Gen. 15 as a late post-P text. See J. Ha, *Genesis 15* (BZAW, 181; Berlin: W. de Gruyter, 1989) and my review of Ha in *BO* 48 (1991), pp. 624–26.

18 For a recent discussion of Gen. 28.10–22 and related texts, see Van Seters, 'Divine Encounter at Bethel'.

19 Here I follow my own scheme of this development, as argued in *Abraham in History and Tradition* and *Prologue to History*.

20 The two episodes of Abraham's dealings with the king of Gerar in Gen. 20 and 21.25–34 are later additions to J that interrupt the narrative. See Van Seters, *The Yahwist*, pp. 134–36.

21 See Westermann, *Genesis 12–36*, pp. 383–84.

22 See Van Seters, *Prologue to History*, pp. 288–95; *idem*, 'Divine Encounter at Bethel'.

23 See now Schorn, *Ruben*, pp. 63–80.

24 Benjamin is not born until after the event in ch. 34.

25 See Van Seters, *Prologue to History*, pp. 280–88; Van Seters, *The Yahwist*, pp. 41–49.

26 See above n. 22.

27 See de Pury, *Promesse divine*.

28 For an extensive review of the literature see Westermann, *Genesis 37–50*; also Van Seters, *Prologue to History*, pp. 311–27; Van Seters, 'The Joseph Story: Some Basic Observations,' in *idem*, *The Yahwist*, pp. 244–66.

29 *Story of Joseph (Genesis 37–50)*.

30 A quite different approach to Gen. 38 has been taken by T. Krüger, 'Genesis 38—ein "Lehrstück" alttestamentlicher Ethik', in R. Bartelmus (ed.), *Konsequente Traditionsgeschichte (Festschrift K. Baltzer;* OBO, 126; Freiburg: University Press; Göttingen: Vandenhoeck & Ruprecht, 1993), pp. 205–26. He suggests a postexilic composition and understanding of the text.

31 See also Blum, *Die Komposition der Vätergeschichte*.

32 Van Seters, 'Confessional Reformulation in the Exilic Period'; *idem, Prologue to History*, pp. 227–45; Römer, *Israels Väter*.

33 Van Seters, 'The Terms "Amorite" and "Hittite" in the Old Testament', pp. 64–81.

34 It seems clear that the Abraham tradition reflected in Ezek. 33.24 still knows nothing of a Babylonian origin for Abraham since this would tend to defeat their claim on the land against the Babylonian exiles.

35 See Van Seters, 'In the Babylonian Exile with J'; *idem*, 'Dating the Yahwist's History: Principles and Perspectives' *Biblica* (forthcoming).

36 See n. 35 above.

37 For what follows, see the details in Van Seters, *The Life of Moses*, and cf. Coats, *Moses: Heroic Man, Man of God*.

38 Childs, *The Book of Exodus*.

39 *Studien zur Komposition des Pentateuch*.

40 For discussion, see *The Life of Moses*, pp. 35–63.

41 Schmid, *Der sogenannte Jahwist*, pp. 44–53.

42 Childs, 'Deuteronomic Formulae of the Exodus Tradition', pp. 30–39.

43 Childs, 'Deuteronomic Formulae of the Exodus Tradition'.

44 See Van Seters, 'Joshua's Campaign'.

45 The references in Joshua that draw a parallel to the Red Sea event are all later additions to the DtrH.

46 Mann, 'The Pillar of Cloud'; *idem, Divine Presence and Guidance*.

47 Van Seters, ' "Comparing Scripture with Scripture" '; *idem, The Life of Moses*, pp. 270–80.

48 Deut. 5.5 looks like an addition to accommodate D to the version in Exodus.

49 See the discussion by E. W. Nicholson, 'The Decalogue as the Direct Address of God', *VT* 27 (1977), pp. 422–33.

50 Nicholson, *God and his People*, pp. 164–78.

51 See *The Life of Moses*, pp. 290–318.

52 See Van Seters, *The Life of Moses*, pp. 361–456.

53 Aurelius, *Der Fürbitter Israels*; Balentine, 'The Prophet as Intercessor'.

54 Redford, *Egypt, Canaan, and Israel*, pp. 408–22.

55 Redford, 'Exodus I 11'; *idem*, 'Pithom'.

56 Holladay, *Cities of the Delta, Part III*; *idem*, 'Maskhuta, Tell el-'.

57 Isa. 40.3-5; 41.17-20; 42.14-17; 43.19-20; 49.9-11; 55.12-13.

58 Isa. 41.14; 43.14; 44.6, 24; 47.4; 48.17; 49.7, 26; 54.5-8.

59 Note the similarity to Second Isaiah.

60 Boorer, *The Promise of the Land*. See my review of Boorer in *BiOr* 54 (1997), pp. 168–71.

61 Van Seters, 'In the Babylonian Exile with J'.

62 Schmid, 'Vers une théologie du Pentateuque'.

63 As I have indicated above, pp. 71–72, in a recent article I have tried to show that the references in J to the 'tent of meeting' are intended as an etiology for the synagogue (meeting place). In Exodus its function is described as a place of prayer, a common term for the synagogue, and it was also closely associated with the elders of the people. See Van Seters, 'The Tent of Meeting in the Yahwist and the Origin of the Synagogue'.

64 R. J. Porter, *Moses and Monarchy: A Study in the Biblical Tradition of Moses* (Oxford: Oxford University Press, 1963).

65 On these prophetic story types see A. Rofé, *The Prophetical Stories* (Jerusalem: Magnes Press, 1988).

66 Aurelius, *Der Fürbitter Israels*; Van Seters, *The Life of Moses*, passim.

67 Balentine, 'The Prophet as Intercessor'.

68 Von Rad, *Old Testament Theology*, II, pp. 231–33.

69 Von Rad, *Old Testament Theology*, II, pp. 260–62.

7

The Priestly Writer (P)

Bibliography

Albertz, R., *A History of Israelite Religion in the Old Testament Period* (trans. J. Bowden; 2 vols.; Louisville, KY: Westminster/John Knox Press, 1994).

Blum, E., *Studien zur Komposition des Pentateuch* (1990).

Cross, F. M., *Canaanite Myth and Hebrew Epic* (1973).

Driver, S. R., *An Introduction to the Literature of the Old Testament* (New York: Meridian, 1957).

Grabbe, L. L., *Judaism from Cyrus to Hadrian. I. The Persian and Greek Periods* (Philadelphia: Fortress Press, 1992).

Lohfink, N., *The Theology of the Pentateuch* (1994).

McEvenue, S. E., *The Narrative Style of the Priestly Writer* (AnBib, 50; Rome: Pontifical Biblical Institute, 1971).

Mowinckel, S., *Erwägungen zur Pentateuch Quellenfrage* (1964).

—— *Tetrateuch-Pentateuch-Hexateuch: Die Berichte über die Landnahme in den drei altisraelitischen Geschichtswerken* (BZAW, 90; Berlin: W. de Gruyter, 1964).

Mullen, E. T., *Ethnic Myths and Pentateuchal Foundations* (1997).

Noth, M., *A History of Pentateuchal Traditions* (1972).

Plöger, O., *Theocracy and Eschatology* (trans. S. Rudman; Richmond, VA: John Knox Press, 1986).

Von Rad, G., *Old Testament Theology* (1962).

Schwartz, B. J., 'The Priestly Account of the Theophany and Lawgiving at Sinai', in M. V. Fox *et al.* (eds.), *Texts, Temples, and Traditions: A Tribute to Menahem Haran* (Winona Lake, IN: Eisenbrauns, 1996), pp. 103–34.

Ska, J. L., 'De la relative indépendance de l'écrit sacerdotal' (1994).

Tengström, S., *Die Toledotformel und die literarische Struktur der priesterlichen Erweiterungsschicht im Pentateuch* (CBOTS, 17; Lund: C.W.K. Gleerup, 1981).

Van Seters, J., *Abraham in History and Tradition* (1975).

—— *In Search of History (1983).*

—— 'The Creation of Man and the Creation of the King', *ZAW* 101 (1989), pp. 333–42.

—— 'Myth and History: The Problem of Origins', in A. de Pury (ed.), *Histoire et conscience historique dans les civilisations du Proche-Orient ancien* (Les Cahiers du CEPOA, 5; Leuven: Peeters, 1989), pp. 49–61.

—— *Prologue to History* (1992).

—— *The Life of Moses* (1994).

—— 'The Tent of Meeting in the Yahwist and the Origin of the Synagogue', *SJOT* (forthcoming).

Vervenne, M., 'The "P" Tradition in the Pentateuch: Document and/or Redaction? The "Sea Narrative" (Ex 13, 17–14, 31) as a Test Case', in C. Brekelmans and J. Lust (eds.), *Pentateuchal and Deuteronomistic Studies* (BETL, 94; Leuven: Peeters, 1990). pp. 67–90.

Vink, J. G., *The Date and Origin of the Priestly Code* (1969).

Whybray, N., *The Making of the Pentateuch* (1987).

Winnett, F. V., 'Reexamining the Foundations' (1965).

Zenger, E., 'Die priesterschriftlichen Schichten ("P")', in Zenger *et al.*, *Einleitung in das Alte Testament*, pp. 89–108.

1. The style, form and structure of P

a. Style

The general characteristics of the Priestly writer's style have become well established over the last century and a half so that they are widely acknowledged in the study of the Pentateuch. They can be seen in the use of fixed formulas, in the stereotyped formulation of narration and in the abundant use of repetition. A good example may be found in the P account of creation in Genesis 1. This narrative stratum also has a strong interest in matters that relate to the cult, to ritual and to the priesthood, both within its narrative history and especially within its law code, hence the name 'Priestly writer'.[1]

b. Form

The form or genre of P as a whole is a matter of controversy.[2] Much depends upon whether one views the whole P corpus as a unity dominated by the large code of law, or a P narrative (Pg) with a legal supplement (Ps), and whether it is dependent upon, and an expansion of, J or an independent source. If the law code is integral to P, then the narrative functions as a kind of prologue, similar to D. If P is primarily a narration of events from creation to the conquest, then the historiographic form predominates. Yet the understanding of P as historiography depends very much upon its close association with J, because without it P is very deficient in content and continuity, as we have seen above. Even though P introduces into the combined narrative a strict absolute chronology, the work is very static, with the various episodes treated as a series of paradigmatic events in the time of the beginnings. For this reason one can speak of the P narrative as myth and its combination with J as the mythologization of the earlier historiography.[3]

Furthermore, while P retains the general historiographic framework of a sequence of events from creation to the conquest, within this are a set of particular events that serve as prologue and explanation of various institutions or laws.

D. S. Mowinckel[4] and J. G. Vink[5] have referred to this aspect of P by characterizing P as a series of 'sophisticated etiologies' that both explain and legitimate customs and institutions in the past and lay down for the present how they are to be maintained. While there are incidental etiologies contained in the earlier strata, virtually the whole of the P narrative is etiological. Thus, the form of P has become a hybrid of those in the earlier literary strata, and this can be seen most clearly in the framing structures employed by P.

c. Structure

When considering the work of J above, we noted the use of genealogy, itinerary and divine promise and blessing as framing structures. These are also used by P but modified and expanded in distinctive ways. The genealogical framework is structured by a series of *toledot* formulas ('These are the generations of . . .') (Gen. 2.4; 5.1; 6.9; 10.1; 11.10, 27; 25.12, 19; 36.1; 37.2) that cover the whole of both the primeval period and the age of the patriarchs.[6] To this genealogical structure P adds a chronology that leads to the reformulation of the genealogies of Seth, between Adam and Noah, and Shem, between Noah and Abraham, into linear genealogies with the length of time in years between the births of the eldest in each generation to create an absolute chronology. In similar fashion, a chronology is introduced into the patriarchal stories with dates of certain events, especially those having to do with births and deaths. This genealogical continuity is carried over to the descendants in Egypt (Gen. 46.8-27) and to the genealogy of Moses and Aaron and the priesthood (Exod. 6.14-27).

In Genesis, P simply relies upon J's itinerary, but in Exodus–Numbers he expands it at various points from the events of the sea to the end of the wilderness journey. He also gives a summary of the route in Numbers 33. To the itinerary notices P attaches a precise date in which the exodus takes place at the beginning of the new religious year and everything is dated from that point.

The theme of the divine promise of land and the blessing of numerous offspring is also carried over from J by P, but with some significant modifications. The blessing of fruitfulness and abundance (in stereotyped formula) is extended back from the patriarchs to include the whole of humanity in Gen. 1.28 and again to the generation after the flood (Gen. 9.1, 7) and then to the patriarchs (Gen. 17.6, 16, 20; 28.3; 35.9, 11; 48.3-4). This part of the promise of numerous offspring was viewed as already fulfilled in Egypt (Gen. 47.27; Exod. 1.7), similar to J. In addition, the more precise promise of nationhood and the land of Canaan is reserved for the patriarchs (Gen. 17.6, 8, 16; 28.3-4; 35.11-12; 48.4), and it is the promise of land that is recalled in P's version of the call of Moses (Exod. 6.4, 8). Beyond this point, P does not return to this theme.

In addition to taking over these structuring elements from J, P has added the schematization of the three main periods of history: the primeval history, the patriarchs and the age of Moses, by associating different designations for the deity with each period. The general term for deity, *Elohim*, is used for the earliest period, that of *El Shaddai* (God Almighty) for the patriarchs and *Yahweh* as the revelation of the divine name to Moses (Exod. 6.2-3). Within J all three types of usage (Elohim, El names, Yahweh) are found without precise distinction as to period of time. Yet one can see how the discussion on the divine name in Exod. 3.12-15 may have led P to introduce such a scheme of revelation.

P also structures his history by introducing laws and institutions as the consequence of certain major events in the history. Thus, the creation of the world in six days with divine rest on the seventh results in the institution of the sabbath as a sacred day (Gen. 1.1–2.3). The flood leads into the laws having to do with the slaughter of animals and homicide (Gen. 9.1-6) followed by a covenant (vv. 8-17). The covenant with Abraham is the occasion for the institution of the practice of circumcision as a sign of the covenant (Gen. 17). The passover comes into existence on the occasion of the last plague and the slaughter of the first-born of Egypt (Exod. 12). The tabernacle and its cult are instituted at Sinai along with other laws as a consequence of the theophany and Moses' stay on the mountain. Various events on the wilderness journey give rise to additional laws, but the preparation for entry into the promised land especially results in several pieces of legislation. While one can find precedence in both J and D for associating covenants and laws with various periods and events, P has integrated them to a much greater degree into the narrative contexts than in the other sources. The laws and covenants become part of the structure of P's history, which has become almost totally etiological.[7]

2. The compositional history of P

The question of how the P corpus was composed can be answered only after one has decided on the form of P, on its comprehensive structure and extent, and on the relationship of P to J and to Deuteronomy and the DtrH. As we have suggested above, these issues are so much under discussion at the present time that it is not possible to deal with all of the issues of the debate here.[8] I will set out my view within the supplementary model in which P is viewed as a compositional stratum that expands and supplements J,[9] but that means that P's work is added to D and DtrH as well. In my view, the compositional history of P is to be explained as a series of expansions of these earlier writings, and in what follows I will try to show how this works.

It should also be noted that throughout the narrative portion of P's work there is very little that does not have a parallel episode in J. With few exceptions, P does not have any additional traditional source of information, apart from the legal corpus that he integrates into the work.

a. P in the primeval history

While P in Gen. 1.1–2.4a offers a parallel account of creation to that of J in Gen. 2.4b-25, he does so in a way that is quite different from that of J. In this one instance he seems to lean heavily upon a different tradition, that of the theogony/cosmogony, which he has rationalized in terms of a single creative deity. As scholars have long observed, hints of the underlying mythological elements may still be observed, and it is this that gives to the account the particular order of events. The creation of the humans (*ʾādām*) in the likeness of the deity is drawn from the Babylonian myth of the creation of the king, which has been democratized.[10] These have all been made to fit a seven-day scheme such that the completion of creation ends in the hallowing of the sabbath as a part of the created order of the world. Since the theogony in antiquity was often structured as a genealogy of the birth of the gods, and since it often stood at the beginning of national histories, the P writer also summarizes his creation account as the 'genealogy' (*tôlĕdôt*) of the heavens and the earth (2.4a) and sets it as a prologue to what follows.

It has long been observed that there is in P a fundamentally different presentation of creation than that found in J, with a different style of presentation, a different order in the various acts of creation, a very different treatment of the creation of the humans, and so on. This has led scholars to the separation of the P and J documents and to argue for their independence based on the degree of contradiction between the two accounts. Independent documents may not be the most appropriate way, however, of understanding the relationship of P to J. Much of P's reordering of the stages of creation is based upon his use of particular mythological sources. Yet in three respects P seems to emphasize revisions of J's presentation. First, the humans were created from the beginning in the image and likeness of the deity, and this likeness was not something that they gained through an act of disobedience (Gen. 1.26-27). This theme is repeated at important points later on (Gen. 5.1; 9.6). Secondly, the whole of creation is declared to be very good (Gen. 1.31) and P does not have any account of how the first pair introduced sin and evil into the world.[11] Thirdly, the account ends with an etiological explanation of the sabbath as part of creation's goodness (Gen. 2.2-3), in contrast to the series of curse etiologies that conclude J's story of the first pair.

The next block of P material is the Seth genealogy in Genesis 5. For the purposes of compositional history, a number of observations are important. First, it would seem very unlikely that the conclusion in Gen. 2.4a, 'This is the genealogy of the heavens and the earth . . .', would be followed immediately by the heading 'This is the book of the genealogy of Adam' in Gen. 5.1. Secondly, there seems to be little reason for the repetition of the statement in Gen. 5.2 about the creation of the humans unless the continuity between P's two blocks had not been interrupted by the J material in 2.4b–4.26. Thirdly, whereas P uses the term 'adam' to mean humans, both male and female in Gen. 1.26-27; 5.1b-2, the genealogy shifts in v. 3

to the meaning of Adam as the first male in the line of descendants. This presupposes the usage in J and cannot be understood without it. The genealogy of Seth borrows heavily from J's genealogy of Seth for the purpose of creating P's chronology. Yet it still retains the anecdote about Noah in 5.29 that clearly reflects J's style of presentation. Everything points to P deliberately constructing this genealogical chronology using J as his source. The length of the ancestors' lives seems to be influenced by the Babylonian tradition of kings who reigned for very long periods before the flood.

The flood story in P is central to the discussion of whether or not P is an independent document. Within this debate much depends upon which texts are assigned to J and which to P.[12] As indicated above, I have attributed Gen. 6.13-16, 22 and 8.1-2, 15-16, 18 to J instead of P. There are two reasons why these texts are assigned to P. First, they use the designation 'god' rather than Yahweh for deity. Since we have seen above that many texts in J use the term 'god', this by itself is not a useful criterion. Secondly, in the early history of Pentateuchal criticism P was held to be the basic document and assigning texts to P was done to make it as complete an account as possible. Since this is in dispute here, there is no longer any reason to do so. The assigning of each text to J or P must be considered on its own merits. Once J has been reconstructed as a consistent, self-contained story, the supplementary character of P becomes clear.

At the end of the Seth genealogy P breaks the previous pattern by having three sons, Shem, Ham and Japhet, all born as triplets in the same 500th year (Gen. 5.32). The triad pattern certainly belongs to J, but the chronology associated with it by P is highly artificial. This is followed in P by the introductory formula, 'This is the genealogy of Noah' (6.9a), then an anecdotal comment on Noah's character (v. 9b) and the statement of his having three sons (v. 10). This sequence is very curious and makes better sense if the introductory formula is used after the J break of 6.1-8 to indicate a new period of history. The remark about Noah as 'righteous' is borrowed from J (7.1), where Noah is singled out within his own generation, but P makes the feature of his piety parallel to the anecdote of Enoch (5.22) within the sequence of generations and not related to the cause of the flood.

The cause of the flood is given in 6.11-12 as the self-corruption of the earth without giving any prior hint as to how this came about. Indeed, so positive is the previous perspective on creation presented by P that this change is inexplicable within P itself. It depends entirely on the prior presentation of J, but it differs from J in focusing not so much on human sin as on the general corruption of all creation, including the animal world, so that they are all involved in the destruction of the flood.

With respect to the number of each kind of animal that entered the ark, there is a difference between J and P. J has additional clean animals because there must be enough of them to allow for the sacrifice at the end of the ordeal. P, however, contradicts this, since the distinction between clean and unclean is not made until the time of Moses. So he has only two of every kind of animal enter the ark. He is so concerned about this 'correction' that he specifically records that only a single pair of both clean and unclean animals came into the ark (7.8-9). There would certainly be no need for such a distinction between clean and unclean in an independent account. It is also the case that P has drastically modified the chronology of J's flood account to make it fit into a single solar year. While P embellishes J's account with this elaborate chronology and in other ways, he does not add anything of significance to the story line and nothing that corresponds to the source of the story in the Babylonian tradition.

Nevertheless, P makes the flood into a great 'historical' divide. While Noah and his sons receive the divine blessing as at creation, their relationship with the animal world has been changed, so that, in addition to the plant world, the animal world is also given to humanity for food, with some restrictions (9.1-7). The laws of homicide are introduced as a control of the violence that leads to the flood. This is followed by an eternal covenant never to bring another flood, with its sign of the rainbow, which parallels the promise of the deity in J (Gen. 8.22). Within 9.1-17 are the formulaic language and structures that are so pervasive in P.

As indicated above, the Table of Nations in Genesis 10 belongs to J's composition and was only modified by P at a few points. The heading 'These are the genealogies of Noah's sons ...', while usually ascribed to P, is a problem. The segmented genealogy does not fit P's usual scheme or chronology. The previous heading for Noah (6.9) would seem to imply more than just one generation, making this one superfluous. The style of the second half of the heading (10.1b) corresponds to that of J. P has a second genealogy of Shem that follows in 11.10-26 that cannot be a part of P's Table of Nations or fit closely with it. It seems to me likely that the formula 'These are the genealogies of ...' is original to the Table of Nations and to J's composition and was borrowed by P as a formula to introduce various parts of his history and chronology.[13]

The Shem genealogy (11.10-26), following J's interval of the Tower of Babel story, borrows material from J's Shem genealogy and creates a chronology from the flood to the time of Abraham. The genealogy of Terah and his sons (11.27-31) was originally part of J's Shem genealogy.[14] It was taken over by P rather artificially by using the formula 'This is the genealogy of Terah' at the beginning, even though Terah is a figure of no consequence in the story. He also fits his chronology to the J genealogy by having all of Terah's three sons born to him as triplets in his seventieth year (11.26), similar to Noah's three sons in his 500th year. The death notice in 11.32 fits P's pattern but obviously rests upon J's remarks in v. 31.

By far the most economical explanation of the relationship of P to J in the primeval history is to see it as an expansion or supplement to J's presentation. Anything else involves the supposition of various redactors, some of whom may be consistent with the style and outlook of P, others of J. They are the invention of those who insist on the independence of a P source, but when they do so it is at the expense of assigning to Rp texts that are part of the fundamental structures and compositional integrity of P.

b. P in the patriarchal stories

The P additions to the patriarchal stories are rather modest, having to do primarily with notations on chronology and birth and death notices. These give an appearance of a basic structural framework, but the larger narrative is not dependent upon them and is often in some conflict or tension with them. They are part of P's embellishments of the older accounts. P does add one narrative about the death and burial of Sarah (Gen. 23) in order to establish a general burial place for all of the patriarchs in Canaan. He also provides a genealogy for Ishmael (Gen. 25.12-17) and Esau (Gen. 36). One cannot simply regard all of these incidental notices as redactional additions by Rp because they are necessary to the whole chronological scheme that pervades P's narrative in Genesis.

What is important for P's treatment of the patriarchs, however, is his modification of J's themes of the divine promises and covenant with Abraham, Isaac and Jacob. With Abraham in particular P repeats the promises (Gen. 17), making them an eternal covenant, like the covenant of Noah, but now with participation in the covenant community conditional upon the observance of circumcision. He also associates with Abraham the revelation of the divine name *El Shaddai*, 'God Almighty'. This covenant, like that of J in Genesis 15, is given in the context of the promise of a son and in response to this Abraham laughs, a motif that is borrowed from the following J story in 18.1-14. The same promise theme is taken up in the addition to J's story of Jacob's stolen blessing, in which P now has Isaac willingly bless Jacob in the name of El Shaddai with the Abrahamic promises (28.1-5). Jacob, in turn, receives further assurances of these blessings and promises in an appearance of El Shaddai to him in Bethel (35.9-15) parallel to the theophany in J (28.10-22). Finally, in P Jacob blesses the sons of Joseph with the divine promises in Egypt, making them equal to the other sons of Jacob (48.3-7). The reason for this is to anticipate this inheritance of land in the final distribution in Joshua 16–17 as two tribes, because Levi does not inherit any tribal land. In every case, the theme of patriarchal promise is built into the P narrative with various parallels and links. In addition, it anticipates the link with Moses in Exod. 6.2-8.

c. P in the exodus story

It is the J history that provides a transition from the patriarchal age to the period of Egyptian oppression and the backdrop for the rescue under Moses (Gen. 50.22-26; Exod. 1.6-7*, 8-12).[15] Into this P has fitted a summary of the extended family of Jacob, who emigrated to Egypt (Exod. 1.1-5; cf. Gen. 46.8-27), but it comes too late for the present context. P supplements J's remark in Exod. 1.7

about the Israelites multiplying and becoming strong by his formulaic phrases about being 'fruitful', 'increasing greatly', and 'filling the land'. The point of such additions is to provide a thematic continuity with the story of creation and the blessing of the patriarchs. Finally, P adds some comment on the theme of oppression (1.13-14), but his addition depends entirely upon the prior statement in J of how this turn of events came about.

The next unit that is commonly identified with P is Exod. 2.23-25, which serves as a clear anticipation of P's call narrative in 6.2-12. Yet there is a problem in the initial remark about the death of the king (2.23a?) that seems to go very closely with 4.19-20 and which in turn is parallel to 4.18 (J). However, few want to ascribe 2.23a? and 4.19-20 to P because of the use of the divine name Yahweh before the self-disclosure in 6.2-3. One might be tempted to regard 2.23a? + 4.19-20 as a continuity into which the whole block of the call narative in 3.1–4.18 has been set.[16] But the reference to the 'rod of God' only makes sense in the context of the call narrative (cf. 4.1-4). The simple solution is to regard the whole of 4.19-23 as the work of P despite the use of Yahweh here. This text is in agreement with P's notion that Moses' task is to perform miracles before Pharaoh, using the divine rod. Of course, it relies upon the prior J story about Moses' sojourn in the land of Midian, the call at the sacred mountain, and on the revelation of the divine name to Moses. There is, therefore, no problem for P to use the name Yahweh from this point onward, even though his own treatment of this revelation is not given until 6.2-3.

Those who take 6.2-12 as the first reference to Moses in P are hard pressed to explain the complete lack of any introduction of Moses in an independent P document. P follows J in highlighting the continuity between the god of the fathers (= patriarchs) and Yahweh, the god of the exodus deliverance. The people's deliverance is to be the fulfillment of the patriarchal promises and the basis of their corporate identity as Yahweh's people. Like J, Moses in P has two tasks. The one is to go and announce deliverance to the people; the other is to confront Pharaoh. In the first task Moses is presented as acting alone. The people do not listen to him because of their cruel bondage. This seems to reflect the results of the first encounter with Pharaoh in ch. 5. The second task is presented as a subsequent commission with the theme of Moses' objections and the appointment of his brother Aaron to help him. This uses motifs from the J call narrative. However, P revises the earlier discussion in 4.15-16, where Moses is like a god, not to Aaron, but to Pharaoh, and where Aaron is his prophet only in their dealings with the Egyptians.

In 7.1-7 P introduces the confrontation with Pharaoh and his court by having Moses and Aaron demand the release of the people, but Pharaoh's refusal leads to repeated 'signs and wonders in the land of Egypt', the plagues. This introduction includes in its purview not just the P plagues, but the whole of the plagues narrative. This is clear from the fact that it is only in the J plagues that Moses and Aaron demand the release of the people. P takes this scheme entirely for granted and uses J's formula about the hardening of Pharaoh's heart and not listening as a summary to his plagues, even when it is not entirely appropriate.[17]

The plagues for P are construed, first of all, as a contest between Moses and Aaron and the magicians, in which the latter must finally admit defeat. In addition to constructing an initial contest in 7.8-13 that is a wonder but not a plague, P adds the contest theme to the first and second plagues and then adds three additional plagues of gnats, boils and darkness, fitting them into the J scheme. The final plague of the death of the first-born is never described in P, even though its presence in the account is demanded by its anticipation in the preparations of the passover. Here P simply relies upon the account of the event in J. While J's account of his seven plagues makes good sense as a self-contained narrative, P's account is completely dependent upon J and cannot be separated from it.

The climax of the story of the plagues in the death of the first-born is the occasion for the institution of yet another cultic practice, the festival of passover. Here P not only regards the passover sacrifice and the eating of unleavened bread as a commemoration of the exodus as in D and J, but he places the first occasion of that festival in Egypt as part of the event and necessary to it (Exod. 12.1-28). This he does even though such observance of the passover stands in considerable tension with the story itself, because the announcement of the final plague and its execution (11.1-8; 12.29-36) do not allow for the festal preparations in 12.1-6 nor for the proper keeping of the rites (12.8-20). This is a clear instance where the paradigmatic myth completely overrides all 'historical' considerations. Yet it is important to note that this is not a case of a law being fitted into a story by some redactional process, because details of the instructions are directly tied to the narration of the event itself (12.11-13). The 'supplementary' injunction in 12.43-49 has the appearance of a rather loose connection with its context and hardly applies to the people's plight in Egypt.

P's remarks on the exodus in 12.40-42, 51 are not a description of the event itself but a summary and comment on J's prior description of the departure. It is also clear from such texts as Exod. 14.1-4 and 15-18 that P's treatment of the crossing of the sea cannot stand as an independent account but was added onto the prior J version. The language of P in the crossing account links it closely with his treatment of the plagues as one final judgment on Pharaoh and his army. It is a feature of P in both the plagues and the sea event that he heightens the miraculous as the sign of the divine presence in the event.

d. P in the wilderness tradition

P has no new traditions to add to the wilderness journey account. In three instances, the manna story in Exodus 16, the failed invasion from the south in Numbers 13–14, and the revolt of Korah, Dathan and Abiram in Numbers 16,

P merely expands the J accounts in terms of his own interests. In the manna story, J presents the event (Exod 16.1a, 2-3*, 4–7, 13b-15, 21, 27-31, 35a) as the way in which the sabbath was first discovered in the wilderness and was a test of divine obedience.[18] For P this is a problem because the sabbath was already established at creation, so his additions in vv. 16-20, 22-26 suggest that the sabbath was already a well-known institution. In the story of the failed mission of the spies and invasion of the land from the south (Num. 13-14), both J and P (following D in Deut. 1.19-46) have a particular interest in the theme of the promised land that was lost to a whole wilderness generation because of their faithlessness. P, in the listing of the spies (13.3-16) and the exoneration of Joshua and Caleb from culpability (14.5-10, 26-38), anticipates their survival into the period of conquest and settlement (Josh. 14.6-15). J's account of the revolt of Dathan and Abiram against the leadership of Moses and Aaron (Num. 16) is expanded to include the opposition of the priestly family of Korah against the supremacy of the Aaronids.

The only new episode in P's wilderness stories is the story about Moses and Aaron striking the rock to produce water for the people (Num. 20.3-13). This episode is modeled on the J murmuring story of Exod. 17.3-7. Both deal with extracting water from the rock at Meribah by striking it with a rod. However, in this case it is not the people who are in the wrong and are punished but Moses and Aaron, who did not follow the exact instructions of Yahweh. As a result, they are punished by being denied the chance of entering the promised land.

e. P in the Sinai pericope

In the P corpus, Sinai becomes the primary location for the giving of the law, which is now contained in Exodus 25–31; 35-40; Leviticus; Numbers 1–10. There is considerable debate about how much of this belongs to Pg and how much to Ps. In general terms, following Noth, one can make a distinction between those parts that seem to be linked most closely with the narrative and those blocks of legal material that have a very loose connection with the narrative context. On this basis what is integral to P's narrative of the Sinai sojourn is its establishment of the cult, primarily the construction of the Tabernacle, the installation of the priesthood and the ordering of the camp for the march to Canaan. This is contained in Exodus 25–31, 35–40; Leviticus 8–10; Numbers 1–10. The rest of the legal material belongs to the supplement and to this we will return below.

The other issue in the Sinai pericope is the extent to which P is present in the narrative of Exodus 19–20, 24 and 34, and therefore the relationship of P to J. It is not too difficult to identify a consistent, unified non-P (= J) narrative in 19.2-11, 13b-19; 20.18-26; 21-23; 24.3-8, 12-15a, 18b. Into this sequence has been spliced priestly material that documentarians assign partly to P, partly to Rp and partly to some other source. This yields the result that 19.1 + 24.15b-18a is made to serve as the entire P prologue to the giving of the law on Sinai, and the rest is considered as redactional addition. That is hardly credible. The obvious and most economical explanation is that P has expanded and 'redacted' the original J account with various additions to make it appropriate as a prologue to his great law code. Thus, J's itinerary notice of 19.2 is given a precise chronology in 19.1. In 19.12-13a, 20-25 P imposes restrictions that prohibit the people from approaching the mountain because the mountain is being treated as a sanctuary. This contradicts J's suggestion that the consecrated 'laity' could ascend the sacred mountain. The Priestly writer could not admit such a possibility.

P also reintroduces from Deuteronomy the declaration of the Ten Commandments from Sinai, which was not in J, but the connection with the context, between 19.25 and 20.18, is very vague. P makes little change in the Decalogue except in the law of the sabbath, which is now grounded in the six days of creation and the sabbath rest (20.11). The importance of this change becomes obvious from 31.12-17 and 35.1-3, where it is indicated that the sabbath is the sign of the eternal covenant between Yahweh and his people. The pattern here follows that of the covenant of Noah in Gen. 9.8-17 and of Abraham in Genesis 17. Many scholars deny that there is any Sinai covenant in P, but P has taken over D's identification of the Decalogue as a covenant declaration and regularly refers to the tablets and the ark in which the tablets were placed as the tablets/ark of the 'testimony' (*'ēdût*), P's special term for covenant. The fact that P also supplements J's covenant ceremony means that he can take this theme of the Sinai covenant for granted. Not only this, but he adds a special covenant meal to J's covenant ceremony in 24.1-2, 9-11 for Moses, Aaron and his two eldest sons as representative of the priesthood and the 70 elders as leaders of the people. In J, these elders are not yet appointed until Num. 11.16-17, 24-25.

For P, the Sinai revelation inaugurates the establishment of the cult, which means first of all the construction of the center of worship, the Tabernacle (*miškān*) and all that goes with it. P skillfully places the revelation of the tabernacle's design during the 40 days when Moses is on the mountain to receive the Tables of the Law (Exod. 25–31), and then the subsequent construction of the Tabernacle (35–40) after J's renewal of the covenant and the reception of the second copy of the laws. The result is an elaborate and sumptuous portable shrine that contrasts rather sharply with J's Tent of Meeting (Exod. 33.7-11), which is merely intended as a portable structure in which the deity could meet and communicate with Moses from time to time. When this happened, the pillar of cloud would stand at the door of the tent while Moses was inside and the deity would then speak with Moses. P takes over this function of the Tent of Meeting and combines it with the Tabernacle. The pillar of cloud and fire becomes the 'glory' that inhabits the Tabernacle/Tent (Exod. 40.34-38) but also comes from time to time to appear at the Tent of Meeting to speak with Moses and Aaron and the people. This conflation of function of the Tabernacle/Tent has made for some confusion in the P account.

P's portrayal of the sojourn at Sinai and of the wilderness period in general is the creation of a great mythic fantasy. In the midst of a barren desert an elaborate cult center is constructed with the most sumptuous and costly furnishings, in which innumerable animals of many kinds are offered in sacrifice and in which serve a complex hierarchy of cult officials. This fantasy is accommodated to the narrative context of life in the desert by the portrayal of a portable temple, but it has no equivalent in reality. There is no hint in the Sinai sojourn of the harsh realities of desert life with its lack of food and water. Even in the manna story, P makes the manna into a miracle food that lasts for the whole of the wilderness period until they reach the land of Canaan (Exod. 16.16-20, 22-26, 32-35). Moses orders a container of it to be kept in perpetuity in the Tabernacle/Temple 'before Yahweh', even before the Tabernacle is built.

f. P and the conquest of the promised land

The thesis advocated by M. Noth[19] that the Tetrateuch, including both J and P, developed independently from that of the whole Dtr corpus from Deuteronomy to 2 Kings meant for Noth that there was no continuation of the P source into Joshua. This was a radical departure from the position held since Wellhausen that P was present in Joshua 13–22. Furthermore, according to Noth all of those texts in the later part of Numbers that anticipated such a conquest of the land, even though they betrayed P stylistic features, were viewed as secondary. This decision by Noth has seriously violated his own principle of drawing a distinction between Pg and Ps by identifying Pg by its connection to the narrative context and Ps by its legal character. A number of scholars, most notably Mowinckel,[20] did not follow Noth's view on this, but the broad acceptance of Noth's thesis on the DtrH has had the effect of redefining P in a radical way.

Those scholars who followed Noth's drastic curtailment of P have continued to debate just where the ending of P should be placed. Noth's choice was to end it with the commissioning of Joshua (Num. 27.12-23) followed by the death of Moses (Deut. 34.7-9).[21] Since we have rejected the thesis of the separate development of the Tetrateuch from the Dtr corpus, there is no reason to limit the P stratum in this way. The strong emphasis on the theme of the promised land in P points to the fulfillment of that theme in the conquest and settlement. If we identify in Numbers all of the Pg material as narrative or as the legal material dependent upon the narrative, we would need to include the camp of the Israelites (1.1–10.10), the departure from Sinai (10.11-28), the mission of the spies (13–14), the rebellion of Korah and the regulation of the priesthood (16–18), water from the rock (20.2-13), the death of Aaron (20.22-29), apostasy of Peor and the Midianites (25.6-18), commissioning of Joshua (27.12-23), war against Midian (31), allotment of the land in Transjordan (32* mixed with J), the wilderness itinerary (33) and preparations for the invasion of Canaan (34–36).

As we saw above, Deuteronomy (and DtrH) uses the theme of conquest to encompass the entire wilderness journey from Horeb to the plains of Moab. J takes this same structure of events and augments it with many other episodes but still retains some treatment of all of the events in D's scheme. Although P declines to deal with many of the conquest events, he still gives a strong militaristic orientation to his narrative.[22] The whole encampment of the Israelites and their march through the desert is treated as the movement of a great army (Num. 1–2; 10.11-28). P takes up the idea of the divine vanguard from J (cf. Num. 10.33-35) and makes it an important feature of his narrative (9.15-23; 10.11-12). The itinerary of P is construed as 'stages' in a military march, with each tribe marching under its own banner. P presents his supplement to J's story of the mission of the spies in Numbers 13–14, which is certainly viewed in P as a military expedition (13.32-33; 14.8-9), even though nothing is said about the abortive attempt to conquer the land from the south. P also says nothing about the actual conquest of the land by the eastern tribes, although he includes a war against the Midianites (Num. 31). This war is not related to the conquest of the promised land, but it allows P to spell out his views of the law of warfare and the claims of the temple on the booty. P's additions to the division of the land among the eastern tribes in Numbers 32 (vv. 2*, 10-12, 28*), with parallels drawn to the spies' mission, indicate that P is well aware of the previous account of the conquest. P further anticipates the conquest by giving his version of the commissioning of Moses' successor but under the authority of the high priest Eleazar. It is through the mediation of Eleazar that Joshua is to receive his divine direction. The census of the tribes of Israel (Num. 26), the boundaries of the promised land (Num. 34), the regulations regarding the cities of refuge (Num. 35; cf. Josh. 20 [Dtr]) and regulations on inheritance (Num. 36) all anticipate the subsequent conquest of the land of Canaan. In my view, P has no independent account of Moses' death but merely embellishes slightly the J version in Deuteronomy 34, adding the remark about the appointment of Joshua in v. 9 in keeping with his report of the event in Numbers 27.

The question of the presence of P in Joshua is strongly debated because it has major implications for the whole understanding of the P work. N. Lohfink[23] has strongly argued for seeing P in Josh. 14.1-2; 18.1; 19.51 because these texts use formulae that connect them with the whole of the P work. These texts and a few other snippets in Joshua cannot be strung together, as Lohfink does, to create a conclusion to a self-contained P work. Even Noth recognized that the allotment of the land to the tribes is a later supplement to the DtrH written in a 'priestly style', but there is no reason to deny it to P. It fits completely with his narrative. This applies also to the allotment of the Levitical cities in ch. 21. The anticipation of the distribution in Numbers 26 and 34–35 suggests that the whole account of the distribution of the land in Joshua 13–19, 21 belongs to P.[24]

P's presentation of the land distribution in Joshua 13–19, 21 means that he was well aware of the DtrH conquest narrative, to which he appended his land allotment. Within the Dtr narrative of the conquest, one can find a number of embellishments in priestly style in the account of the crossing of the Jordan and the processional march around Jericho.[25] There is also an episode in Josh. 22.7-34 that is obviously appended to the Dtr unit in 22.1-6, in which the eastern tribes are sent back with Joshua's blessing to their own region after the conquest is over. The appended unit in vv. 7-34 contains many hints of P style and perspective. It deals with the issue of the true boundaries of the promised land as the holy land and how those outside of this region, represented by the eastern tribes, can remain loyal to the worship of Yahweh. To this issue we will return.

Beyond the book of Joshua there are other texts within the DtrH corpus that strongly suggest the possibility of priestly addition or elaboration. The matter is very much in dispute and cannot be taken up in detail here. One example will suffice. It would not be surprising to find the presence of a Priestly writer in the account of the construction of Solomon's temple if it were the case that P's work in the Pentateuch and Joshua was a supplement to the DtrH. The list of objects made of gold in 1 Kgs 7.48-50 looks like just such an embellishment. However, it is in the additions to the account of the dedication of the temple (1 Kgs 8) that P's presence is most obvious. Within the context of Solomon bringing up the ark to the new temple the P writer includes the bringing up of the 'Tent of Meeting and all the holy vessels that were in the tent' (8.4) to establish a continuity with the Tabernacle in the wilderness. D and DtrH do not know of any such Tent of Meeting. Again, when the ark is placed by the priests in the temple and they come out, it states that 'a cloud filled the house of Yahweh so that the priests were not able to stand to minister because of the cloud; for the glory of Yahweh filled the house of Yahweh' (8.10-11). This corresponds very closely with the description of the completion of the Tabernacle and the descent of the glory into it in Exod. 40.34-35. There are few scholars who would deny that 1 Kgs 8.10-11 is a priestly supplement to the DtrH. But if that is the case, then why not elsewhere in DtrH and in the whole literary relationship of P to J and D/DtrH?

3. The social setting of P

a. The problem of P's origin

The attempt to ascertain the social setting of the P narrative and its meaning or intention within that context is dependent upon a number of factors. Much rests upon the perceived relationship of P to the non-P (J) material of the Tetrateuch and to Deuteronomy and DtrH. The older documentary method construed the relationship as one of evolution from the simple agricultural/nature religion of the early monarchy (J) to the centralized Jerusalem cultus of the late Judahite kingdom (D), to the theocratic concentration of priestly authority and elaborate cultus of the Second Temple reconstruction. This evolutionary scheme suggested that P's social context should be understood primarily in comparison with D as a priestly response to this reform movement.

Concerning the dating and provenance of P, there has been fairly strong opinion that it is to be associated with the late exilic or early postexilic periods with a general *terminus ad quem* considered to be the rebuilding of the Second Temple in 515 BCE. This view of an early Persian period date is strongly supported by those who follow Noth in the view that there is no reference to settlement in P and that the narrative ends in the wilderness, symbolic of the author's location in the exile. Such reforming priests could perhaps be found among the disciples of Ezekiel.

At the same time, P is also associated with the work of Ezra and his promulgation of the law under the authority of the Persian government (Ezra 7) about 400 BCE. If the law being brought to Jerusalem and imposed by Ezra is the Priestly Code, as many assume, then there is a considerable time gap between its composition and its promulgation. It is also supposed that this act of bringing the law to Jerusalem had something to do with the combination of the three main sources J (or JE) and P with D to form the Pentateuch. In such a scenario the work of Ezra has more to do with the final 'redaction' of the Pentateuch than with P itself.

Likewise, of central importance to the discussion over the last fifty years has been the role of the Persian administration in the promulgation of the law as reflected in Ezra 7. It is possible to dismiss the chapter as expressive of the Chronicler's bias, and there are certainly some elements in the unit that are to be attributed to his outlook. At the same time, there is enough evidence of Persian intervention in the religious affairs of its subject peoples in cooperation with local religious authorities to lead one to believe that the text of Ezra reflects a set of events that took place at that time.[26] A parallel to this can be seen in the so-called Passover Papyrus (Cowley EP 21), which dates to the fifth year of Darius II (419 BCE). This letter seems to decree certain regulations for the keeping of the passover and feast of unleavened bread in the Jewish garrison in Elephantine (Yeb) in Egypt.[27]

Some observations about this example, however, should be noted. First, the instructions resemble those of P but they seem to reflect an earlier stage than the versions in the P strata. If this is correct, it would suggest that there was a long process of formation of the legal tradition in the exile/diaspora that was still continuing in the late Persian period before the formation of the P narrative. Secondly, this and other examples of Persian intervention have to do with matters of law and regulation of the local cult and hardly reflect the authorization of such an extensive corpus as the whole of P. This is particularly the case if P is historiography and if it extends beyond the P Code in Numbers and includes a substantial addition to Joshua. Thirdly, I think it would be better to dissociate the support of Persian authority from the whole problem of the Pentateuch's canonization. It is not possible to decide when the first five books were treated as a unit distinct from the historical books that followed and there is nothing in the account of Ezra that suggests such a distinction.

Another issue in the discussion is related to the genre of P and its function in a particular social setting. Is P to be understood as a historiographic work that legitimates the origins of certain customs, institutions and practices in the distant past, or is it a programmatic work that prescribes and reforms practices for the future? The legitimation function may be understood as appropriate to a situation in which the rights and privileges of one religious authority or group are contested by another within the land of Palestine. The programmatic function may be the esoteric preoccupation of visionaries in the exile/diaspora far removed from the harsh realities of life in the land. If one looks within the Pentateuch, one can find certain oppositions reflected in the sources, such as the nationalism of D as compared with the more universal outlook of J and P, and this could be paired with the historical distinction between the homeland and the exile/diaspora. Or, one could emphasize the distinction between lay and priest, especially in the non-P/P dichotomy of the Tetrateuch. In the Persian period as reflected in Nehemiah, there is also the tension between the north (Samaria) and the south (Judah/Jerusalem), coupled with attitudes of tolerance or intolerance towards certain norms of orthodoxy. This range of possibilities has spawned a number of different scenarios for the social context of P.

The older documentary approach highlighted the differences between D and P in the discussion of this social tension in exilic/postexilic times. The non-P (J) material was considered only as a body of older traditions that may or may not be shared by P in its own tradition history. The recent critique of the documentary method, with its radical redating of the non-P stratum of the Tetrateuch to the exilic[28] or even the postexilic[29] periods, has called for a basic reappraisal of this relationship. It now becomes clear that the contrast between non-P (KD/J) and P is as important as that between D and P. Compared with the documentary method, the two-composition method of Blum and the supplementary method of Van Seters have much in common in their re-evaluation of the social setting and intention of P. At the very least, the time period between P and non-P has been greatly reduced and the use of the earlier stratum by P and its conscious composition as a theological and ideological response to the earlier work is recognized by both methods. Nevertheless, there are some important disagreements that stem from the differences in literary method. Due to space limitations, I will set out my own view of the broad parameters in the discussion of this subject based on my supplementary method of analysis and indicate where it might differ from the other positions.

The historical setting of P is governed first and foremost by virtue of the fact that it is a supplement to J in its fullest and most complete form. I have argued that J is post-D/DtrH and belongs to the late exilic period, contemporary with Second Isaiah, and this obviously means that P is later and belongs to the Persian period.

This also means that P is dependent upon, and later than, the prophetic tradition that includes Ezekiel and Second Isaiah, with which it has a number of points of affinity. Comparison should also be made with Haggai and Zechariah at the beginning of the Second Temple period and Malachi in the late Persian period. For reasons already indicated in the remarks about the Passover Papyrus, a date in the late Persian period fits best. This also means that P is considerably later than the D corpus of Deuteronomy to 2 Kings and the Dtr edition of Jeremiah.

It is at this point that the most important distinction arises between the two-composition method of Blum and Albertz[30] and my own view. By characterizing the non-P version of the Tetrateuch as a D composition, these scholars blur the distinction between the non-P stratum of the Tetrateuch and D/DtrH and then compare the whole of D in Genesis–2 Kings to P. This inclusive D work and P are dated to the same early Persian period and are viewed as rival presentations of the sacred history, one from a lay-theological perspective and one from a reform-priestly perspective. The final Pentateuch is a compromise document that was hammered out under the Persian imperial authority as a binding edict for the Jews within the western province of Syria (Trans-Euphrates). This means that everything in P is read in such a way as to relate to this lay/priest dichotomy and the political/religious struggle between these two parties.[31]

I cannot accept this reconstruction for a number of reasons. First, it is wrong in my view to regard the J corpus in the Pentateuch as Deuteronomistic and reflective of the perspective of D/DtrH. The differences are often as great between J and D as they are between J and P. There are three major compositions to be reckoned with in the discussion, not two. Secondly, these three strata belong to three quite different historical and social settings and are successive. They are not contemporary documents that have been combined by an editorial committee but are the result of supplementation after the lapse of time and new circumstances. P is at least a century later than the whole corpus of non-P (= J) in the Tetrateuch. This completely undermines the notion that the documents themselves reflect the two sides of party struggle. This is not to deny that there was in both the exilic and postexilic periods considerable diversity in theology and piety and that much of the biblical literature reflects such diversity. Indeed, the 'final' Pentateuch did not put an end to it. Yet, I find it preferable to discuss D/DtrH as a work related to the early exile, J as a product of the late exile, and P as a work of the Second Temple reconstruction, without implying that there is a strict evolution of religion through these three phases. Even so, J often represents a middle position between D and P and indicates the impact of the exile upon the theology of J as compared with D. J reflects a diaspora religion before the rebuilding of the temple and the reinstitutionalization of the priesthood and its cultus that is so strongly presented by P. It is the transformation of J's form of 'lay' theology as reflected in the Tetrateuch that is the primary objective of P. His additions to D are rather minimal.

Furthermore, Blum follows Noth in limiting P to the Tetrateuch and thereby excludes the settlement theme of Joshua and the problem of the relationship with DtrH. Here I follow Vink and Mowinckel in regarding the theme of land settlement in Joshua as of the greatest importance to the work of P. This means that P's composition was understood from the outset as a revision of the historiographic tradition from Genesis to 2 Kings and was not produced as a 'compromise' legal document to win the backing of the Persian administration.[32] The latter view has the curious consequence of conflating the whole period from 515 to 400 BCE into some vague middle period unrelated to any particular set of conditions or circumstances.

Another scenario for the origin of the Pentateuch is proposed by E. T. Mullen.[33] He, too, sees the Persian authorities as primarily responsible for the urge to create a Jewish ethnic identity based upon a foundation document. In this case, Mullen makes a major distinction between D/DtrH and the Tetrateuch in both historical and social context but no basic source or strata distinction within the Tetrateuch, which, like Whybray,[34] is treated as a single composition, whatever its 'traditional' sources may have been. The Tetrateuch, therefore, is not the work of a specific Pentateuchal strata P but an elite scribal class linked to both the Persian administration and the reconstructed temple community. They are responsible for composing the Tetrateuch out of sources that correspond to the J and P strata and of combining this with the DtrH to form the 'Primary History' from Genesis to 2 Kings. At the same time, Mullen suggests that those who created the Primary History destroyed it by creating the Pentateuch as a separate entity out of part of it. He argues that it is these same scribes who 'detached Deuteronomy from its position as a prologue [to DtrH] and encapsulated it into a new document [the Pentateuch] that would satisfy Persian requirements'.[35]

I cannot accept this position of Mullen on the creation of the 'Primary History' or the Tetrateuch or the Pentateuch. Mullen uses disagreements over the Documentary Hypothesis and lack of consensus about source division as an excuse for treating the Tetrateuch synchronically, but there is very strong agreement that non-P and P can and should be viewed as quite distinct from each other in the Tetrateuch. Furthermore, it is J (non-P) who is responsible for the construction of the history from creation to the plains of Moab as an extension of the DtrH. And this was done before the Persian period and without any political influence from authorities in Babylon. P follows entirely the broad outline established by J. Finally, there is no evidence that the Persians were interested in other people's ethnicity or even in their own. I have seen little evidence that before the Hellenistic period any of the other Near Eastern nations had any clear sense of their own ethnicity. The Persian authorities may have wished to see well-governed and cohesive communities within their realm and may have supported specific measures to bring that about. However, the idea that the Persian authorities were somehow behind the creation of Jewish ethnicity goes beyond all of the evidence of Persian involvement in local affairs and has nothing to commend it.

In contrast to Blum and Albertz, as a working hypothesis I would view P as reflecting the historical conditions of the late Persian period, about 400 BCE. I believe that it was a work composed in the Babylonian diaspora with concerns for both the diaspora context and events that were taking place in the Palestinian homeland. Against Mullen and others, I see no reason to suppose that Ezra and his priestly colleagues had any role in the Persian administration or were specially trained by the Persian chancellory. They received support from the authorities for 'law and order' but beyond that they reflect no commitment to the support of the Persian empire. Taking my cue from Mowinckel and Vink that P represents a series of etiologies that explain and legitimate priestly thought and practice and set out a program for cultic reform, I will set out a number of themes in P that seem to me to be related to this new historical and cultural setting.

b. Identity and covenant in P

P inherited from D a nationalistic form of identity of Israel as the people of Yahweh living in the land, given by covenant agreement on the condition of absolute loyalty and obedience to his laws. P inherited from J an ethnic form of identity based on the divine election of the forefathers Abraham, Isaac and Jacob and an unconditional covenant of promises of land and nationhood. These are now combined in a new form of identity, that of the 'congregation', the religious community, which is also ethnic through the covenant of Abraham. The covenant is in the nature of an eternal promise (*bĕrît ʿôlām*) that implies the continuous existence of the community-people, but participation within this group is conditioned upon observance of the 'sign' of circumcision. Identity, while it is based on ethnicity, is still one of choice and this reflects the experience of the diaspora situation.

While the Abrahamic covenant affirms strongly the ethnic component of the identity, it is the Sinai covenant, with its sign of sabbath observance, that establishes the cultic-religious element as the congregation of Yahweh. This is also an eternal covenant, an institution that requires observances as the condition of participation. The etiology of the sabbath is grounded in the creation of the cosmos so that sabbath observance is recognition of Yahweh as the creator deity. This is the theological legacy of Second Isaiah above all. The sabbath is the sign of the divine order of things and its violation is taken with the utmost seriousness.

The people are regularly identified as a 'congregation' (*ʿēdâh*) or 'assembly' (*qāhāl*) and in this way they are constituted as a cultic community circumscribed by a complex set of restrictions and regulations. This is the religious temple-community of the homeland and the worshiping community of the diaspora, extended to embody the people as a whole. Within this community the priestly hierarchy play an important role. They offer a realm of protection from the dangers of the sacred and so function as intermediaries in matters of the cult, such as sacrifice, which have to do with contact or proximity to the deity. The danger is constantly emphasized, even for the priests, when two of Aaron's sons die because they offered incense with unholy fire (Lev. 10.1-11). The rebellion of Korah (Num. 16) also illustrates the same threat within the priesthood.

This raises the question of a fundamentally different understanding of the religious community from that suggested in J. For J, the people as a whole were holy and a 'kingdom of priests', such that they could be specially consecrated and approach the sacred mountain (Exod. 19.3-6, 10-11, 13b). This special consecration is recognized by the covenant of Sinai in which all the people are sprinkled with the sacrificial blood (Exod. 24.3-8). Only Moses as prophet acts as a mediator to communicate with the deity, but P has replaced Moses' mediatory role by the priesthood. In P, the sacred mountain is off limits to the people upon pain of death (Exod. 19.12-13a, 20-25), and it is only the priests who consecrate themselves. In P's installation of Aaron and his sons as priests in an elaborate ceremony (Lev. 8), it is Aaron and his sons alone whose garments are sprinkled with the sacrificial blood. It is also the priesthood that takes over the mediatorial role of Moses through the sacrificial system. Furthermore, as we saw above, P has combined J's simple Tent of Meeting, which was for Moses' use, with the elaborate Tabernacle, which is the center of the religious community, the activity of the priesthood and the sacrificial cult. What is important to note is that P is in dialogue with J and not with D in his conception of the religious community.

If J is to be associated with the Babylonian exile and P also stems from the Babylonian diaspora somewhat later, then how can we account for the shift from the lay orientation of J to the priestly transformation of P? After the destruction of the temple in 586 BCE there was a serious dislocation of the priesthood and those in the exile had little opportunity to engage in the cult. If there were religious gatherings in the exilic communities they were largely of a lay character under the control of the elders, the meeting place (synagogue), perhaps with prophetic leadership, and this is still the situation in the time of J about 540 BCE.[36] Aaron, 'the Levite', does not have any strictly cultic function in J, but he does 'speak for Moses', that is, his task is to explain the words of Moses to the people (Exod. 4.14-16, 30-31). With the restoration of the temple in 515 BCE, however, the role of the priesthood and the sacrificial cult was revived. Among the priests in the exile, the legal and cultic traditions were maintained and developed and these take up much that is preserved in the Holiness Code and the P supplement. In J, there is no place for a future monarchic state. This is a radical departure from DtrH, with its hope of a continuing Davidic rule. But for J, as for Second Isaiah, the Davidic covenant has been democratized. The authority exercised in the community is now a council of elders, legitimated by the etiology of the seventy elders endowed with Moses' spirit in Num. 11.16-17, 24-25. The Jerusalemite community of the early Second Temple period still thought in terms of a revival of the Davidic monarchy, but with a diarchy of high priest and king (see Haggai and

Zechariah). P clearly rejects the notion of any monarchy and makes the political leader (Joshua) subservient in authority to the high priest. P retains the secular authority of the elders and they are occasionally referred to together with the high priest. But for P the monarchy has been replaced by the high priest. It has also been noted that the priestly vestments and installation by anointing resemble the investiture of royalty.

c. The promised land and settlement of the tribes

As I have argued above, P affirms in the strongest way the promise of the land of Canaan to the patriarchs. The limits of this land (Josh. 13.2-6) are more modest than those claimed in the Dtr tradition and in J (Gen. 15.18-21). While P supplements the DtrH narrative of the conquest at a number of points and, therefore, can hardly be viewed as irenic,[37] the primary focus is upon the settlement of the land by the tribes. He presents the settlement of the land west of the Jordan as taking place in two phases. In the first, the tribes of Judah and Joseph (Ephraim and Manasseh) receive their allotment while the military camp of Joshua is still set up in Gilgal (Josh. 14–16). The second phase is presented as taking place a long time after the conquest and the settlement of Judah and Joseph, when the land lay 'subdued' before the Israelites and the administrative center of the land is now represented by the Tent of Meeting at Shiloh (Josh. 18–19). Here Joshua, the civil leader, acts in consort with Eleazar, the priest, in the distribution of the territory to the remaining seven tribes.

The question that obviously presents itself is why P introduces such a distinction when it is certainly not suggested by the course of the conquest in Joshua 10–11. Vink, I believe, has rightly understood this to be etiological and programmatic for the historical period to which P relates.[38] It parallels the situation in the late Persian period in which Judah and Joseph (Samaria) have long been established in their territories and the Second Temple has been set up in Jerusalem, the successor of Shiloh, with its diarchy of high priest and governor. What it seems to advocate is a resettlement of these largely peripheral regions by 'Israelites' from the diaspora.

If this suggestion is correct, then it seems to relate closely to the situation of Ezra's return and was probably composed in close association with that event. Given the tensions and animosities of the previous period, in which attempts were made to drive a wedge between Samaria and Judah, the whole import of this theme in P is to consider the land as the inheritance of all the tribes. The Joseph tribes are treated equally with that of Judah. It is also suggested that after so long a period of resettlement there still remains much land to be settled by homesteading 'Israelites' both in the north and the south (Josh. 18–19). A major aspect of Ezra's mission seems to have been the return of a large group from Mesopotamia in a kind of second exodus (Ezra 8). This may suggest a policy of the Persian government to build up its control of this strategic area by a loyal population group.

If P seems to be much more tolerant of the Israelites of the north than had been the case with the extreme nationalists under Nehemiah, then what was its attitude to places of worship outside of Jerusalem? The fact that P says so little about the issue of centralization has led to very different appraisals of its setting. On the one hand, P establishes a strict hierarchy with a high priest and certain activities that are limited to him alone, so that the one central sanctuary at least has pre-eminence over all others. On the other hand, there are certain observances and festivals that could be conducted at other places of worship or even in the home, most notably passover, which are permitted in a form that modifies the centralization of D. There is also the P story of Joshua 22 in which the issue of centralization of worship is strongly debated. Here the story offers an etiology for those places of worship outside of the promised land that constituted non-sacrificial 'altars of witness'.[39]

d. The Tabernacle and the 'glory' (*Kābôd*) of Yahweh

It has long been recognized that an important element of P's theology is the notion of the deity's presence as represented by his 'glory' (*kābôd*).[40] This is in contrast to D, who prefers to speak of the 'name' of Yahweh as symbolic of the divine presence in the chosen sanctuary. The notion of the resplendent glory probably derives from the cultic tradition of Jerusalem (see Psalms and Isa. 6.3) and comes to the fore especially in Ezekiel (Ezek. 1–3). This prophet not only describes the glory but states that prior to the destruction of the temple it left its abode to take up sanctuary with the exiles (Ezek. 10–11). In the exilic and postexilic prophets one finds a great preoccupation with the coming or return of the glory to his people and his temple.[41]

It is clear that P has taken over much of his description of the glory and its association with the cloud from Ezekiel (Exod. 16.10; 24.16-17; 40.34-38; Num. 17.7 [16.42]; cf. Ezek. 1.4, 28; 10.4, 18-19, 22-23). For both P and Ezekiel, the glory has its abode in the Tabernacle/Temple and yet is not limited to it. P especially has combined the concept of the glory with J's use of the pillar of cloud and fire as a vanguard and gives it the same association with the Tent of Meeting. It is the divine presence that both accompanies the people and that dwells in the Tabernacle as the focal point of the cult. This presence as devouring fire requires the protection of the regulations of holiness and the gradations of priestly sanctity. At the same time that the whole cultus is constructed to serve the glory of Yahweh, the glory also comes or manifests itself to the 'congregation' in moments of necessity to save the people but also in acts of judgment to punish the evil-doers.

This programmatic treatment of the theme of the coming of Yahweh's glory and its presence among his people may be set over against the tendency in Jewish eschatology, as reflected in much late prophecy, that sees the coming of the glory in increasingly cataclysmic terms.[42] The tendency was to read into certain political events the 'signs' of the coming of the glory and kingdom of Yahweh. P seems to address this concern with the coming of the glory by placing it at the heart of the cult as the means by which the glory of Yahweh will dwell with his people and benefit them. This programmatic approach could be perceived as a way of providing some order and control over a rather volatile element within Judaism of the Persian period.

4. Conclusion

The P narrative (Pg) comes at the end of a long process of theological reflection as a revision of the national tradition of J and DtrH and represents the restoration of priestly authority and ideology. It establishes within this historiography a number of sophisticated etiologies to support its own institutions and priestly traditions. But it also seeks a programmatic restructuring of the cultic institutions in Jerusalem along the lines of its presentation of the Tabernacle cultus and priesthood. These reforming priests are from Babylonia with support from the Persian administration, as the story of Ezra indicates, even if the details are somewhat exaggerated. The turbulent periods of Nehemiah and Bagoas, governors of Judah, were the occasion for the mission of Ezra. It is possible that Malachi reflects something of the state of affairs before Ezra's coming and the anticipation of the changes that he will bring about (Mal. 3.1-4). The situation called for intervention by the prosperous and politically influencial Jews of Mesopotamia and the priestly elite who were still in that region.[43]

I think that it is incorrect to suggest that the Persian administration authorized the composition of the P corpus or the Pentateuch. They were primarily concerned with the establishment and maintenance of order in religious and civil matters, and if the documents that the reforming priests brought to Jerusalem *contained* the law, that was all that mattered. I also think it unlikely that the whole of P was written for this single occasion. Yet the P narrative (Pg) is a single unified composition written in the late Persian period and reflecting the general circumstances and ideological issues of that time.

Notes

1 In the older 'Introductions' to the Hebrew Bible one can find useful lists of distinctive terms and features characteristic of the P source. See Driver, *An Introduction to the Literature of the Old Testament*, pp. 126–59.

2 Zenger, 'Die priesterschriftlichen Schichten ("P")', pp. 89–96; Schwartz, 'The Priestly Account of the Theophany and Lawgiving at Sinai'; Ska, 'De la relative indépendance de l'écrit sacerdotal'.

3 Lohfink, *The Theology of the Pentateuch*, pp. 149–63; Van Seters, 'Myth and History'.
4 *Tetrateuch-Pentateuch-Hexateuch*, pp. 78–86.
5 *The Date and Origin of the Priestly Code*, pp. 69–73.
6 Tengström, *Die Toledotformel*.
7 For further discussion of Priestly style, see McEvenue, *The Narrative Style of the Priestly Writer*.
8 Vervenne, 'The "P" Tradition in the Pentateuch'.
9 Cross, *Canaanite Myth and Hebrew Epic*, pp. 293–325.
10 Van Seters, 'The Creation of Man'.
11 For a somewhat different view see N. Lohfink, 'Original Sin in the Priestly Historical Narrative', in *The Theology of the Pentateuch*, pp. 96–115.
12 Van Seters, *Prologue to History*, pp. 160–65.
13 See Tengström, *Die Toledotformel*, pp. 19–25.
14 Emerton, 'Genesis XI 27–32'.
15 There is a recent tendency in Pentateuchal studies to attribute the earliest connection between Genesis and Exodus to P (so also Winnett, 'Reexamining the Foundations') and to see these verses as post-P, but I would strongly resist this move.
16 See Blum, *Studien zur Komposition des Pentateuch*, pp. 20–22.
17 Van Seters, *The Life of Moses*, pp. 100–11.
18 See Van Seters, *The Life of Moses*, pp. 181–91.
19 *A History of Pentateuchal Traditions*.
20 *Erwägungen zur Pentateuch Quellenfrage*.
21 See also Blenkinsopp, *The Pentateuch*, pp. 229–32. Yet if P extends to Josh. 18–19 for Blenkinsopp (p. 237), then Noth's scheme will not work for him.
22 Here I must part company with the viewpoint of Lohfink, who argues that there is no war in the Priestly historical narrative. 'The Strata of the Pentateuch and the Question of War', *The Theology of the Pentateuch*, pp. 195–210.
23 *The Theology of the Pentateuch*, pp. 199–201.
24 See Van Seters, *In Search of History*, pp. 331–37; also Vink, *The Date and Origin of the Priestly Code*, pp. 63–68.
25 See Van Seters, *In Search of History*, pp. 324–31.
26 See Albertz, *A History of Israelite Religion*, pp. 464–93; and for a somewhat different view, Grabbe, *Judaism from Cyrus to Hadrian*, I, pp. 94–98.
27 A translation is published in *ANET*, p. 491. See the discussion in Vink, *The Date and Origin of the Priestly Code*, pp. 37–63.
28 Van Seters, *Abraham in History and Tradition*.
29 Blum, *Studien zur Komposition des Pentateuch*.
30 See nn. 26 and 29 above.
31 See Albertz, *A History of Israelite Religion*, pp. 464–93.
32 Albertz, *A History of Israelite Religion*, pp. 464–70.
33 *Ethnic Myths and Pentateuchal Foundations*, pp. 57–86.
34 *The Making of the Pentateuch*.
35 *Ethnic Myths and Pentateuchal Foundations*, p. 86. Since earlier on the same page Mullen rejects the use of the terms Tetrateuch, Pentateuch, Hexateuch, I find this statement quite contradictory. See also pp. 315–25.
36 Concerning the origin of the synagogue in the Neo-Babylonian period sees Van Seters, 'The Tent of Meeting in the Yahwist and the Origin of the Synagogue', *SJOT* (forthcoming).
37 Contra Lohfink, *The Theology of the Pentateuch*, pp. 195–224.

38 *The Date and Origin of the Priestly Code*, pp. 63–68.
39 See Vink, *The Date and Origin of the Priestly Code*, pp. 73–77; are these non-Priestly places of worship intended to reflect the synagogues? See J. Van Seters, 'The Tent of Meeting in the Yahwist and the Origin of the Synagogue', *SJOT* (forthcoming).
40 Von Rad, *Old Testament Theology*, I, pp. 234–41.
41 See M. Weinfeld, 'kabod', *TDOT*, VII, pp. 34–36.
42 Weinfeld, 'kabod'. See also Plöger, *Theocracy and Eschatology*, pp. 30–37, 106–17.
43 See Vink, *The Date and Origin of the Priestly Code*, pp. 59–61.

8

Law in the Pentateuch

Bibliography

Alt, A., 'The Origin of Israelite Laws' (1934).
Boecker, H. J., *Law and the Administration of Justice in the Old Testament and Ancient East* (trans. J. Moiser; Minneapolis: Augsburg, 1980).
Budd, P. J., *Leviticus* (NCBC; Grand Rapids: Eerdmans, 1996).
Clark, W. M., 'Law', in John H. Hayes (ed.), *Old Testament Form Criticism* (San Antonio, TX: Trinity University Press, 1974), pp. 99–139.
Crüsemann, F., *The Torah: Theology and Social History of Old Testament Law* (trans. W. Mahnke; Philadelphia: Fortress Press, 1996).
Driver, G. R., and J. C. Miles (eds.), *The Babylonian Laws* (2 vols.; Oxford: Oxford University Press, 1952–55).
Houtman, C., *Das Bundesbuch: Ein Kommentar* (Leiden: E.J. Brill, 1997).
Jepsen, Alfred, *Untersuchungen zum Bundesbuch* (BWANT, 3.5; Stuttgart: W. Kohlhammer, 1927).
Levinson, B. M., *Deuteronomy and the Hermeneutics of Legal Innovation* (Oxford: Oxford University Press, 1997).
Morgenstern, Julian, 'The Book of the Covenant', *HUCA* 5 (1928), pp. 1–151.
—— 'The Book of the Covenant, Part II', *HUCA* 7 (1930), pp. 19–258.
—— 'The Book of the Covenant, Part III', *HUCA* 8–9 (1931–32), pp. 1–150.
Nicholson, E. W., *Deuteronomy and Tradition* (1967).
Patrick, D., *Old Testament Law* (Atlanta: John Knox Press, 1985).
Pfeiffer, R. H., *Introduction to the Old Testament* (1941).
Rad, G. von, *Old Testament Theology*, I (1962).
Roth, M. T., *Law Collections from Mesopotamia and Asia Minor* (Atlanta: Scholars Press, 1995).
Van Seters, J., 'Cultic Laws in the Covenant Code (Ex 20.22–23.33) and their Relationship to Deuteronomy and the Holiness Code', in M. Vervenne (ed.), *Studies in the Book of Exodus: Redaction-Reception-Interpretation* (BETL, 126; Leuven: Peeters, 1996), pp. 319–46.
—— 'The Law of the Hebrew Slave', *ZAW* 108 (1996), pp. 534–46.
—— *A Law Book for the Diaspora* (2003).
—— 'Revision in the Study of the Covenant Code and a Response to my Critics', *SJOT* 21 (2007).
Weinfeld, M., *Deuteronomy and the Deuteronomic School* (1972).
Zimmerli, W., *I Am Yahweh* (ed. W. Brueggemann; trans. D. W. Scott; Atlanta: John Knox Press, 1982).

1. Introduction

As I indicated at the outset, about one-half of the Pentateuch consists of law in one form or other. All of the laws, with the exception of a few in Genesis, are attributed to Moses by tradition, and most of them to the time that Israel spent at Horeb/ Sinai. The laws, however, belong to all three strata of the Pentateuch (D, J and P) and consist of many different types, reflecting a long tradition of laws and customs from many different periods of Israelite history. These laws have undergone many changes and modifications that can be seen from the comparison of laws dealing with the same subject in the different sources and codes.

In making the case for his new version of the Documentary Hypothesis, Wellhausen placed great emphasis upon identifying the appropriate historical and social setting of the laws in each source and their relationship to each other as the surest way of arriving at the dating of the sources. Scholars are generally agreed that the laws, above all, reflect the time of their incorporation into the narrative, when such statutes and regulations were in vogue within the contemporaneous society. Thus, it is the law of centralization in Deuteronomy that dates D as a whole. The P Code is viewed against the background of the reconstruction of the Second Temple. Within the non-P (J) corpus, the Covenant Code (Exod. 21-23) contains a set of humanitarian laws that are viewed as influenced by the reforming prophets of the eighth century and dated by Wellhausen accordingly. While there has been greater emphasis since Wellhausen on the older legal traditions within the various codes, the relative dating of the codes has not changed and is still the primary basis for dating much of the literary strata. To this issue we will return.

2. Types of laws

With the rise of the form-critical study of the Pentateuch, the German scholar Albrecht Alt sought to establish a broad classification of the various types of laws and their origin and social setting.[1] He was not the first nor the only one to do so,[2] but his work gained special prominence and is the point of departure for most discussion on types of laws in the Pentateuch. His typology is still useful if modified by a consideration of the subsequent discussion.[3]

a. Casuistic/case law

This type of law sets forth a case or instance of an infraction and then prescribes the penalty. This has the form, 'If a man does thus and thus, and this causes the following damages, then he must pay ...' Examples of this kind may be found in Exod. 21.18–22.16[17]. This form of law is common to other Near Eastern law codes,[4] many of which are much older than Israelite law and often deal with the same subjects. The content of these laws reflects urban and rural life in the land of Canaan. This is civil law, appropriate for life in Israel during the monarchy and later periods. Alt was of the opinion that, at the time of its origin in the land, Israel inherited this legal tradition from the Canaanites. Such laws could be adjudicated by law courts administered by local judges to settle property and personal injury disputes.

b. Apodictic laws

This form of law states an absolute demand. It may be expressed in various ways: (a) a direct address command: 'You shall not kill/steal/etc.' (Exod. 20.13-17); (b) a curse: 'Cursed is the one who does . . .' (Deut. 27.15-26), related to the sphere of religious sanction; (c) an indirect general principle: 'whoever does . . . shall be put to death' (Exod. 21.12-17), which has been associated by some with criminal law and the administration of justice by the state. These three forms of apodictic law are often found in short series, such as the Ten Commandments. Alt believed that the absolute demands of the apodictic forms of law originated from the sphere of primitive Israelite religion and only secondarily came into combination with the 'Canaanite' casuistic law in the period of settlement and the rise of the state. Alt further believed that the *lex talionis* of 'an eye for an eye and a tooth for a tooth' (Exod. 21.23-24) was also of primitive Israelite origin and was used to correct the adopted Canaanite law.

c. Humanitarian laws

This type of law is more in the nature of moral guideline, since it urges a mode of behavior that cannot be regulated by the courts. It often takes the form of a command supported by a motivation clause: 'You shall not wrong a stranger or oppress him, for you were stangers in the land of Egypt' (Exod. 22.21). Such laws reflect the influence of the ethical preaching of the eighth-century prophets. They are generally held by scholars to belong to a later phase in the development of biblical law.

d. Cultic laws

These laws have to do with the regulation of religious matters associated with formal worship. In the older codes they take the form of commands or statutes to the people as a whole to fulfill certain obligations, such as the keeping of religious festivals and holy days. The oldest exemplars of this type were thought to be those in Exod. 23.12-19 and 34.17-26. Again, these are marked by the brevity of injunctions in a short series. By contrast, the Priestly Code includes a large body of elaborate instructions directed primarily to the priests, having to do with their duties, forms of sacrifice, food laws, details on the keeping of festivals, etc. This now constitutes the largest body of laws in the Pentateuch.

In the form-critical analysis of law, the general principle that was followed by most scholars after Alt was that the primitive Israelite form of law was a short series of prohibitions or instructions that were believed to reflect the primitive oral culture out of which they arose. Any modifications of the series of laws by motivation clauses or by qualifications were regarded as secondary expansions. This did not apply so much to the casuistic laws, which were the inheritance of a long legal tradition. However, the recovery of 'original' apodictic series and other collections was a major preoccupation of the literary criticism of Hebrew law.

The form-critical model of legal development is based upon an understanding of the early history of Israel that has become highly problematic. Thus, it is not at all clear that one can assume a primitive nomadic Israel, with its distinctive religious prohibitions, encountering an alien Canaanite culture, with its long-established civil law system, and forming an amalgam that is currently reflected in the laws of Exodus 21–23. There has been an increasing tendency to view the 'earliest' laws as later in date and as having less emphasis on the distinction between Israelite and Canaanite. Nevertheless, the form-critical habit of distinguishing types of laws and levels of editing and redaction persists in most studies of Hebrew law.

3. The law codes

The practice of compiling collections of laws into codes is very ancient in the Near East, and a number of codes—the most famous being Hammurabi's—have come to light through archaeology.[5] Some of these codes have laws that are very similar to the casuistic/civil laws of the type discussed above. The purpose of such law codes has been a matter of considerable debate. Whether they were intended to serve as precedent for the administration of justice, or as the product of scholars and scribal schools, or as royal edicts to address certain abuses, is difficult to determine. Within the Pentateuch there are a number of codes some of which contain civil law but which are otherwise quite different from Near Eastern law codes so that their function is even more disputed.

The biblical codes contain a number of laws that are parallel to each other, but with some modifications. This has led to much discussion about how one set of laws is related to, and develops from, the previous set of laws. So long as one followed the order of sources in the Documentary Hypothesis, the line of development and the order of discussion of the law codes was never in dispute. Only in the debates over the priority of P to D did some scholars attempt to change the order of direction. With the revision of Pentateuchal criticism and the admission by a number of scholars that the non-P strata of the Pentateuch, which contains the so-called Covenant Code of Exod. 22.22–23.33, may be later than D, one would have expected some reconsideration of the relationship of this code to that of Deuteronomy. Until now that has not happened and the course of the discussion has continued much as before.[6] However, for the present study I will continue to follow the supplementary model in which D precedes J and deal with the law codes in that order.

a. The D code (Deuteronomy 12–26)

As we have seen, this code is especially concerned with religious and social reform in its emphasis on the centralization of worship in the one chosen place. This religious reform is most strongly reflected in the laws of 12.1–16.17, beginning with the law of the central altar and the centralization of all sacrifice in ch. 12, and with making the worship of another god a capital offense in ch. 13. D's concept of Israel as a chosen and holy people is related to regulations about mourning rites and to the consumption of clean and unclean animals (14.1-21).[7] This is followed more loosely by religious and ethical obligations and institutions having to do with the tithe (14.22-29), the law of debt release and release of slaves (15.1-18), the law of firstlings (15.19-23) and the festival calendar (16.1-17). Within this group of laws religious reform predominates and some would limit the Josianic proto-D to this collection.

The group of laws in 16.18–20.20 are often viewed as an ideal or utopian constitution arising from the centralization reform. These laws have to do with the administration of justice (16.18-20; 17.8-13), the monarchy (17.14-20), the priesthood (18.1-8) and the prophet (18.15-22). Chapter 19 deals with the setting up of cities of refuge to which the manslayer may flee (vv. 1-13) and the procedures governing homicide as well as other court procedure regulations (vv. 15-21). The ideology of holy war is set out in a detailed 'law' in chs. 20 and 21.10-14. It should be noted, however, that interspersed within these laws are those in 17.2-7 and 18.9-14 that have to do with religious reform as dealt with in ch. 13.

The rest of the D code (chs. 21–25) is a mixture of civil, humanitarian and religious laws and regulations, as discussed above, with a minimum of Deuteronomic editing. One should note that the laws dealing with debt release and the Hebrew debt-slave in 15.1-18 have little to do with religious reform and centralization and belong more properly with the subject matter of ch. 22. Furthermore, the law having to do with a war captive (21.10-14) fits the category of social legislation as well as making a connection back to the law of warfare in ch. 20. There are numerous other interconnections that make it difficult to separate these blocks chronologically or ideologically from each other.

The code concludes with two liturgical confessions (26.1-15) and a declaration of the covenant (26.16-19).

1. Literary-critical evaluation of the laws. As we have seen above with Deuteronomy as a whole, there are many literary levels in the text and this applies also to the law code. The task that faces the scholar is to find and apply a set of criteria by which to make the necessary distinctions between the different diachronic levels and hands without proliferating these to the point of absurdity. Some of these criteria may be set out in a general way, although their application is by no means uniform and has led to a variety of views and opinions about what is the oldest code of laws and which laws are later, what is preexilic and Josianic and what is exilic or post-exilic. Nevertheless, it should be emphasized that the largest part of the code is 'Deuteronomic' in perspective in a way that is quite distinct from all the other codes, and this fact would seem to impose on scholars certain limits regarding its compositional and historical horizon.

2. *Form and content.* The first obvious distinction that can be made within the laws is between those of chs. 12–20 and those that follow in 21–25. Those of the earlier chapters have to do with extensive treatment of particular subjects that are particularly appropriate to the themes and concerns of D and the reforms. Those in 21–25 tend to be shorter units that are much less closely related and often viewed for this reason as an appendix or later extension. Yet the matter is not so simple, since one can still find distinctive D elements and themes in some of the later laws of the code as well. Likewise, corresponding to this division in content is the tendency towards a difference in legal form. In the laws of chs. 12–20 the form of apodictic commands on important religious or cultic matters and extended instructions in the pseudo-casuistic 'if-you' style predominate. Within the laws of chs. 21–25 the casuistic or impersonal form is much more common, although even here the second person address frequently modifies the 'older' form of the laws.

3. *Redactional expansion in the laws.* There are a number of ways that scholars have tried to identify later redactional expansions, especially by Dtr, within the laws. First, it is widely held that the older stratum of D laws uses the second singular form of address, whereas the later levels use either the plural or a mixture. Secondly, some try to identify a particular language, a terminology and a perspective reflected in DtrH that can be found distributed throughout the laws and used to separate a later stratum. This is especially the case where laws are given historical introductions that seem to presuppose the account of the conquest under Joshua, or similar historical allusions. Yet such historical references may be slight and suggest no more than familiarity with an exodus-settlement tradition, such as is already present in Hosea and Amos. Furthermore, since Dtr derives much of its language and perspective from D, making a clear distinction between them is difficult and leaves room for considerable difference of opinion. Thirdly, where the text becomes syntactically awkward or the subject of a law is interrupted by quite different material, one may suspect redactional expansion. Yet a counterbalance to this may be considerations having to do with whether the law is a combination of sources or the result of corruption during transmission. The homogeneity and cohesiveness of each individual unit and the general principles of how laws were

put together must be used in each particular case. Fourthly, if one makes a distinction between the basic D Code as belonging to the pre-exilic, Josianic period and the Dtr additions as exilic, then the criterion of the social and historical fit of the laws in one period or the other comes into consideration. However, if the first Dtr redaction already belongs to the late pre-exilic period, then such a criterion becomes harder to apply.

4. *Historical and social setting of the D code.* The parts of the code that have been used by scholars to date the core of Deuteronomy to the Josianic period have to do primarily with the laws of centralization of worship, the laws against the worship of other gods (12–13; 17.2-7; 18.9-14; cf. 2 Kgs 23.4-14, 24), and the revision of the festival calendar (16.1-17; cf. 2 Kgs 23.21-23). Nevertheless, there is still much debate about whether these laws were formulated before that event and gave rise to it, whether they arose as justification for Josiah's actions, which may have been as much political as religious, or whether they are a later formulation, as late as the exilic period, by which DtrH construed the reform measures of Josiah's time in retrospect.[8]

Centralization is also thought to have important social implications on Israelite institutions of law and government.[9] This may be seen in the establishment of a regular judiciary (Deut. 16.18-20) and a central court (17.8-13) with 'Levitical priests and the judge who will be in office at that time' who will decide the difficult cases. One form of explanation has been a tendency to connect these laws with a reform of the judicial system in 2 Chron. 19.4-11.[10] In my judgment the Chronicler has simply used the law of Deuteronomy, but revised it according to his own ideological perspective.[11] Therefore, 2 Chron. 19.4-11 should not be used to explain this situation. The idea that there was a supreme court consisting of Levitical priests and a 'judge' does not seem to be reflected in any of the sources having to do with the Judahite monarchy, especially from the eighth century onwards. A second form of explanation is to see the appointment of professional judges and a central judicial authority for cases beyond the competence of local authorities as a major social shift away from the local clan control of the elders and the local sanctuaries to a centralized religious and judicial control.[12] Yet this view relies on comparison with the role of elders in the latter part of Deuteronomy, even in those laws, such as the setting up of the cities of refuge in 19.1-13, which were necessitated by the centralization reform. In 21.1-9 judges, elders and Levites all act in consort.

The problem with the notion of a constitutional reform in D is that it has a certain utopian quality that is not reflected in any reality of the late monarchy. The law of the king in 17.14-20 certainly does not reflect royal power in the time of Josiah or later, and the privileges of the Levites at the central sanctuary in 18.6-8 are specifically denied in 2 Kgs 23.9. Furthermore, the cities of refuge in 19.1-13 presuppose the extensive conquest of Joshua and the possession of a large territory that hardly seems to correspond to that of the late monarchy. Either these laws were formulated in anticipation of a reform that never was completely implemented or they reflect a later exilic ideal in the event of some future restoration.

The clue to understanding this part of the code may lie in identifying the office of 'the judge who will be [in place] in those days'. We know from the example of Phoenician cities that in the Neo-Babylonian period a 'judge' (*sft*) might act as a supreme magistrate or governor in the absence of a king. If this is what is in mind, then a similar situation existed after the demise of the Judahite monarchy in the figure of Gedaliah the governor. The judge also has some affinities with the presentation of the pre-monarchic 'judges' of the book of Judges and the figure of Samuel. By contrast, the law regarding the king in 17.14-20 seems to portray a very modest role in comparison with Dtr's notion of the dynastic promise to David and the more exalted role of the king in DtrH. Moreover, the discussion about the true and false prophets (18.15-22) is dependent upon the description of the Horeb theophany and the etiology of prophecy through the mediation of Moses (ch. 5). This seems to reflect the special concerns of the late monarchy in the time of Jeremiah and may well be a Dtr addition.

As has often been noted, there is in the D Code a strong element of humanitarian concern for the poor and needy and an ideal of brotherhood in the civil legislation.[13] This seems to reflect the concerns of the eighth-century prophets. When this is taken together with the special concerns of Hosea for reform of religion in terms of exclusive worship of Yahweh, the abolition of 'foreign' elements and the reform of the priesthood, a date for the development of this legal tradition in the north following the fall of Samaria and continuing until its migration to the south and 'discovery' in the time of Josiah seems most likely.[14] What seems clear from the law code is that it represents an extended process of expansion and revision from the early, pre-D collections of laws to the 'publication' of the code in connection with Josiah's reform and subsequent additions by Dtr and even by the priestly tradition.

b. The Covenant Code (Exodus 20.22–23.33)

1. *Form and content.* The Covenant Code (CC) is J's version of the law. The name is derived from the statement in Exod. 24.7, which refers to a 'book of the Covenant' as the written version of the laws given by the deity to Moses. J's terminology is taken from Dtr, who refers to the D Code as 'the book of the law' or 'the words of the covenant' (Deut. 29) or 'the book of the covenant' (2 Kgs 23.2). In D there are two sets of laws and two covenants: the words of the covenant declared by the deity at Horeb and inscribed on the stone tablets, and the book of the law written by Moses and given to the people in the land of Moab. In J these have been combined into one covenant at Sinai/Horeb, which is then written in a book by Moses and also inscribed on tablets of stone by the deity (24.4, 7, 12). This means that the

content of the Ten Commandments and the other laws have also been combined by J into a single code.

Regarding the type of laws contained in it, the casuistic/civil law predominates. They deal with matters of everyday life, property, personal injury, etc. (21.2-11; 18-22.16[17]). There are apodictic series of the type 'the one who does ... shall be put to death' (21.12-17; 22.18-19[19-20] and of the type of absolute religious demands, 'You shall not ...' (20.23; 22.17[18], 27-30[28-31]). There are also humanitarian laws (22.20-26[21-27]; 23.4-10) that are clearly exhortations to charity, but within the other categories of laws the humanitarian element often plays a dominant role. Finally, there are obligations related to the sabbath and the festival calendar (23.12-19).

A number of laws in this code are directly parallel to some in the D Code, and this raises the question of the relationship between the two codes. A prime example is the law having to do with the Hebrew slave in Exod. 21.2-11, for which there is a parallel in Deut. 15.12-18. It is almost universally assumed in critical scholarship that the DC version represents a revision of CC. In my own comparison of these examples, however, I have argued that J's law is a later revision and modification of the law in D to cover a wider range of cases of the enslavement of Hebrews by foreigners in the exilic period.[15]

Furthermore, one can see in a number of cases where CC (J) assumes the body of law in DC and only includes additional cases or new applications of the law. Thus, it was pointed out by R. H. Pfeiffer[16] that CC contains only one law that has to do with marriage in Exod. 22.15-16 [16-17]. The DC has an extensive treatment of marriage laws in Deut. 22.13-29. Only in the very last of these, regarding the rape of a virgin (vv. 28-29), is the situation parallel to that in CC. And yet the latter deals with an additional situation, that of the father's refusal to give his daughter to the violator, which is an extension of the laws in DC. The same may be seen in the case of the laws of D regarding lost goods (Deut. 22.1-4). If the domestic animal of one's fellow Israelite ('brother') is lost and is found wandering, then it is to be returned. In the same way one must help one's fellow with a large fallen animal to set it on its feet again. In CC this neighborly obligation is assumed and extended to include also the animals of one's 'enemy' (Exod. 23.4-5). Even the animals of those beyond the circle of fellow Israelites should be treated kindly. There can be no question, in my mind, that CC supplements and comes later than DC.[17]

In the account of the covenant renewal in Exod. 34.10-27 there is a summary version of the larger J code. It contains a short prologue of exhortation to loyalty to Yahweh (vv. 11-16), a command against molten images (v. 17) and a list of ritual laws (vv. 18-26) parallel to those in 23.12-19. These have often been ascribed to different sources, but I consider them both as the work of J.

2. *The historical and social setting of the Covenant Code.* There has been a long-standing tendency for scholars to view CC as a corpus of laws that has a very long

history of development distinct from that of the present narrative source in which it is imbedded.[18] Its incorporation into the Sinai pericope and the occasional evidences of lateness, particularly in the closing admonition of 23.20-33, which contains language similar to Deuteronomy 7, are attributed to a Dtr redactor. This scenario is still based upon a defense of the Documentary Hypothesis and the firm belief that CC is the earliest body of law in the Pentateuch.

In my view, both the narrative context of the Sinai pericope and the laws of CC belong to the same post-D author, J. It is very likely the case that both J and the DC supplement in Deuteronomy 22 had access to a very similar body of civil law, but J only includes material from it that is not found in DC. Thus, J includes laws of personal liability and property (Exod. 21.18–22.14[15]) not covered by DC, and DC covers marriage laws that are not in J. Yet where parallels exist between the two codes, CC consistently contains the later version. In the case of this corpus of laws, unlike those of DC, I believe that they all belong to the same compositional level and are the work of J in the exilic period. The code, in my view, is formulated to regulate life in the Jewish community of the Babylonian exile.

There are in CC a number of subtle clues to this social context. The first is in the law of the altar in Exod. 20.24-26. This is usually taken to be evidence of its pre-D dating because of the supposed reference to a plurality of cult places in v. 24b. Apart from this, the rest can be understood as referring to a single altar, similar to those mentioned in Deut. 27.5-8; Josh. 8.30-35, both post-D additions. The problematic text in Exod. 20.24b that reads in the Hebrew text 'In every place where I invoke my name …' cannot be correct and has led to many forced interpretations. The text should read, 'In every place where you invoke my name, I will come to you and bless you.' This is in keeping with all of the other uses of the verb 'to invoke' (*zkr*) the name of a deity (see Exod. 23.13). What this means is that even if an altar is (re)constructed in Jerusalem, the deity will still heed the prayers of those worshiping in the exile and will bless them.[19]

The laws regarding male and female Hebrew slaves in Exod. 21.2-11 have been expanded to include not just those who become slaves through debt, as in DC, but also Hebrews who are purchased as chattels by other Hebrews from foreigners.[20] They, too, should be given their freedom after seven years of service. This is a situation that is reflected in Neh. 5.1-9, where it is this law and not the one in Deuteronomy that is being abused. The 'sale' of a daughter into marriage without dowry is a custom that has Mesopotamian parallels and perhaps best reflects that milieu.

In the humanitarian law discussed above (Exod. 23.4-5), the animal of the enemy that is lost and recovered by the Israelite cannot refer to an animal of a foreign land wandering about in Israel or Judah. It is more likely that it refers to the animals of the Babylonians in the immediate region of the exilic community. The law has been extended to deal with relations between the Jews and non-Jews (= the enemy) in their new social context.

The CC says very little about community officials. It makes no allowance for a king. In place of the latter, it mentions the *nasi* (22.27[28]), which is the term used in Ezekiel for the leader of the restored community (Ezek. 44-48) and very likely the term used of the leaders in the exilic communities. It is usually taken as a late gloss but there is no compelling reason to do so. Absent from the cultic and festival regulations is any reference to priests, as is the case throughout J. The requirements of this law are uncomplicated, not because of the primitive character of the society as Wellhausen and others supposed, but because the conditions of the exilic communities required such simplicity. The most appropriate setting for the CC would be the synagogue, whose origin and setting in the Babylonian diaspora is discussed above (see pp. 71–72).

c. The Holiness Code (Leviticus 17–26)

As we saw above, this is a collection of laws that belongs to P and is usually associated with P[s], although it has long been regarded by most Pentateuchal scholars as earlier in date than the rest of the P corpus.[21] Its major concern is for holiness (thus called by scholars the 'Holiness Code'). It is also priestly in outlook, language and content. The code belongs to the exilic period and has close affinities with the language and perspective of the prophet Ezekiel, a priest and leader of the Jewish community in exile in Babylon. Originally, it was an independent code before it took its place within the P Code.

1. *Form and content.* This block of laws is the most diverse in the P code, covering a variety of subjects and types of laws. Some of the laws have to do with cultic and priestly regulations (Lev. 17; 21–22; 24.1-9) and with festivals (23). Others deal with sexual mores (18) and with a mixture of requirements and offences both religious and ethical (19–20; 24.10-23). There are also laws legislating sabbatical and jubilee years having to do with relief from debts (25). This last leads into a final discourse containing promises of blessing and threats of punishment and concluding with the prospect of hope beyond the predicted judgment in the exile (26).

It will be clear from this summary of the content that there is no clear organization and arrangement of the material in this code in its present form. Much of the cohesion rests upon the use of language, the repetition of clichés and formulae throughout the code. There are frequent references to the past experience in Egypt as motivation for keeping certain laws.[22] Similarly, there are anticipations of their entry into the land of Canaan that the deity is giving them as the basis for laws.[23] These two features are also prominent in Deuteronomy. In addition, there are frequent references to 'keeping' or 'doing' or 'walking in' the 'ordinances', 'statutes', 'laws', 'commandments', 'covenant',[24] which is typical of Deuteronomic parenetic style. Quite distinctive of the Holiness Code, HC, is the use of the self-designation formula 'I am Yahweh/Yahweh your god' and the statement that Yahweh is the one who 'sanctifies' or 'separates' his people from the other nations and who therefore demands their holiness.[25]

Within the HC is an intrusion of priestly materials from a later stratum that introduces a change in perspective. Instead of Moses being called upon to address the laws to the people, they are addressed to Aaron and his sons,[26] and much of what follows is of quite a different character from the rest of HC but similar to the P code. This strata also introduces some narrative that relates the laws more particularly to the P wilderness setting, as in ch. 24. In addition, there are two levels of instructions regarding the festivals in ch. 23 and in some of the other laws. All of this makes the code complex and less homogeneous than if it were the work of one period and stratum.

2. *The social and historical context of the Holiness Code.* The social and historical context of HC may be ascertained first through the internal dating of the code by the content of ch. 26. This gives a vivid portrayal of the disaster of the Babylonian invasion and destruction of Judah and Jerusalem and the plight of the exiles. All of this is viewed as divine judgment for disobedience to the deity's laws in a style and language that is very reminiscent of Deuteronomy 28 and the exhortation in Deuteronomy generally. It ends on a note of hope in a restoration through repentance and divine forgiveness. The covenant with the forefathers was not ultimately abrogated and life in the land, after a period of sabbath rest for the land, will resume.

Not only is HC similar to DC in the form of the epilogue (ch. 26) as promise of blessing and threat of judgment, but, as we have seen above, it shares with DC much of the same language and formulas. In this respect it stands closer to DC than all the rest of the P strata. For those who argue for the priority of P, HC becomes the latest addition to P, but for those who regard P as late, HC becomes the earliest part of P; that is the view followed here. It is a response to Deuteronomy from a more priestly perspective, one that shares a viewpoint similar to that of Ezekiel. With DC it shares some of the same laws and same mixture of types but in a different 'revised' version. This can be seen most clearly in the case of the laws on the sabbath year, the year of jubilee and redemption from debt of property or personal enslavement (Lev. 25), which may be compared with the seven-year edict of release of debt and the release of Hebrew slaves in Deuteronomy 15. The DC version is the earlier, which builds upon the broader Near Eastern practice of a periodic edict of debt forgiveness and also sets limits for serviture from debt. HC has idealized the year of release into a sabbath year for broader humanitarian concerns (Lev. 25.1-7, 18-24) and has extended the application of the laws covering impoverishment for debt beyond those of DC (25.25-28, 35-55). At a second level of editing, the idea of a jubilee year is introduced and then applied to the laws of debt in a way that is entirely artificial and unworkable. Since HC speaks in the closing discourse of the land from which the people has been exiled as 'enjoying its sabbaths while it lies desolate' (Lev. 26.43), one wonders if the jubilee is not meant to cover the period of exile so that returnees after such a long absence may still have a claim on their land.

If HC is later than DC and a modification of some of its laws, then the question of how it relates to CC arises, especially if, as I have argued, CC is also later than DC. There is less overlap between CC and HC, but enough to establish the relationship between them. In the law of the Hebrew/Israelite slave in Lev. 25.39-46 and Exod. 21.2-11, the latter law assumes the right to buy chattel slaves, as in HC but not in DC. However, CC extends this provision to buying Hebrew chattel slaves and not just foreigners and then makes a distinction between the two types of chattel slaves. The Hebrew slave thus purchased is to be treated in a way similar to the Hebrew debt slave and released in seven years.

Similarly, the *lex talionis*, 'eye for an eye', which deals with personal injury, was regarded by Alt as part of Israel's primitive law and its presence in CC (Exod. 21.23-24) as a reason for considering this code to be early. However, it is very loosely attached to a law having to do with an injury to a pregnant woman (Exod. 21.22-24). Its parallel is found in HC (Lev. 24.18-20) in a fuller form, where the connection with personal injuries is made much more explicit. CC assumes the fuller law in HC. Furthermore, in Exod. 21.23-24 the law states 'you shall give [*ntn*] life for life, eye for eye', which suggests that the community and not the offender is to pay the penalty. In the previous verse, the offender is the one who must give, that is, pay (*ntn*). The switch in subject is very awkward and confusing and has led to much discussion. Yet the sense of the text becomes immediately clear from the HC parallel in Lev. 24.20, which states the principle: 'As he [the offender] has inflicted [*ntn*] injury on a person, so it must be inflicted [*ntn*] on him'. Here the Hebrew verb *ntn* clearly has the force of 'punish', which is what is required in Exod. 21.23. The direction of dependence is therefore established; CC came after HC.[27]

If this is correct, it suggests that the sequence of law codes, DC, HC, CC represents a process of collection and revision that extended from the late monarchic period through the exile and reflects both 'lay' and 'priestly' perspectives on the law. The law also made the transition from the Judahite homeland through the upheaval of the state's demise to its domestication in Babylonia and the exilic communities there.

d. The Priestly Code

Unlike the other codes or collections of laws that we have discussed above, the 'P Code' (PC) is not a collection of laws that can be easily separated from its narrative context, being often imbedded in it as part of the narrative action. The initial passover law (Exod. 12.1-28) is made part of the events of the exodus night itself with 'supplementary' regulations and instructions included at other later points in the work. The inauguration of the cult with the building of the Tabernacle (Exod. 25–31, 35–40) and the consecration of the priests (Lev. 8–11) is the etiology and legitimation of a particular form of temple worship, even though the Tabernacle is not a blueprint for later times and the events of the priestly consecration are not repeatable in this form.

Into P's larger etiological narrative have been fitted blocks of legislative and regulatory material. Such is the HC, as we have seen. Scholars are also persuaded that the Manual of Offerings (Lev. 1–7) and the Manual of Purity (Lev. 11–15) are older collections of priestly lore that have come down from earlier (pre-exilic?) times.[28] They are loosely attached to their present context. The degree to which the rest of P is supplemental and the relationship of the various legal sections within the narrative frame depends upon one's decision of P's limits, and that is much debated as we have seen above.

It remains to say something about the place of HC in the development of the P strata. As indicated above, there were two quite different responses to the Deuteronomic reform. The one was priestly (HC) and the other was lay (J), with the one preceding the other by only one or two decades. The priestly reforming tendencies that are evident in HC very likely continued. With the re-establishment of the temple, however, there is a decided emphasis towards the elevation of the priesthood and a new focus on the temple as the center of religious activity. Most of the concerns for civil and humanitarian matters reflected in the other codes are no longer addressed, or they are simply assumed by P. This is a long way from the other codes and from the prophetic inspiration that gave rise to them.

As I indicated in the previous chapter, it is with J that the P Code must be primarily compared. Out of the very simple Tent of Meeting in J with its single attendant, Joshua, the P Code constructs an elaborate portable temple with a very complex cultus and vast body of priestly personnel of various ranks. Aaron, the Levite, with no priestly function in J, becomes the high priest and founder of the whole sacerdotal system in PC. In J the Levites (Exod. 32.25-29) are honored with the one specifically cultic role of pronouncing the blessing in the divine service, but they are demoted to second rank in PC and it is the Aaronid priests who take over all the priestly functions, including the blessing of the people (Num. 6.22-27). Only the priests can invoke the divine name for blessing (cf. Exod. 20.24 J). Even the role of Moses as mediator and intercessor on behalf of the people is replaced by that of Aaron as the high priest who makes atonement for the people.

A very large part of the PC is taken up with the subject of sacrifices (Lev. 1–7; 14.10-32; 17; 22.17-30; 27; Num. 18–19) and the closely related subject of ritual cleanness and the matter of holiness (Lev. 11–15; and frequently throughout). It is not possible to review here the many theories about the social and religious meaning of sacrifice in general or in Israel in particular.[29] What is often assumed in such discussions of sacrifice is that the elaborate presentations of the sacrificial system in PC are representative of Israelite society over an extended historical period. However, such assumptions are confronted by radically different presentations and attitudes to sacrifice, the officiants and the recipients, in the different codes and sources. Earlier generations of scholars, such as Wellhausen and Robertson Smith, attempted an evolutionary-historical explanation related to their dating of sources and their identification of primitive survivals in later materials. This approach has been largely replaced by functionalist methods with little concern for historical or cultural discontinuities within the Pentateuchal tradition.

It is, therefore, precisely the immediate juxtaposition of PC to CC and the J source that seems to me so important for the understanding of the cult in P. For J, living in the exile, the cult in the form of the annual festivals and certain traditional sacrifices could be continued with little or no cultic personnel and the presence and blessing of the deity could always be invoked in prayer quite apart from the altar (Exod. 20.24).[30] Taking up a theme from DC and HC, J emphasizes that all the people are holy, a 'kingdom of priests', and originally consecrated as such at Sinai (Exod. 19.6; 24.3-8). It is over against this understanding of the cult and what it means to be holy and what is acceptable to Yahweh that one must see the PC treatment of holiness and sacrifice.

While P has clearly inherited a great body of traditional sacrifices, he has set much of it out in such a way as to make the whole sacrificial system highly complex and the role of the professional priests indispensable. There are now many gradations in holiness within the whole cultic community and the people are confined to the outer fringes, with their direct participation in the cult greatly restricted. A large part of the sacrificial system is interpreted in terms of offerings for sin, intentional and unintentional, and atonement is gained through the intervention of the priests.[31] Many of the 'gift' offerings are interpreted as specifically for the maintenance of a large body of priests and temple personnel. The communal aspect of festival offerings, so strongly emphasized in DC and CC, is also largely absorbed into this priestly system of sacrifices (Lev. 23; Num. 28), and to it has been added a new appointed feast, the day of atonement, the most sacred of all (Lev. 16; Num. 29).

The system whereby a sacrificial offering was judged by a cultic official as acceptable or unacceptable, or an animal clean or unclean, certainly belonged to the older tradition of cultic practice and is reflected in both D and J, as well as in the prophetic literature. J seems to suggest in the Cain and Abel story (Gen. 4) that whether an offering is acceptable or unacceptable is of little consequence so long as one does what is good, which is the primary means of acceptance before Yahweh. The PC, however, makes the sacrificial system and the priestly role in acceptance by the god indispensable. In this way, participation within the cultic community and its activity was completely controlled by the priests.

Some have suggested that the 'lay' approach, as reflected in J, and the sacerdotal scheme of P were combined in a compromise in the Pentateuch. However, the story of the rebellion of Korah, Dathan and Abiram in Numbers 16–17 suggests otherwise. J's original story of the rebellion of Dathan and Abiram against the leadership of Moses and Aaron has been turned into a struggle by the proponents of the holiness of all the people, supported by some Levites (?), and the rights of the Aaronid priests. For P, all persons who advocate such views are condemned to destruction. In the face of such controversy, the complete destruction of the whole people can only be averted by the intervention of the atonement of the high priest with his censer. The rod of the high priest Aaron that budded and which was miraculously chosen by Yahweh was preserved as a relic for the future, thus confirming the future high priests of such a position.[32]

The PC is not simply a repository of priestly tradition nor a manual on current practice, although both may be partially the case. It is very much an ideological document that seems to elevate the priesthood of the Second Temple to supreme political and religious authority. It is a challenge to other forms of political leadership and other understandings of worship and theology. This was not a peaceful, ecumenical process and one only gets glimpses of the struggle. The strategy of P was not to produce a separate, rival document, but to augment the traditional text as an interpretive expansion. The massive PC legal addition is effective primarily by overwhelming the older legislation, particularly in matters of the cult. It is perhaps ironic that Aaron, 'the Levite', who, in J, is to interpret the words of Moses, according to P has done so in a way that could scarcely have been imagined by the earlier writer.

4. The Ten Commandments, Exodus 20.1-17 (P) = Deuteronomy 5.6-21 (D)

The Ten Commandments (literally 'ten words') is a set of laws that stands apart from the codes. The Decalogue is regarded in D as the direct utterance by the deity at Horeb (Sinai) to all Israel. These laws were then copied by the deity on two tablets of stone that Moses received from Yahweh when he later ascended the mountain. The rest of the laws were all mediated through Moses to the people because they were afraid to hear the voice of the god directly. The two versions of the Ten Commandments (one by D and one by P) are almost identical, with only slight differences in wording, except for the law of the sabbath. The D version is the older. It combines within it various types of laws: strong religious sanctions against the worship of other gods, idolatry and misuse of the divine name for evil purposes, regulations about observance of the sabbath, moral injunction on the honoring of one's parents and a series of apodictic commands regarding basic social behavior. These are intended as a summation of the most basic principles of Israelite religion and ethics.

There is no separate version of the Ten Commandments in J. Instead, J included its primary elements within the Covenant Code. P, however, has restored the Ten

Commandments as a separate group of laws given at Sinai, at the same time making some slight revisions, particularly in the law of the sabbath. In D, the sabbath is a national law linked with the exodus; in P it is a universal law linked with creation. This is picked up again by P, where the sabbath is made the sign of the covenant between the people and the deity (Exod. 31.12-17).

The Ten Commandments continue to have a special status in Judaism and Christianity, but they should be viewed within the context of the ancient world and not be too quickly modernized. The first command, for example, does not strictly advocate monotheism but requires that Yahweh should be the only deity worshiped by Israel. The precise wording 'alongside of me' perhaps arises out of a rejection of any consort for Yahweh. It is known that some Israelites considered the goddess Asherah as Yahweh's consort. However, what the law does not make clear is whether Yahweh could be identified or assimilated with other deities, such as the creator god El. Furthermore, the second command rejects any representation of the deity as a carved image, a statue or any likeness of any creature to represent the deity. Since deities were sometimes represented in the form of animals, like the bull to symbolize strength and fertility, as was the case with the god Baal, this seems to be an attempt to avoid such associations. Again, the third command against taking the name of the deity in vain does not mean profanity in the modern sense, but the use of the divine name to curse or injure someone—swearing to another's injury or making a false or meaningless oath. The Ten Commandments were not intended to cover the whole of religious and moral teaching; nor should one make a distinction between them as universal and timeless and the 'other' laws as more temporally and socially restricted. In fact, most of the laws in the Ten Commandments are found in the other codes as well. Finally, while scholars have long recognized that the law codes do not reflect life in the wilderness and date them long after the 'time of Moses', there is still a tendency by some to consider the Ten Commandments, or some earlier version, as coming from Moses. But as with the other codes, the laws reflect the settled life in the land of Canaan (see nos. 4, 5, 10). Like all the laws, the Ten Commandments were ascribed to Moses because he becomes the symbol of the divine mediation of law and the social and religious orders of life, and his lifetime is viewed as the 'constitutional' age of ancient Israel.

Notes

1 Alt, 'The Origin of Israelite Laws'.
2 See Jepsen, *Untersuchungen zum Bundesbuch*; Morgenstern, 'The Book of the Covenant', 'The Book of the Covenant, Part II', 'The Book of the Covenant, Part III'. See the useful review by Clark, 'Law', pp. 105–16.
3 See Clark, 'Law', pp. 99–139; Boecker, *Law and the Administration of Justice*; Patrick, *Old Testament Law*.

4 See the recent new translations in Roth, *Law Collections*; also in *ANET*, pp. 159–98, 523–28.

5 See Roth, *Law Collections;* and *ANET*, pp. 159–98, 523–28. Also Driver and Miles (eds.), *The Babylonian Laws*.

6 An exception is the series of recent studies by myself: Van Seters, 'Cultic Laws in the Covenant Code; *idem*, 'The Law of the Hebrew Slave'; *idem*, 'Some Observations on the Lex Talionis in Exodus 21.23-25', in S. Beyerle, G. Mayer and H. Strauss (eds.), *Recht und Ethos im Alten Testament: Gestalt und Wirkung* (Festschrift Horst Seebass zum 65. Geburtstag; Neukirchen-Vluyn: Neukirchener Verlag, 1999), pp. 27–37; *idem*, 'The Law on Child Sacrifice in Exod 22, 28b-29', *ETL* 74 (1998), pp. 364–72.

7 Some scholars regard this as a later addition, based on the P code.

8 2 Kgs 23:24 looks like a late addition to make the reform conform more closely with the demands of Deut. 18.9-14.

9 Levinson, *Deuteronomy and the Hermeneutics of Legal Innovation*.

10 See A. D. H. Mayes, *The Story of Israel between Settlement and Exile* (London: SCM Press, 1983), pp. 268–69; Crüsemann, *The Torah*, pp. 90–98. The primary reason for the development of this view was to account for the parallel in Exod. 18, which was ascribed to E and dated to the ninth century BCE.

11 So also Wellhausen, *Prolegomena*, p. 191.

12 See Levinson, *Deuteronomy and the Hermeneutics of Legal Innovation*, pp. 98–143.

13 See Weinfeld, *Deuteronomy and the Deuteronomic School*, pp. 282–97; L. Perlitt, ' "Ein einzig Volk von Brüdern": Zur deuteronomischen Herkunft der biblischen Bezeichnung "Bruder" ', in D. Lührmann and G. Strecker (eds.), *Kirche* (Festschrift G. Bornkamm; Tübingen: J.C.B. Mohr, 1980), pp. 27–52.

14 Nicholson, *Deuteronomy and Tradition*.

15 See 'The Law of the Hebrew Slave'; *idem, A Law Book for the Diaspora,* 82–95; *idem*, 'Revision in the Study of the Covenant Code and a Response to my Critics', *SJOT* 21 (2007), pp. 5–28.

16 *Introduction to the Old Testament*, pp. 212–13.

17 Van Seters, *A Law Book for the Diaspora*, pp. 82–171.

18 See Houtman, *Das Bundesbuch*, pp. 7–48.

19 A similar perspective is already anticipated in such exilic texts as 1 Kgs 8.46-53 and Deut. 4.7.

20 Van Seters, 'The Law of the Hebrew Slave'; see n. 15 above.

21 The auguments against viewing HC as a separate early source are reflected in Crüsemann, *The Torah*, pp. 277–82, or as a late addition (Blenkinsopp, *The Pentateuch*, p. 224). Both of these positions I consider as untenable.

22 Lev. 18.3; 19.34, 36; 22.33; 23.43; 25.38, 42, 55; 26.13, 45.

23 Lev. 18.3, 24-28; 19.23; 20.22-24; 23.9; 25.2, 38.

24 Lev. 18.4, 26, 30; 19.19, 37; 20.8, 22; 22.31; 25.18; 26.3, 14, 15, 21, 23, 27, 42, 43, 46.

25 See Zimmerli, *I Am Yahweh*, pp. 2–7.

26 Lev. 17.2; 21.1, 16, 24; 22.2, 17.

27 See further Van Seters, 'Lex Talionis in Exod 21.23-25'.

28 See Budd, *Leviticus*, pp. 12–20.

29 See the useful survey by Budd, *Leviticus*, pp. 24–34.

30 See Van Seters, *The Life of Moses*, pp. 280–82.

31 See von Rad, *Old Testament Theology*, I, pp. 250–72.

32 Of course, with the destruction of the First Temple and the disappearance of the ark, there was no way to disconfirm this statement.

9

Conclusion

The governing assumption of this guidebook is that the interpretation of the Pentateuch cannot dispense with the initial task of understanding its compositional history. The basic demands of any reader for unity, consistency and coherence require some explanation for those many points in the text when these requirements for making sense of the text break down or are seriously violated. The long history of literary criticism of the Pentateuch has given rise to the conviction that the best explanation for such problematic features in the text in most cases is the hypothesis that the Pentateuch is a combination of sources or authors and that within such works the expectations of unity, consistency and coherence are more easily satisfied. As we have seen, the one point at which there is still considerable disagreement is on the unity of the Tetrateuchal sources. Many scholars in the past argued that P provided the basic unity for the whole and that a fragmented non-P source was used to fill in the narrative content. I have argued that it was the J source that was the unified narrative and that P was never a unity but composed from the start as a supplementation to the earlier work.

Furthermore, exegetes will invariably need to interpret certain texts of one author in relation to texts of another author that use the same language or address the same themes or that stand in marked contrast or contradiction to each other. When the interrelationship of various parts of the Pentateuch is viewed diachronically, then the relative chronology of its various parts and the interplay between them becomes a major task of historical criticism. Yet, as I have tried to make clear, the particular model that one adopts for explaining that textual interrelationship, whether documentary with redactors or supplementary without redactors or the fragmentary-block model with final amalgamation, makes a major difference in the way in which the texts of the Pentateuch are understood.

In distinction from other recent guidebooks on the Pentateuch, I have advocated the supplementary model of accounting for J's relationship to the prior corpus of D/DtrH and P's relationship to the combined work of both. While there may still be a few late additions (e.g. Gen. 14) that are not easily integrated into any of these major compositions, I strenuously resist the use of a plurality of redactors to account for the combination of documents or the random insertion of texts as an adequate or useful scholarly explanation of the Pentateuch's compositional history.

The same supplementary method is at work to some extent within these three literary layers, that is, within Deuteronomy and the development of Deuteronomy by Dtr, within J, especially in the patriarchal narratives in Genesis, and within P and the relationship of Pg to Ps. In spite of this complication, however, the supplementary method using three major sources greatly simplifies and clarifies the compositional history of the Pentateuch.

Within the trilogy of authors P designated as Deuteronomist, the Yahwist and the Priestly Writer, it is the Yahwist who has been most seriously misunderstood and the most fragmented in recent years. J has therefore been the primary focus of my own study and the work that is treated at the greatest length here. The dating of J long before Deuteronomy resulted in a completely different understanding of this work from the one advocated here. The Yahwist as historian of Israelite antiquities, theologian and ideologue of Israelite identity, and lawgiver of a revisionist code must be read in relationship to D/DtrH, which he supplements, and in the period of the exile between Ezekiel and Second Isaiah.[1] In this way, the so-called Dtr redaction of the Tetrateuch completely disappears.

The problems of the P source's interrelationship with the other two sources has been debated on two different levels. On the one hand, there is the discussion of the literary relationship, dependent or independent, with J. On the other hand, there is the ideological and theological comparison of P with D/DtrH as the most important way of placing P in its appropriate context and explicating its theological perspective. I have argued, however, that P's relationship to J (which is not to be subsumed under D)[2] also involves P's direct response to J's exilic spirituality and theology and its most important challenge. P's supplement is primarily attached to J because J calls for the greatest priestly revision. This interrelationship P and J has been obscured in recent discussion by the invention of yet another post-P redactor to whom various blocks of J texts have been attributed. Clarity in the discussion of the literary relationship between an exilic J and a postexilic P will greatly aid in the understanding of P as an ideological and theological response to the earlier corpus.

My current analysis has also run counter to another prevailing tendency, which is to see the beginnings of the Pentateuch's canonization in the final stages of the its composition. It is suggested that Deuteronomy represents the beginning of a process in which the document was understood as both authoritative and final: 'You shall not add to the word that I command you, nor take from it' (Deut. 4:2; 13:1 [12:32]). This statement, which, strictly speaking, applies only to the laws, is a common Near Eastern formula associated with such legal and wisdom texts. These words hardly seem to have served as much of a deterrent to the addition of many more laws.[3] The idea that there was a specific redactional process or activity that tried to define and limit the Pentateuch as a work distinct from the historical books that followed is a piece of scholarly speculation that cannot be demonstrated. None of the Pentateuchal sources end with the death of Moses but all continue into, or make additions to, the book of Joshua. Furthermore, all three sources have their own accounts of the appointment of Joshua as Moses' successor, whose task was to finish the conquest begun by Moses. There is simply no way around this obvious fact.[4] That is not to deny that at each stage of their development, these writings acquired a high degree of respect and authority. However, the process of canonization is a much later phenomenon and has nothing to do with the history of the Pentateuch's composition.

The process of Pentateuchal expansion came to an end, not by the decree of some foreign power, such as the Persian government, but because the priestly caste was largely successful in gaining the necessary authority over the religious community in Jerusalem and thus over the religious texts that governed its life. Few additions were made after the P revision. One, however, is perhaps significant, and that is Genesis 14, stemming from the Hellenistic period.[5] In the story recounted there Abraham pays homage to the priest-king of Jerusalem, the prototype of the Hellenistic high priests, especially the Maccabean kings. It is clear that the books that made up the Pentateuch remained firmly under the control of the priestly authority in Jerusalem.

Notes

1   See Van Seters, 'In the Babylonian Exile with J'.
2   So Blum and Albertz.
3   Contra Blenkinsopp, *The Pentateuch*, p. 233.
4   Blenkinsopp, *The Pentateuch*, pp. 229–32.
5   Van Seters, *Abraham in History and Tradition*, pp. 296–308.

Bibliography

Ahlström, G., *The History of Ancient Palestine* (Philadelphia: Fortress Press, 1993).

Albrektson, B., *History and the Gods: An Essay on the Idea of Historical Events as Divine Manifestations in the Ancient Near East and Israel* (Lund: C. W. K. Gleerup, 1967).

Albertz, R., *A History of Israelite Religion in the Old Testament Period* (trans. J. Bowden; 2 vols.; Louisville, KY: Westminster/John Knox Press, 1994).

—— 'Der Beginn der vorpriesterlichen Exodus-komposition (K^{EX}): Eine Kompositions- und Redaktionsgeschichte von Ex 1-5,' *TZ* 67 (2011): pp. 223–62.

Albright, W. F., *From the Stone Age to Christianity* (Baltimore: The Johns Hopkins University Press, 1940).

—— 'Abram the Hebrew: A New Archaeological Interpretation', BASOR 163 (October 1961), pp. 36–54.

—— *Yahweh and the Gods of Canaan* (Garden City, NY: Doubleday, 1968).

Alt, A., 'The Origin of Israelite Laws' (1934), in *idem, Essays*, pp. 79–132.

—— 'The God of the Fathers' (1929), in *idem, Essays*, pp. 1–66.

—— *Essays on Old Testament History and Religion* (Oxford: Basil Blackwell, 1966).

Aly, W., *Volksmärchen, Sage und Novelle bei Herodot und seinen Zeitgenossen* (Göttingen: Vandenhoeck & Ruprecht, 1921).

Aurelius, E., *Der Fürbitter Israels: Eine Studie zum Mosebild im Alten Testament* (ConBOT, 27; Stockholm: Almqvist & Wiksell, 1988).

Baden, J. S., *J, E, and the Redaction of the Pentateuch* (Tübingen: Mohr Siebeck, 2009).

Balentine, S. E., 'The Prophet as Intercessor: A Reassessment', *JBL* 103 (1984), pp. 161–73.

Baltzer, K., *Das Bundesformular* (WMANT, 4; Neukirchen-Vluyn: Neukirchener Verlag, 1964); ET *The Covenant Formulary* (trans. D. E. Green; Oxford; Basil Blackwell, 1971).

Barr, J., *Holy Scripture, Canon, Authority, Criticism* (Philadelphia: Westminster Press, 1983).

Barton, J., *Reading the Old Testament* (Philadelphia: Westminster Press, 2nd edn, 1997 [1984]).

—— *Oracles of God* (Oxford: Oxford University Press, 1986).

Beidelman, T. O., 'W. Robertson Smith', *EncRel*, XIII, pp. 366–67.

Berge, K., *Reading Sources in a Text: Coherence and Literary Criticism in the Call of Moses* (ATSAT, 54; St Ottilien: EOS Verlag, 1997).

Blenkinsopp, J., *The Pentateuch* (New York: Doubleday, 1992).

—— 'An Assessment of the Alleged Pre-Exilic Date of the Priestly Material in the Pentateuch', *ZAW* 108 (1996), pp. 495–518.

Blum, E., *Die Komposition der Vätergeschichte* (WMANT, 57; Neukirchen-Vluyn: Neukirchener Verlag, 1984).

—— *Studien zur Komposition des Pentateuch* (BZAW, 189; Berlin: W. de Gruyter, 1990).

—— 'Gibt es die Endgestalt des Pentateuch?', in J. A. Emerton (ed.), *Congress Volume: Leuven, 1989* (VTSup, 43; Leiden: E. J. Brill, 1992), pp. 46–57.

Boecker, H. J., *Law and the Administration of Justice in the Old Testament and Ancient East* (trans. J. Moiser; Minneapolis: Augsburg, 1980).

Boorer, S., 'The Importance of a Diachronic Approach: The Case of Genesis–Kings', *CBQ* 51 (1989), pp. 195–208.

—— *The Promise of the Land as Oath* (BZAW, 205; Berlin: W. de Gruyter, 1992).

Braulik, G., 'Deuteronomy and the Birth of Monotheism', in *idem, The Theology of Deuteronomy* (trans. U. Lindblad; N. Richland Hills, TX: BIBAL Press, 1994), pp. 99–130.

Brenner, M., *The Song of the Sea: Ex. 15:1–21* (BZAW, 195; Berlin: W. de Gruyter, 1991).

Budd, P. J., *Leviticus* (NCBC; Grand Rapids: Eerdmans, 1996).

Campbell, A. F., and M. A. O'Brien, *Sources of the Pentateuch: Texts, Introduction, Annotations* (Philadelphia: Fortress Press, 1993).

Carr, D. M., *Reading the Fractures of Genesis: Historical and Literary Approaches* (Louisville, KY: Westminster/John Knox Press, 1996).

Childs, B. S., 'A Study of the Formula, "Until This Day" ', *JBL* 82 (1963), pp. 279–92.

—— 'Deuteronomic Formulae of the Exodus Tradition', in *Hebräische Wortforschung* (VTSup, 16; Leiden: E. J. Brill, 1967), pp. 30–39.

—— *The Book of Exodus* (OTL; Philadelphia: Westminster Press, 1974).

—— *Introduction to the Old Testament as Scripture* (Philadelphia: Fortress Press, 1979).

Clark, W. M., 'Law', in John H. Hayes (ed.), *Old Testament Form Criticism* (San Antonio, TX: Trinity University Press, 1974), pp. 99–139.

Clements, R. E., *Abraham and David* (SBT, 2.5; London: SCM Press, 1967).

Clifford, R. J., *The Cosmic Mountain in Canaan and the Old Testament* (HSM, 4; Cambridge, MA: Harvard University Press, 1972).

Coats, G. W., *Genesis with an Introduction to Narrative Literature* (FOTL, 1; Grand Rapids: Eerdmans, 1983).

—— *Moses: Heroic Man, Man of God* (JSOTSup, 57; Sheffield: JSOT Press, 1988).

Cross, F. M., *Canaanite Myth and Hebrew Epic* (Cambridge, MA: Harvard University Press, 1973).

Crüsemann, F., 'Die Eigenständigkeit der Urgeschichte: Ein Beitrag zur Diskussion um den "Jahwisten" ', in J. Jeremias and L. Perlitt (eds.), *Die Botschaft und die Boten* (Festschrift H. W. Wolff; Neukirchen-Vluyn: Neukirchener Verlag, 1981), pp. 11–29.

—— *The Torah: Theology and Social History of Old Testament Law* (trans. A. W. Mahnke; Philadelphia: Fortress Press, 1996).

Dearman, A. (ed.), *Studies in the Mesha Inscription and Moab* (Archaeology and Biblical Studies, 2; Atlanta: Scholars Press, 1989).

Dever, W. G., 'Temples and Sanctuaries—Syria-Palestine', *ABD*, VI, pp. 378–80.

De Vries, Jan, *Perspectives in the History of Religions* (Berkeley: University of California Press, 1977).

Dozaman, T. B. and K. Schmid (eds.), *A Farewell to the Yahwist? The Composition of the Pentateuch in Recent European Interpretation* (Atlanta: SBL, 2006).

Driver, G. R., and J. C. Miles (eds.), *The Babylonian Laws* (2 vols.; Oxford: Oxford University Press, 1952–55).

Driver, S. R., *Deuteronomy* (ICC; New York: Charles Scribner's Sons, 1895).

—— *An Introduction to the Literature of the Old Testament* (New York: Meridian, 1957).

Dundes, A. (ed.), *The Study of Folklore* (Englewood Cliffs, NJ: Prentice-Hall, 1965).

Eissfeldt, O., *The Old Testament, an Introduction* (trans. P. R. Ackroyd; New York: Harper & Row, 1965 [1964]).

Emerton, J. A., 'The Priestly Writer in Genesis', *JTS* 39 (1988), pp. 381–400.

—— 'The Source Analysis of Genesis XI 27–32', *VT* 42 (1992), pp. 37–46.

Engnell, I., *A Rigid Scrutiny: Critical Essays on the Old Testament* (trans. John T. Willis; Nashville: Vanderbilt University Press, 1969).

Finley, M. I., 'Myth, Memory and History', in *idem, The Use and Abuse of History* (New York: Viking Press, 1975).

Fishbane, M., *Biblical Interpretation in Ancient Israel* (Oxford: Oxford University Press, 1985).

Fohrer, G., *Introduction to the Old Testament* (trans. D. E. Green; Nashville: Abingdon Press, 1968 [1965]).

Frankena, R., 'The Vassal Treaties of Esarhaddon and the Dating of Deuteronomy', *OTS* 14 (1965), pp. 122–54.

Friedman, R. E., *Who Wrote the Bible?* (Englewood Cliffs, NJ: Prentice-Hall, 1987).

—— 'Torah (Pentateuch)', *ABD,* VI, pp. 605–22.

Galling, K., *Die Erwählungstraditionen Israels* (BZAW, 48; Berlin: W. de Gruyter, 1928).

Gertz, J. C., K. Schmid, and M. Witt (eds). *Abschied vom Jehwisten: Die Komposition des Hexateuch in der jüngsten Diskusion* (BZAW 315; Berlin: de Gruyter, 2002).

Geus, C. H. J. de, *The Tribes of Israel: An Investigation into Some of the Presuppositions of Martin Noth's Amphictyony Hypothesis* (Assen: Van Gorcum, 1976).

Grabbe, L. L., *Judaism from Cyrus to Hadrian. I. The Persian and Greek Periods* (Philadelphia: Fortress Press, 1992).

Gressmann, H., *Mose und seine Zeit* (FRLANT, 1; Göttingen: Vandenhoeck & Ruprecht, 1913).

Gunkel, H., *Genesis* (HKAT, 1.1; Göttingen: Vandenhoeck & Ruprecht, 3rd edn, 1910); ET *Genesis* (trans. M. E. Bittle; Macon, GA: Mercer University Press, 1997).

—— *The Folktale in the Old Testament* (Sheffield: Sheffield Academic Press, 1987 [1917]).

—— 'Geschichtsschreibung im A.T.', *RGG,* II, pp. 1348–54; 2nd edn, II, pp. 1112–15.

Ha, J., *Genesis 15* (BZAW, 181; Berlin, W. de Gruyter, 1989).

Hadley, J. M., 'Yahweh and "His Asherah": Archaeological and Textual Evidence for the Cult of the Goddess', in W. Dietrich and M. Klopfenstein (eds.), *Ein Gott allein?* (Freiburg: University Press, 1994), pp. 235–68.

Haran, M., *Temple and Temple Service in Ancient Israel* (Oxford: Clarendon Press, 1978).

Harrelson, W., 'Myth and Ritual School', *EncRel,* X, pp. 282–85.

Harris, W. V., *Ancient Literacy* (Cambridge, MA: Harvard University Press, 1989).

Hendel, R. S., *The Epic of the Patriarch* (HSM, 42; Atlanta: Scholars Press, 1987).

Hiebert, T., *The Yahwist's Landscape: Nature and Religion in Early Israel* (Oxford: Oxford University Press, 1996).

Hobsbawm, E., and T. Ranger (eds.), *The Invention of Tradition* (Cambridge: University of Cambridge Press, 1983).

Hoftijzer, J., *Die Verheissungen an der drei Ertzväter* (Leiden: E.J. Brill, 1956).

Holladay, J. S., Jr, 'Religion in Israel and Judah under the Monarchy: An Explicitly Archaeological Approach', in P. D. Miller, Jr *et al.* (eds.), *Ancient Israelite Religion* (Philadelphia: Fortress Press, 1987), pp. 249–99.

—— *Cities of the Delta, Part III: Tell el-Maskhuta. Preliminary Report on the Wadi Tumilat Project 1978–79* (ARCE Reports, 6; Los Angeles: Undena Publications, 1982).

—— 'Maskhuta, Tell el-', *ABD,* IV, pp. 588–92.

Houtman, C., *Der Pentateuch* (Kampen: Kok, 1994).

—— *Das Bundesbuch: Ein Kommentar* (Leiden: E.J. Brill, 1997).

Jackson, B. S., 'Revolution in Biblical Law: Some Reflections on the Role of Theory and Methodology', *JSS* 50 (2005), pp. 83–115.

Jepsen, A., *Untersuchungen zum Bundesbuch* (BWANT, 3.5; Stuttgart: W. Kohlhammer, 1927).

Jeremias, J., *Theophanie: Die Geschichte einer alttestamentlichen Gattung* (WMANT, 10; Neukirchen-Vluyn: Neukirchener Verlag, 1965).

Kang, S. M., *Divine War in the Old Testament and in the Ancient Near East* (BZAW, 177; Berlin: W. de Gruyter, 1989).

Kaufmann, Y., *The Religion of Israel: From its Beginnings to the Babylonian Exile* (trans. and abr. M. Greenberg; Chicago: University of Chicago Press, 1960).

Kirkpatrick, P. G., *The Old Testament and Folklore Study* (JSOTSup, 62; Sheffield: Sheffield Academic Press, 1988).

Klatt, W., *Hermann Gunkel: Zu seiner Theologie der Religionsgeschichte und zur Entstehung der formgeschichtliche Methode* (FRLANT, 100; Göttingen: Vandenhoeck & Ruprecht, 1969).

Knight, D. A., *Rediscovering the Traditions of Israel* (Missoula, MT: Scholars Press, 1973).

Knoppers, G. N., *Two Nations under God: The Deuteronomistic History of Solomon and the Dual Monarchies* (2 vols.; HSM, 53; Atlanta: Scholars Press, 1994).

Koch, K., 'P-Kein Redaktor: Erinnerung an zwei Eckdaten der Quellenscheidung', *VT* 37 (1987), pp. 446–67.

Krüger, T., 'Genesis 38—ein "Lehrstück" alttestamentlicher Ethik', in R. Bartelmus (ed.), *Konsequente Traditionsgeschichte* (Festschrift K. Baltzer; OBO, 126; Freiburg: University Press; Göttingen; Vandenhoeck & Ruprecht, 1993), pp. 205–226.

Levenson, J., *Sinai and Zion: An Entry into the Jewish Bible* (San Francisco: Harper & Row, 1985).

Levinson, B. M., *Deuteronomy and the Hermeneutics of Legal Innovation* (Oxford: Oxford University Press, 1997).

—— 'Is the Covenant Code an Exilic Composition? A Response to John Van Seters', in J. Day (ed.), *In Search of Pre-exilic Israel* (JSOTS 406; London: T & T Clark, 2004), pp. 272–325.

Lohfink, N., *Das Hauptgebot: Eine Untersuchung literarischer Einleitungsfragen zu Dtn 5–11* (AnBib, 20; Rome: Pontifical Biblical Institute, 1963).

—— 'Deuteronomy', in *IDBSup*, pp. 229–32.

—— 'The Cult Reform of Josiah of Judah: 2 Kings 22–23 as a Source for the History of Israelite Religion', in P. D. Miller *et al.* (eds.), *Ancient Israelite Religion* (Philadelphia: Fortress Press, 1987), pp. 459–75.

—— 'Deuteronomium und Pentateuch', in *idem* (ed.), *Studien zum Deuteronomium,* III (Stuttgart: Katholisches Bibelwerk, 1990), pp. 13–38.

—— *The Theology of the Pentateuch* (trans. L. M. Maloney; Philadelphia: Fortress Press, 1994).

Lohfink, N. (ed.), *Das Deuteronomium Entstehumg, Gestalt und Botschaft* (BETL, 68; Leuven: Peeters, 1985).

Long, B. O., *The Problem of Etiological Narrative in the Old Testament* (BZAW, 108; Berlin: W. de Gruyter, 1968).

Mann, T., 'The Pillar of Cloud in the Red Sea Narrative', *JBL* 90 (1971), pp. 15–39.

—— *Divine Presence and Guidance in Israelite Traditions: The Typology of Exaltation* (Baltimore: The Johns Hopkins University Press, 1977).

Mattingly, G. L., 'Moabite Religion and the Mesha' Inscription', in A. Dearman (ed.), *Studies in the Mesha Inscription and Moab (Archaeology and Biblical Studies,* 2; Atlanta: Scholars Press, 1989), pp. 232–37.

Mayes, A. D. H., *Deuteronomy* (NCBC; Grand Rapids: Eerdmans, 1979).

—— *The Story of Israel between Settlement and Exile* (London: SCM Press, 1983).

McCarthy, D. J., *Old Testament Covenant: A Survey of Current Opinions* (Richmond, VA: John Knox Press, 1972).

McEvenue, S. E., *The Narrative Style of the Priestly Writer* (AnBib, 50; Rome: Pontifical Biblical Institute, 1971).

McKenzie, S. L., and S. R. Haynes (eds.), *To Each its Own Meaning: An Introduction to Biblical Criticisms and their Meanings* (Louisville, KY: Westminster/John Knox Press, 1993).

Miller, P. D. et al. (eds.), *Ancient Israelite Religion* (Philadelphia: Fortress Press, 1987).

Minette de Tillesse, G., 'Section "tu" et sections "vous" dans le Deutéronome', *VT* 12 (1962), pp. 29–87.

Morgan, R., and J. Barton, *Biblical Interpretation* (Oxford: Oxford University Press, 1988).

Morgenstern, J., 'The Book of the Covenant', *HUCA* 5 (1928), pp. 1–151.

—— 'The Book of the Covenant, Part II', *HUCA* 7 (1930), pp. 19–258.

—— 'The Book of the Covenant, Part III', *HUCA* 8–9 (1931–32), pp. 1–150.

Mowinckel, S., *Erwägungen zur Pentateuch Quellenfrage* (Oslo: Universitetsforlaget, 1964).

—— *Tetrateuch-Pentateuch-Hexateuch: Die Berichte über die Landnahme in den drei altisrealitischen Geschichtswerken* (BZAW, 90; Berlin: W. de Gruyter, 1964).

Mullen, E. T., Jr, *Ethnic Myths and Pentateuchal Foundations* (Atlanta: Scholars Press, 1997).

Na'aman, N., 'The Debated Historicity of Hezekiah's Reform in the Light of Historical and Archaeological Research', *ZAW* 107 (1995), pp. 179–95.

—— 'Sources and Composition in the History of Solomon', in L. K. Handy (ed.), *The Age of Solomon* (Leiden: E.J. Brill, 1997), pp. 57–80.

Nicholson, E. W., *Deuteronomy and Tradition* (Oxford: Basil Blackwell, 1967).

—— 'The Decalogue as the Direct Address of God', *VT* 27 (1977), pp. 422–33.

—— *God and his People* (Oxford: Oxford University Press, 1986).

—— *The Pentateuch in the Twentieth Century: The Legacy of Julius Wellhausen* (Oxford: Oxford University Press, 1998).

Niditch, S., *Oral World and Written Word: Ancient Israelite Literature* (Louisville, KY: Westminster/John Knox Press, 1996).

Niemann, H. M., 'The Socio-Political Shadow Cast by the Biblical Solomon', in L. K. Handy (ed.), *The Age of Solomon* (Leiden: E.J. Brill, 1997), pp. 252–99.

Noth, M., *Überlieferungsgeschichtliche Studien* (Tübingen: Max Niemeyer, 2nd edn, 1957); pp. 1–110 were translated as *The Deuteronomistic History* (JSOTSup, 15; Sheffield: JSOT Press, 1981).

—— *Überlieferungsgeschichte des Pentateuch* (Stuttgart: W. Kohlhammer, 1948); ET *A History of Pentateuchal Traditions* (trans. B. W. Anderson; Englewood Cliffs, NJ: Prentice-Hall, 1972).

—— 'Geschichtsschreibung im A.T.', *RGG,* 3rd edn, II, pp. 1498–1504.

Olyan, S. M., *Asherah and the Cult of Yahweh in Israel* (SBLMS, 34; Atlanta: Scholars Press, 1988).

Otto, E., a review of J. Van Seters, *A Law Book for the Diaspora*, in RBL, published on its website July 2004 and with a German version in *Biblica* 85 (2004), pp. 273–77.

Patrick, D., *Old Testament Law* (Atlanta: John Knox Press, 1985).

Pearson, L., *The Early Ionian Historians* (Oxford: Oxford University Press, 1939).

—— *The Local Historians of Attica* (APAPM, 11; Philadelphia: American Philological Association, 1942).

—— *The Greek Historians of the West* (Atlanta: Scholars Press, 1987).

Perlitt, L., *Vatke und Wellhausen* (BZAW, 94; Berlin: W. de Gruyter, 1965).

—— *Bundestheologie im Alten Testament* (Neukirchen-Vluyn: Neukirchener Verlag, 1969).

—— ' "Ein einzig Volk von Brüdern": Zur deuteronomischen Herkunft der biblischen Bezeichnung "Bruder"', in D. Lührmann and G. Strecker (eds.), *Kirche* (Festschrift G. Bornkamm; Tübingen: J.C.B. Mohr, 1980), pp. 27–52.

Pfeiffer, R. H., *Introduction to the Old Testament* (New York: Harper & Brothers, 1941).

Plöger, O., *Theocracy and Eschatology* (trans. S. Rudman; Richmond, VA: John Knox Press, 1986).

Porter, R. J., *Moses and Monarchy: A Study in the Biblical Tradition of Moses* (Oxford: Oxford University Press, 1963).

Preus, J. S., *Explaining Religion: Criticism and Theory from Bodin to Freud* (New Haven: Yale University Press, 1987).

Preuss, H. D., *Deuteronomium* (ErFor, 164; Darmstadt: Wissenschaftliche Buchgesellschaft, 1982).

—— 'Zum deuteronomistische Geschichtswerk', *TRu* 58 (1993), pp. 229–45.

Pury, A. de, *Promesse divine et légende culturelle dans le cycle de Jacob* (2 vols.; Paris: J. Gabalda, 1975).

—— 'Erwägungen zu einen vorexilischen Stämmejahwismus: Hos 12 und die Auseinandersetzung um die Identität Israels und seines Gottes', in W. Dietrich and M. A. Klopfenstein (eds.), *Ein Gott allein?* (Freiburg: University Press, 1994), pp. 413–39.

Pury, A. de, and T. Römer, 'Le pentateuque en question: Position du problème et brève histoire de la recherche', in A. de Pury (ed.), *Le pentateuque en question* (Geneva: Labor et Fides, 1989), pp. 9–90.

Rad, G. von, *Das formgeschichtliche Problem des Hexateuchs* (BWANT, 4.26; Stuttgart: W. Kohlhammer, 1938); ET 'The Form-Critical Problem of the Hexateuch', in *idem, The Problem of the Hexateuch and Other Essays* (trans. E. W. T. Dicken; Edinburgh: Oliver & Boyd, 1966), pp. 1–78.

—— 'The Beginning of Historical Writing in Ancient Israel' (1944), in *idem, The Problem of the Hexateuch and Other Essays,* pp. 166–204.

—— *Studies in Deuteronomy* (trans. D. M. G. Stalker; SBT, 9; London: SCM Press, 1953).

—— *Deuteronomy* (OTL; Philadelphia: Westminster Press, 1966).

—— *Old Testament Theology* (trans. D. M. G. Stalker; 2 vols.; New York: Harper & Row, 1962).

—— *Genesis* (Philadelphia: Westminster Press, rev. edn, 1972).

Redford, D. B., 'Exodus I 11', *VT* 13 (1963), pp. 401–18.

—— *A Study of the Biblical Story of Joseph (Genesis 37–50)* (VTSup, 20; Leiden: E. J. Brill, 1970).

—— 'Pithom', *LÄ* 4 (1982), pp. 1054–58.

—— *Egypt, Canaan, and Israel in Ancient Times* (Princeton, NJ: Princeton University Press, 1992).

Rendtorff, R., *Das überlieferungsgeschichtliche Problem des Pentateuch* (BZAW 147; Berlin: W. de Gruyter, 1977).

Rofé, A., *The Prophetical Stories* (Jerusalem: Magnes Press, 1988).

Rogerson, J., *Old Testament Criticism in the Nineteenth Century: England and Germany* (London: SPCK, 1984).

Römer, T., *Israels Väter: Untersuchungen zur Väterthematik im Deuteronomium und in der deuteronomistischen Tradition* (OBO, 99; Freiburg: University Press; Vandenhoeck & Ruprecht, 1990).

—— 'Transformations in Deuteronomistic and Biblical Historiography: On "Book-Finding" and Other Literary Strategies', *ZAW* 109 (1997), pp. 1–12.

Rose, M., *Deuteronomist und Jahwist* (ATANT, 67; Zürich: Theologischer Verlag, 1981).

Roth, M. T., *Law Collections from Mesopotamia and Asia Minor* (Atlanta: Scholars Press, 1995).

Rudolph, K., 'Religionsgeschichtliche Schule', *EncRel* XII, pp. 293–96.

Rudolph, W., *Der 'Elohist' von Exodus bis Joshua* (BZAW, 68; Berlin: W. de Gruyter, 1938).

Schmid, H. H., *Der sogenannte Jahwist* (Zürich: Theologischer Verlag, 1976).

—— 'Vers une théologie du Pentateuque', in A. de Pury (ed.), *Le pentateuque en question* (Geneva: Labor et Fides, 1989), pp. 361–86.

Schmid, K., *Erzväter und Exodus: Untersuchungen zur doppelten Begründung der Ursprünge Israels innnerhalb der Geschichtsbücher des Alten Testaments* (WMANT 81; Neukirchen-Vluyn: Neukirchener Verlag, 1999).

Schmidt, B. B., 'The Aniconic Tradition: On Reading Images and Viewing Texts', in D. V. Edelman (ed.), *The Triumph of Elohim: From Yahwisms to Judaisms* (Kampen: Kok, 1995), pp. 96–105.

Schmitt, H-C., *Arbeitsbuch zum Alten Testament*, 3rd edn (Göttingen: Vandenhoeck and Ruprecht, 2011).

Schorn, U., *Ruben und das System der zwölf Stämme Israels* (BZAW, 248; Berlin: W. de Gruyter, 1997).

Schulte, H., *Die Entstehung der Geschichtsschreibung im alten Israel* (BZAW 128; Berlin: W. de Gruyter, 1972).

Schwartz, B. J., 'The Priestly Account of the Theophany and Lawgiving at Sinai', in M. V. Fox *et al.* (eds.), *Texts, Temples, and Traditions: A Tribute to Menahem Haran* (Winona Lake, IN: Eisenbrauns, 1996), pp. 103–34.

Seitz, G., *Redaktionsgeschichtliche Studien zum Deuteronomium* (BWANT, 5.13; Stuttgart: W. Kohlhammer, 1971).

Sharpe, E. J., *Comparative Religion: A History* (New York: Charles Scribner's Sons, 2nd edn, 1975).

Ska, J. L., 'De la relative indépendence de l'écrit sacerdotal', *Bib* 75 (1994), pp. 396–415.

Smith, J. Z., 'In Comparison a Magic Dwells', in *idem, Imaging Religion* (Chicago: University of Chicago Press, 1982), pp. 19–35.

—— 'When the Bough Breaks', in *idem, Map Is Not Territory* (Chicago: University of Chicago Press, 1978), pp. 208–39.

Smith, W. Robertson, *The Religion of the Semites* (New York: Meridian, 1956 [1889]).

Sparks, K. L., *Ethnicity and Identity in Ancient Israel* (Winona Lake, IN: Eisenbrauns, 1998).

Tengström, S., *Die Toledotformel und die literarische Struktur der priesterlichen Erweiterungsschicht im Pentateuch* (CBOTS, 17; Lund: Gleerup, 1981).

Thomas, R., *Oral Tradition and Written Record in Classical Athens* (Cambridge: Cambridge University Press, 1989).

—— *Literacy and Orality in Ancient Greece* (Cambridge: Cambridge University Press, 1992).

Thompson, T. L., *The Historicity of the Patriarchal Narratives* (BZAW, 133; Berlin: W. de Gruyter, 1974).

Ühlinger, C., *Weltreich und "eine Rede": Eine neue Deutung der sogenannten Turmbauerzählung (Gen 11, 1–9)* (OBO, 101; Freiburg: University Press; Göttingen: Vandenhoeck & Ruprecht, 1990).

Van Seters, J., 'Confessional Reformulation in the Exilic Period', *VT* 22 (1972), pp. 448–59.

—— 'The Terms "Amorite" and "Hittite" in the Old Testament', *VT* 22 (1972), pp. 64–81.

—— 'The Conquest of Sihon's Kingdom: A Literary Examination', *JBL* 91 (1972), pp. 182–97.

—— *Abraham in History and Tradition* (New Haven: Yale University Press, 1975).

—— 'The Yahwist as Theologian? A Response', *JSOT* 3 (1977), pp. 15–20.

—— 'Recent Studies on the Pentateuch: A Crisis in Method', *JAOS* 99 (1979), pp. 663–73.

—— *In Search of History: Historiography in the Ancient World and the Origins of Biblical History* (New Haven: Yale University Press, 1983).

—— 'Joshua 24 and the Problem of Tradition in the Old Testament', in W. B. Barrick and J. R. Spencer (eds.), *In the Shelter of Elyon: Essays in Honor of G. W. Ahlström* (JSOTSup, 31; Sheffield: JSOT Press, 1984), pp. 139–58.

—— 'Etiology in the Moses Tradition: The Case of Exodus 18', *HAR* 9 (1985), pp. 355–61.

—— ' "Comparing Scripture with Scripture": Some Observations on the Sinai Pericope of Exodus 19–24', in G. M. Tucker, D. L. Peterson and R. R. Wilson (eds.), *Canon, Theology, and Old Testament Interpretation: Essays in Honor of Brevard S. Childs* (Philadelphia: Fortress Press, 1988), pp. 111–30.

—— 'The Creation of Man and the Creation of the King', *ZAW* 101 (1989), pp. 333–42.

—— 'Myth and History: The Problem of Origins', in A. de Pury (ed.), *Histoire et conscience historique dans les civilizations du Proche-Orient ancien* (Les Cahiers du CEPOA, 5; Leuven: Peeters, 1989), pp. 49–61.

—— 'Joshua's Campaign and Near Eastern Historiography', *SJOT* 2 (1990), pp. 1–12.

—— Review of *Genesis 15* (BZAW, 181; Berlin: W. de Gruyter, 1989), by J. Ha, in *BO* 48 (1991), pp. 624–26.

—— 'The So-called Deuteronomistic Redaction of the Pentateuch', in J. A. Emerton (ed.), *Congress Volume: Leuven, 1989* (VTSup, 43; Leiden: E.J. Brill, 1992), pp. 58–77.

—— *Prologue to History: The Yahwist as Historian in Genesis* (Louisville, KY: Westminster/John Knox Press; Zürich: Theologischer Verlag, 1992).

—— *The Life of Moses: The Yahwist as Historian in Exodus-Numbers* (Louisville, KY: Westminster/John Knox Press; Kampen: Kok, 1994).

—— 'The Theology of the Yahwist: A Preliminary Sketch', in I. Kottsieper et al. (eds.), *'Wer ist wie du, Herr, unter den Göttern?': Studien zur Theologie und Religionsgeschichte sraels* (Festschrift Otto Kaiser; Göttingen: Vandenhoeck & Ruprecht, 1995), pp. 219–28.

—— 'Cultic Laws in the Covenant Code (Ex 20:22–23:33) and their Relationship to Deuteronomy and the Holiness Code', in M. Vervenne (ed.), *Studies in the Book of Exodus: Redaction-Reception-Interpretation* (BETL, 126; Leuven: Peeters, 1996), pp. 319–46.

—— 'The Law of the Hebrew Slave', *ZAW* 108 (1996), pp. 534–46.

—— Review of *The Promise of the Land as Oath* (BZAW, 205; Berlin: W. de Gruyter, 1992), by S. Boorer, in *BO* 54 (1997), pp. 168–71.

—— 'Some Observations on the Lex Talionis in Exod 21:23–25', in S. Beyerle, G. Mayer and H. Strauss (eds.), *Recht und Ethos im Alten Testament: Gestalt und Wirkung* (Festschrift Horst Seebass zum 65. Geburtstag: Neukirchen-Vluyn: Neukirchener Verlag, 1999), pp. 27–37.

—— 'The Law on Child Sacrifice in Exod 22,28b–29', *ETL* 74 (1998), pp. 364–72.

—— 'Divine Encounter at Bethel (Gen 28,10–22) in Recent Literary-Critical Study of Genesis', *ZAW* 110 (1998), pp. 505–13.

—— 'In the Babylonian Exile with J: Between Judgment in Ezekiel and Salvation in Second Isaiah', in B. Becking and M. C. A. Korpel (eds.), *The Crisis of Israelite Religion: Transformations of Religious Tradition in Exilic and Post-Exilic Times* (OTS, 42; Leiden: E.J. Brill, 1999), pp. 71–89.

—— 'The Court History and DtrH: Conflicting Perspectives on the House of David', in A. de Pury and T. Römer, eds. *Die sogenannte Thronfolgegeschichte Davids: Neue Einsichten und Anfragen,* (OBO 176; Freiburg, Switzerland: Universitätsverlag, 2000), pp. 70–93.

—— *A Law Book for the Diaspora: Revision in the Study of the Covenant Code* (Oxford: Oxford University Press, 2003).

—— 'The Patriarchs and the Exodus: Bridging the Gap Between Two Origin Traditions', in R. Roukema, (ed.), *The Interpretation of Exodus: Studies in Honour of Cornelis Houtman* (Leuven: Peeters, 2006), pp. 1–15.

—— 'The Report of the Yahwist's Demise Has Been Greatly Exaggerated!', in Dozaman and Schmid (eds.), *A Farewell to the Yahwist?* (2006), pp. 143–57.

—— *The Edited Bible: The Curious History of the 'Editor' in Biblical Criticism* (Winona Lake, IN: Eisenbrauns, 2006).

—— 'Revision in the Study of the Covenant Code and a Response to my Critics', *SJOT* 21 (2007), pp. 5–28.

—— 'The Israelites in Egypt (Exodus 1–5) within the Larger Context of the Yahwist's History', in idem, *The Yahwist: A Historian of Israelite Origins* (Winona Lake, IN: Eisenbrauns, 2013), pp. 267–89.

—— 'Dating the Yahwist's History: Principles and Perspectives', *Biblica* (forthcoming).

—— 'The Tent of Meeting in the Yahwist and the Origin of the Synagogue', *SJOT* (forthcoming).

Vervenne, M., 'The "P" Tradition in the Pentateuch: Document and/or Redaction? The "Sea Narrative" (Ex 13,17–14,31) as a Test Case', in C. Brekelmans and J. Lust (eds.), *Pentateuchal and Deuteronomistic Studies* (BETL, 94; Leuven: Peeters, 1990), pp. 67–90.

—— 'The Question of "Deuteronomistic" Elements in Genesis to Numbers', in F. G. Martinez *et al.* (eds.), *Studies in Deuteronomy in Honor of C. J. Labuschagne on the Occasion of his 65th Birthday* (VTSup, 53; Leiden: E. J. Brill, 1994), pp. 243–68.

Veyne, P., *Did the Greeks Believe their Myths?* (Chicago: University of Chicago Press, 1988).

Vink, J. G., *The Date and Origin of the Priestly Code in the Old Testament* (Leiden: E. J. Brill, 1969).

Volz, P., and W. Rudolph, *Der Elohist als Erzähler: Ein Irrweg der Pentateuchkritik?* (BZAW, 63; Berlin: W. de Gruyter, 1933).

Wahl, H., *Die Jakob Erzählungen* (BZAW, 258; Berlin: W. de Gruyter, 1997).

Wallace, H. N., *The Eden Narrative* (HSM, 32; Atlanta: Scholars Press, 1985).

Weinfeld, M., *Deuteronomy and the Deuteronomic School* (Oxford: Oxford University Press, 1972).

—— 'Divine Intervention in War in Ancient Israel and in the Ancient Near East', in H. Tadmor and M. Weinfeld (eds.), *History, Historiography and Interpretation* (Jerusalem: Magnes Press, 1983), pp. 121–47.

—— *Deuteronomy 1–11* (AB, 5; New York: Doubleday, 1991).

—— 'kabod', *TDOT,* VII, pp. 34–36.

Weippert, M., ' "Heiliger Krieg" in Israel und Assyrien', *ZAW* 84 (1972), pp. 460–93.

Wellhausen, J., *Prolegomena to the History of Ancient Israel* (trans. J. S. Black and A. Menzies; Edinburgh: A. & C. Black, 1885).

West, M. L., *The Hesiodic Catalogue of Women: Its Nature, Structure and Origins* (Oxford: Oxford University Press, 1985).

Westermann, C., 'Arten der Erzählung in der Genesis', in *idem, Forschung am Alten Testament* (TBü, 24; Munich: Chr. Kaiser Verlag, 1964), pp. 9–91; ET *The Promises to the Fathers* (Philadelphia: Fortress Press, 1980), pp. 1–94.

—— *Genesis 1–11* (trans. J. J. Scullion; Minneapolis: Augsburg, 1984).

—— *Genesis 12–36* (Minneapolis: Augsburg, 1985).

—— *Genesis 37–50* (Minneapolis: Augsburg, 1986).

Whaling, F. (ed.), *Theory and Method in Religious Studies* (Berlin: W. de Gruyter, 1995).

Whybray, R. N., 'The Joseph Story and Pentateuchal Criticism', *VT* 18 (1968), pp. 522–28.

—— *The Making of the Pentateuch: A Methodological Study* (JSOTSup, 53; Sheffield: Sheffield Academic Press, 1987).

—— *Introduction to the Pentateuch* (Grand Rapids: Eerdmans, 1995).

Winnett, F. V., *The Mosaic Tradition* (Toronto: University of Toronto Press, 1949).

—— 'Reexamining the Foundations', *JBL* 84 (1965), pp. 1–19.

Zenger, E., et al., *Einleitung in das Alte Testament* (ST, 1.1; Stuttgart: W. Kohlhammer, 1995).

Zimmerli, W., *I Am Yahweh* (ed. W. Brueggemann; trans. D. W. Scott; Atlanta: John Knox Press, 1982).

Index of References

Index of Authors